CULTURAL DIVERSITY
and Families

EXPANDING PERSPECTIVES

EDITORS

Bahira Sherif Trask
University of Delaware

Raeann R. Hamon
Messiah College

SAGE Publications
Thousand Oaks ▪ London ▪ New Delhi

For information:

Sage Publications, Inc.
2455 Teller Road
Thousand Oaks, California 91320
E-mail: order@sagepub.com

Sage Publications Ltd.
1 Oliver's Yard
55 City Road
London EC1Y 1SP
United Kingdom

Sage Publications India Pvt. Ltd.
B-42, Panchsheel Enclave
Post Box 4109
New Delhi 110 017 India

Printed in the United States of America.

Library of Congress Cataloging-in-Publication Data

Cultural diversity and families: expanding perspectives /
[edited by] Bahira Sherif Trask, Raeann R. Hamon.
    p. cm.
Includes bibliographical references and index.
ISBN-13: 978-1-4129-1542-7 (pbk.)
    1. Family—United States. 2. Family—Study and teaching.
3. Multiculturalism—United States. I. Sherif Trask,
Bahira. II. Hamon, Raeann R.

HQ536.C853 2007
306.8508'0973—dc22   2006025669

This book is printed on acid-free paper.

07   08   09   10   11   10   9   8   7   6   5   4   3   2

Acquisitions Editor:	Cheri Dellelo
Editorial Assistant:	Anna Mesick
Project Editor:	Tracy Alpern
Copy Editor:	Cate Huisman
Typesetter:	C&M Digitals (P) Ltd.
Proofreader:	Anne Rogers
Indexer:	Maria Sosnowski
Cover Designer:	Glenn Vogel

Contents

Preface

The idea for this book was born out of a growing dissatisfaction on the part of the editors with the current materials available on cultural diversity and families. While most social science disciplines recognize the inclusion of diversity issues as integral to their fields, most available texts approach the topic by presenting the characteristics, practices, and values of specific racial or ethnic groups as immutable facts that do not change over time or place. Intragroup variability and the dynamic relationship between individuals and their cultural contexts (the concept of agency) are overlooked. This book attempts to move the dialogue about culturally diverse families to a new level by discussing topically the issues that affect culturally diverse families instead of organizing the information by racial and or ethnic groups.

Cultural diversity is an integral part of American family life. Currently 1 in 10 Americans is foreign born, 1 in 8 speaks a language besides English at home, and 1 in 5 is in either the first or second generation of a family to be born in this country. More than one-fourth of the current population is African American, Latino, Asian, or American Indian, and approximately one-third of all American children are non-White. By 2050, people of color are predicted to replace Whites as the majority in the United States. In the field of family science, the concept of *family,* which originally unified the discipline, has been replaced by the understanding that there are multiple forms of families and that families differ over time and within varying social, cultural, political, and economic contexts. Issues of diversity have reshaped our understanding of family and the family science field.

The impact of cultural diversity is complex: Individuals do not fall neatly into categories or typologies, nor does group membership necessarily mean that group characteristics are relevant in a particular case. Individuals and their families must be understood in the context of historical differences with respect to access to power, resources, and status and with respect to the culture of various groups. Furthermore, many individuals who have multiple religious, ethnic, or class affiliations are not captured under our current systems of categorization. How useful and accurate is our current knowledge about families? How do we best train students to understand issues facing diverse families? How do we provide the kind of services that are needed by culturally diverse families?

This book proposes to break new ground by investigating how concepts of cultural diversity have shaped the study of families from theoretical and applied perspectives. It investigates the impact of cultural diversity on the study of families in order to transcend simplistic categorizations that have juxtaposed White families in opposition to families of color and vice versa. It consciously emphasizes cultural aspects over racial impacts on family life so as not to reinforce the myth that race is a biological truth.

In summary, this book

- delineates the increasing cultural diversity of American families and examines the impact of these demographic changes for the social sciences;
- outlines the unique experiences of culturally diverse families in the United States in order to enhance understanding, direct future family research, and serve these families through responsive policy and practice;
- identifies shared family experiences across groups; and
- discusses implications of cultural diversity for future family research.

This text is divided into three sections: history and trends in the study of culturally diverse families, family life in culturally diverse families, and contextual issues and culturally diverse families.

Part I: History and Trends in the Study of Culturally Diverse Families

We set the stage with a discussion about the historical tensions in the study of culturally diverse families. Family science has long grappled with the complexity of understanding the experiences of families that deviate from the traditional White suburban families that form the basis for so much of the accepted research and theorizing. We then examine the current and projected demographic situation with respect to American families and offer theoretical approaches to studying culturally diverse families.

Part II: Family Life in Culturally Diverse Families

The second part of the book explores issues facing culturally diverse families from a thematic perspective. By focusing on experiences that are shared by all families such as gender issues, economics, marital relationships, childrearing, work-family issues, and intergenerational relationships and aging, we emphasize commonalities among families. However, by discussing these topics as they manifest themselves—sometimes quite similarly and at other times quite differently—in various groups and contexts, we also highlight the fact that there are multiple interpretations and experiences of commonly shared family issues.

Part III: Contextual Issues and Culturally Diverse Families

The latter part of the book focuses on the impact of cultural diversity for the interface between families and various social systems, service delivery, education, public policy, and ethics. It highlights the fact that as the demographics of our society change, our scholarly understanding of family diversity needs to be applied to better serve individuals in the families and communities in which they live.

We hope that this book begins to accomplish our goal of transforming the discourse on diversity and families by arguing that a more nuanced discussion about this relationship is necessary. Furthermore, while we are aware of the heterogeneity that exists among families, we are also arguing that families, no matter what their cultural roots, share common experiences and are impacted by the circumstances and the time in which they live.

Acknowledgments

We would like to thank all of our contributors who have made this such an excellent work.

In addition, Sage Publications would like to acknowledge the following reviewers:

Deborah Gentry, Illinois State University

Mark Hutter, Rowan University

Karen Kopera-Frye, University of Nevada, Reno

Teresa McDowell, University of Connecticut

Laurie Ellis McLeod, University of Wisconsin–Madison
Glenna Adell Mosby, University of Tennessee
Susan D. Talley, Utah State University–Uintah Basin
Ruben P. Viramontez Anguiano, Bowling Green State University
Ani Yazedjian, Texas State University–San Marcos

—Bahira Sherif Trask and Raeann R. Hamon

PART I

History and Trends in the Study of Culturally Diverse Families

1

Historical Trends in the Study of Diverse Families

Pearl Stewart and Katia Paz Goldfarb

This chapter describes major trends that have guided the study, interpretation, and understanding of diverse families. Historically in the study of families, the concept of diversity has been viewed only in terms of race and ethnicity, and both these terms were interwoven with the concept of culture. Research on family diversity has examined structure, function, norms, and values as well as discussed the ethnic, racial, and cultural aspects of families. However, there has been a failure to integrate the two discussions in ways that would portray the complexity of family diversity. Current definitions of family diversity tend to reference the extent to which families do or do not follow the western European model of the nuclear family. Baca Zinn and Eitzen (1988) describe that model as "a white, middle-class, monogamous father-at-work/mother-at-home family living in a suburban one family home" (p. 181). These trends in the understanding and study of diverse families have impacted attitudes and policies that affect diverse families.

After a brief discussion of terms and contexts relevant to the study of diverse families, this chapter will review and discuss several approaches from which diverse families have been studied. The chapter will then address the tendency to ignore the variation within specific groups. The next section will address the failure to study diverse families with the same degree of depth or frequency as families that meet the norm. Finally, we will advance a broader and more contemporary view of family diversity.

Defining Concepts and Context

In order to provide background, context, and a common language for this discussion, there are several terms that must be defined. Those terms include *family, family diversity, culture* and *cultural diversity, race,* and *ethnicity.*

The need to define family is at the heart of family science; otherwise, the failure to conform to a prescribed definition of family leads to immediate assumptions of pathology or to a failure to include essential family members in research and practice. A definition of *family* that allows virtually all family types to be acknowledged and accepted as valid would include shared biological, legal, cultural, and/or emotional ties and some sense of a future together (Anderson & Sabatelli, 2003; Davidson & Moore, 1996; Munro & Munro, 2003).

Historically, the study of families began with the assumption that the western European nuclear family model was normative. Families that diverged from that model were seen as inherently deviant, and that deviance was assumed to be embedded in the cultures of those family groups (Staples, 1971). In the context of this chapter, *family diversity* refers to the variety of ways that families are structured and function to meet the needs of those defined as family members. For example, extended families may view the rearing of children as a group responsibility, while nuclear families may vest that responsibility with the biological parents.

An understanding of the nature and importance of *culture* is also essential to the study of diverse families. Culture is a dynamic process that impacts our interaction with others and is passed from generation to generation (Barrera & Corso, 2002). It is "the cluster of learned and shared beliefs, values . . . practices . . . behaviors. . . . symbols . . . and attitudes . . . that are characteristic of a particular group of people" (Gardiner & Kosmitzki, 2005, p. 4). While culture has been historically defined in terms of race and ethnicity, individuals joined by factors such as sexual orientation, religion, and disability status may also be said to possess distinct cultures (Aulette, 2002). *Cultural diversity* speaks to differences in the beliefs, practices, and attitudes that exist in families and individuals because of cultural backgrounds. For example, one cultural perspective might require that elder care be provided directly by family members, while another perspective may view nursing home care as an appropriate method to meet that caregiving obligation.

While the terms *race* and *ethnicity* are certainly connected and intertwined, they are not interchangeable. The term *race* refers to socially defined categories based upon physical characteristics such as skin color. While it was long believed that there was a biological basis to racial categories, recent research has demonstrated that individuals assigned to different racial categories do not differ significantly at a biological level (Lamanna & Reidman, 2006). Ethnicity is a concept that refers to a group's "commonality of ancestry and history, through which have evolved shared values and customs over the centuries" (McGoldrick, Giordano, & Garcia-Preto, 2005, p. 2). Ethnicity speaks to a group's culture and all of the processes and issues that culture invokes.

Approaches to Studying Diverse Families

The cultural deviant, the cultural equivalent, and the cultural variant approaches were advanced by Walter Allen (1978) to describe research approaches to African American families, but they can be equally applicable to the study of other marginalized groups. The *cultural deviant* approach sees diverse families as having distinct characteristics and views those characteristics as negative or pathological. The *cultural equivalent* approach views all families as being essentially the same with diverse families having no distinctive characteristics. Some scholars who hold this view (e.g., Scanzoni, 1971) maintain that any differences among families are due to differences in social class rather than to cultural considerations. Like cultural deviant approaches, *cultural variant* approaches recognize culturally diverse families as having distinctive characteristics. However, cultural variant models attach no inherent pathology to those differences. In general, the cultural deviant approach has dominated the literature on diverse families.

Family Diversity as Deviance

Prior to the mid-1960s, diverse families were almost universally viewed as deviant and in need of repair (Staples, 1971; Staples & Mirande, 1980). *White ethnics,* such as Irish, Polish, and Italians, and various *socioreligious ethnic minorities,* such as Mormons, Amish, Muslims, and Jews, were expected to assimilate into the nuclear family model (Mindel, Haberstein, & Wright, 1998). Adherence to this model required men (husbands) to function as the primary or only earner and be the family's link to the larger society, while women were to remain in the home and maintain the role of nurturer and caregiver (Baca Zinn, 2000). Families that were racially or ethnically diverse were sometimes unwilling, based upon cultural mores, or unable, based upon societal barriers, to adhere to these rules. For example, African American women have always been part of the workforce, and their contributions to family finances were and continue to be essential to the survival of the family, even in the presence of two parents (Geschwender & Carroll-Seguin, 1990; McGoldrick, Giordano, & Pearce, 1996). While limited research is available about Asian Indian or Southeast Asian populations prior to 1980 (Staples & Mirande, 1980), research that examines the historical work patterns of these groups indicates that both women and, in the case of family-owned businesses, children were actively involved in work outside the home (Wong, 2002). This is clearly in violation of roles prescribed by the nuclear family model.

Family diversity is also an important issue with respect to the decision-making processes that guide family life. The nuclear family model has been the primary family system for those of western European descent since the Middle Ages, and the primary aim of decision-making is to advance the goals of the conjugal unit (Sudarkasa, 1997). Conversely, the extended family system tradition common to those of African, Latino, Southeast Asian, Asian Indian, or American Indian descent emphasizes blood, conjugal ties, and social ties, and decision-making is focused on advancing the goals of the entire unit (Dilworth-Anderson & McAdoo, 1988; Segal, 1998; Stewart, 2004). Those extended ties represent a significant and essential source of social and practical support (Sotomayor, 1991) but can interfere with the advancement of nuclear family goals.

Frazier's (1939, 1957) research on African American families and Sutton and Broken Nose's (1996) research on American Indians stress the ways in which context influences family structure and function and affects the way others define these groups. Frazier believed that slavery and persistent racism resulted in the loss of connection with the African kinship patterns and traditions that defined appropriate patterns of marriage and family obligation. He observed that disconnection led to disorganization and dysfunction in African American families (Mathis, 1978; Staples & Mirande, 1980). Work by Sutton and Broken Nose (1996) reveals a similar experience for American Indian populations whose children were forcibly removed and placed in state-run boarding schools, expunging their traditions for future generations. While American Indian families have been an almost nonexistent group in the literature of family diversity, the limited research that exists has perpetuated stereotypes of American Indians as lazy, alcoholic, exotic, and submissive (Kawamoto & Cheshire, 1997).

Implications of Deviance Approaches

The use of deviance models to study diverse families influenced both policy and practice. For example, in the 1950s, research on Mexican and

Mexican American families highlighted the family characteristics that deviated from the western European norm and determined that those deviations "predisposed Mexican-origin families to deficiency" (Baca Zinn & Wells, 2000, p. 253). The controversial and influential report issued by Daniel Patrick Moynihan (1965) held that the matriarchal nature of the African American family was responsible for the breakdown of those families and that the breakdown was the impetus for the problems (poverty, crime, single-parent families, teen pregnancy) in African American communities (Baca Zinn & Eitzen, 2005; Staples, 1971). Although Southeast Asian families have been a part of the United States more prominently since the mid-1800s, very few studies focused on them until the mid-1970s. These studies were characterized by comparisons of findings for Southeast Asian families with those for American families of European origin (Ishii-Kuntz, 2000).

Traditionally, diverse families were studied with a view toward identifying the root causes of problems inherent in the culture and structure of these families rather than understanding family processes and development (Dilworth-Anderson & McAdoo, 1988) and their relationship to societal factors. The feeling was that by understanding family processes of "normal" families, diverse families could be brought closer to the norm through appropriate interventions (Dilworth-Anderson & McAdoo, 1988).

Cultural Variant Approaches

While long-term negative effects were keenly felt by African American families, the Moynihan report set the stage for scholars to challenge the depiction of all diverse families and to call for a different approach to studying these groups (Billingsley, 1968; Hill, 1972). It was when African American researchers began to study African American families and to analyze data collected from the perspective of African Americans that African American families began to be viewed as resilient entities that had survived in the midst of problems. These scholars used *cultural variance* approaches to question "key assumptions of what was normative for families across cultural groups and to offer new paradigms and models for understanding the nature of black family life" (Taylor, Jackson, & Chatters, 1997, p. 3). The 1980s witnessed a focus on the adaptive features of African American families (Taylor, Chatters, Tucker, & Lewis, 1990). There was an insistence that racially diverse families be evaluated in context rather than in comparison to the middle-class White standard. This broader view of interpreting the lives of diverse families allowed for a move away from problem-focused study. And, while it is important to focus on the problems facing diverse families, a strict focus on problems leaves little time or space to acknowledge the levels of strength and resilience demonstrated over time or to examine the strategies used by diverse families to address the problems with which they were faced (Berardo, 1990; Taylor, Jackson, & Chatters, 1997). The trend toward focusing on diverse families as more than the problems they faced allowed researchers to view diverse families as entities unto themselves. Researchers began to recognize that diverse families are not unidimensional. They are groups with complex and multidimensional social characteristics. These more culturally sensitive and comprehensive models of understanding allowed for a deeper, more nuanced view of the development and functioning of ethnically and racially diverse families.

Lack of Attention to Diversity in Textbooks and Scholarly Journals

The lack of attention to diverse populations has been manifest in both family science textbooks and scholarly journals. There is a need to address the failure to study culturally diverse families with the same degree of depth and frequency that is applied to families that meet the norm. This failure has taken the form of a general lack of research and writing on the issue, a lack of depth in the research, inadequate or inappropriate analysis of the data, and a lack of visibility for the research and writing that does exist (Taylor, Chatters, Tucker, & Lewis, 1990).

Textbooks

Peters (1974) examined the extent to which African American families were included in available and adopted family science textbooks as well as the extent to which that inclusion represented and reinforced negative myths about African American families. When diverse families are included, they are typically confined to one chapter. In 1997, *Family Relations* journal published a special section on family textbooks (Dwyer & Youngblade, 1997, pp. 197–226). The editors, Dwyer and Youngblade, stated the importance of the dialogue and critiques presented in this series. It was indeed provocative and informative. However, the issue of lack of depth and frequency in which families from ethnic minority groups are described was not a focus of criticism.

More recently, a study of family science textbooks (Mann, Grimes, Kemp, & Jenkins, 1997) indicated that though coverage of racially or ethnically diverse families increased between 1960 and 1990, much of that coverage remained problem focused. One specific point raised was that racially or ethnically diverse families were generally linked to poverty, thus giving the false impression that ethnically diverse families are, on the whole, impoverished. Many instructors are ill equipped to adequately teach about ethnically and racially diverse families due to the unavailability of inclusive textbooks. Benokraitis (2002) summarizes the problems that exist in trying to find textbooks with relevant information about ethnic families in the United States:

> The books typically devoted much space to European American families. . . . The books tended to focus on low-socioeconomic households—especially those in black and Latino communities—but I was interested in increasing students' awareness of healthy family processes across and within ethnic households. (p. vii)

Scholarly Journals

While each decade produces larger amounts of research with respect to culturally diverse families, the tendency toward invisibility must still be addressed. Both the 1980 (Staples & Mirande) and 1990 (Taylor, Chatters, Tucker, & Lewis) decades in review identified the invisibility of African American families in the research literature as a problem. Staples and Mirande (1980) reported that the years between 1960 and 1970 produced five times more African American family literature than published in total before 1970. Likewise, there was a tremendous increase in the amount of work produced about Latino families during the 1970s. Asian and American Indian families were rarely studied during this period.

Graham's (1996) 20-year content analysis of six American Psychological Association journals, covering the period between 1970 and 1990, described an actual decrease in research on African American families. More-recent studies have also demonstrated the disparity between the demographic growth of the Latino population in all areas of the United States and the number of research articles published about this specific group (Rodriguez & Morrobel, 2004; Rodriguez, Morrobel, & Villarruel, 2003). Gonzalez-Kruger, Umaña-Taylor, Goldfarb, and Villarruel (2003) did a review of eight of the top family research journals between 1992 and 2002, paying particular attention to the inclusion of Latino populations in studies. The coverage of exclusive research on the Latino population ranges from one article to ten articles per journal in that decade. Fang, McDowell, Goldfarb, and Gonzalez-Kruger's (in press) content analysis of 10 top refereed family science journals found a grim picture for research focusing on Asian American families. Research on diverse families is still mainly comparative to White families.

While one must acknowledge the continuing increase in the amount of research being conducted on families fitting ever broader definitions of diversity, it is noteworthy that the results of that family research often appears in journals relating specifically to those groups (e.g., *Journal of Homosexuality, Journal of Black Studies, Hispanic Journal of Behavioral Sciences, Journal for the Scientific Study of Religion*) rather than in more broadly based family science journals. When such work appears in family oriented journals, it is often in the form of a special issue rather than as an integrated part of the family literature.

Assumptions of Sameness (Homogeneity)

Fallacy of Monolithic Identity

When diverse families are visible in the literature, there is a tendency to view those families as homogeneous within groups (Baca Zinn & Eitzen, 2005). Stanfield and Rutledge (1993) described the belief that those sharing the same cultural, racial, or ethnic background can be studied or acted upon without regard for other factors as the *fallacy of monolithic identity*. They go on to provide a possible explanation for the continuation of this belief:

> To recognize that people of color [diverse families] have ranges of identities is to acknowledge their humanity in a way that is threatening to the status quo, in that it disturbs the social, political, and economic arrangements of the dominant group. (p. 21)

This mind-set has significant implications for the study of culturally diverse families. First, it promotes and allows for a simplistic understanding of family life within these groups. The assumption that all group members experience life in the same way disregards social factors crucial to the understanding of family life. African American families encompass those of Haitian, Jamaican, and Trinidadian backgrounds as well as immigrants from various African countries. For these distinct groups, issues related to slavery, emancipation, and urbanization (Taylor, 2000) as well as poverty, oppression, discrimination, and identity are experienced differently. And, "however useful the terms Latino and Hispanic may be as political and census identifiers, they mask extraordinary diversity" (Baca Zinn & Wells, 2000, p. 253). Mexican, Chicano/a, Puerto Rican, Cuban, Dominican, Salvadoran, and other groups from Central and South America experience family life in very distinctive ways. Immigration, language barriers, intergenerational relationships, location, socioeconomic status, and migration are some of the issues that affect these groups differently. To add to the complexity under the Latino/Hispanic label, we need to consider families from Spain that share the language but not the North/Central/South American experiences as well as families from Brazil that share these experiences but do not share the language.

The literature portrays the Asian American family as the ideal ethnic or immigrant family, perpetuating the notion that the group shares a single identity (Ishii-Kuntz, 2000). There are several significant reasons that this is problematic. First, Chinese, Korean, Japanese, Filipino, Vietnamese, Cambodian, Laotian, and Hmong groups have not experienced family life the same way. For example, Japanese American families that lived through the internment during World War II had different assimilation and acculturation experiences than newer immigrants. Second, there are marked distinctions between South Asians and Southeast Asians. South Asian groups have varying experiences in their countries of origin and in the United States. They are only recently being examined as a division apart from Southeast Asians, and studies have barely begun on the ethnic groups that compose the South Asian category (Baptiste, 2005; Gupta & Pillai, 2002).

Stereotyping and Its Impacts

The perception that there is no variation within ethnic groups sets the stage for the development of stereotypes. The stereotypes that have developed about those of African, Latino, and American Indian descent have been largely negative (Taylor, Jackson, & Chatters, 1997). For example, in the early days of studying family diversity, theories about the functioning of the African American family were put forth with little or no thought given to variations in social class, geography, or educational level, while studies of family life among Americans of European descent were deemed incomplete without making such distinctions. Consequently, the results of studies on African American families of low socioeconomic status were merely applied to all African Americans. This created and reinforced the assumption that all African Americans were of low socioeconomic status and faced the same issues. Until fairly recently, African American families who were middle class or without identified problems have been virtually invisible to all but a few family scholars, and their unique issues have remained largely unaddressed (Billingsley, 1992; Dilworth-Anderson & McAdoo, 1988; Tatum, 1999; Toliver, 1998).

The depiction of American Indians as lazy, alcoholic, and dependant may be the reality of some American Indian families, but this view is biased and misleading without a historical understanding. "First the Spanish colonization and its active agenda of 'conversion' and then the U.S. policies of extermination" (Grinberg & Saavedra, 2000, p. 438) influenced the rupture of family values and traditions, and this rupture perpetuates a blame-the-victim attitude.

Similarly, Latinos are often perceived as dirty and lazy, and all Latino men are perceived as macho. Parrillo (1996) speaks of the need to include the history of American acquisition of land in the Southwest as a relevant context when conducting or interpreting research on Mexican Americans. Latino parents are seen as disinterested and indifferent to their children's education (Goldfarb, 1998). Cuban immigrants are seen as a very powerful political and economic force in Florida. Puerto Ricans are regarded as second-class citizens who continue to struggle to combine the cultures of the island and mainland. "Puerto Rican American household are sometimes perceived to be unstructured collections of people who are gathered together as a manifestation of social disorganization rather than as a reaction against it" (Carrasquillo, 1997, p. 167).

While stereotypes have been less negative for some of Southeast Asian descent, these individuals, too, are impacted with respect to lifestyle and study. Being viewed as the "model minority" with "high levels of educational attainment, low crime rates, and an absence of juvenile delinquency and mental health problems" (Ishii-Kuntz, 1997, p. 125) has masked the problems and needs of those who do not meet those expectations. In addition, like members of other diverse groups, Southeast Asians face discrimination in the workplace and are subject to the glass ceiling. The deeply ingrained stereotypes and prejudices are hard to overcome, even when they depict an ethnic group as intelligent, overachievers, and hard working. There needs to be a better understanding of how society has constructed these views and of their impact on family life for Southeast Asian American families.

There is tremendous variation between and within groups. The lives, behaviors, and experiences of members of culturally diverse groups may be impacted by factors such as geography, religion, educational level, social class, age, acculturation, language, or overt racial characteristics (Boyd-Franklin, 2003; Carter & McGoldrick, 1999; McGoldrick, Giordano, & Pearce, 1996). The myth of sameness also ignores or masks the distinctions among ethnics of European descent. Recent work has begun to provide descriptions of the variations among ethnic groups of European descent (Benokraitis, 2002; Hines, Preto, McGoldrick, Almeida, & Weltman, 1999; Mindel et al., 1998).

Emerging Perspectives

As trends began to change, the approach to the study of family diversity moved from seeing ethnic families as "merely cultural artifacts" (Baca Zinn &

Eitzen, 2005, p. 63) to an understanding that contextual factors impact families. The interrelationships among family structure, culture, ethnicity, race, gender, and social class started to shape some of the more critical research on family diversity. Parallel to these changes, the definition of family was also being transformed. A monolithic, static, and idealistic form of family has been challenged, and definitions that reflect the historical diversity in family structure are emerging. There is acknowledgment that family definition, structure, and function are influenced by economic, social, and political contextual factors (Coontz, 2000; Munro & Munro, 2003; Skolnick & Skolnick, 2005). At the practical level, a cadre of researchers who represent diverse groups has taken leadership in studying family diversity within more contextual and critical perspectives.

Certain aspects of feminist thought did much to broaden the study of diverse families. "Diversity, inequality and conflict are now woven throughout family science, replacing the old themes of family uniformity, convergence and consensus" (Baca Zinn, 2000, p. 49). While a feminist perspective added a level of positive depth to the study of racially and ethnically diverse families, some aspects of the feminist model were at odds with the experience of African American and other women of color. Traditional feminist thought focused on the male domination and oppression of women but virtually ignored the issues created by oppression based upon race and, to some extent, social class. For women of color, the family often represented a place of strength and refuge from inequality and oppression, rather than a primary source of repression (Baca Zinn, 2000).

Redefining Diversity

As the study of diverse families evolves, continued attention will need to be paid to the definitions of diversity. Narrow definitions that attend only to broad categories connected to race and ethnicity are no longer appropriate. While the broadening of the definition of family diversity is necessary in many respects, one specific area to be addressed is that of families that are headed by or include members that are gay, lesbian, bisexual, or transgendered. As was the case for families that are racially, ethnically, or culturally diverse that were compared to the White, middle-class, nuclear family, much of the research conducted regarding gay and lesbian families has compared them to heterosexual families. This has left "much of the experience of these families yet to be investigated" (Lambert, 2005, p. 43). While specific journals, such as the *Journal of Homosexuality,* have been introduced to address issues related to these individuals, their presence in family science literature and textbooks continues to be sparse. Discussions about the impact of same-sex marriage have brought issues of marriage and family to the forefront. In addition, since members of the gay, lesbian, bisexual, or transgendered community cross racial, ethnic, and socioeconomic lines, one cannot assume that their unique issues will be addressed in the study of other groups.

Another topic that is even more neglected in the literature is that of issues related to racially mixed people. Graham (1996) eloquently describes the problems surrounding the U.S. Census Bureau's "check one" racial and ethnic classifications. She states, "We will not sit still for discrimination so that government numbers will not be disturbed. Omission of multiracial people is a form of discrimination" (p. 48). The 2000 U.S. Census permitted checking of more than one box. This change is a clear example of awareness and legitimization of multiple group membership. In order for multiracial people to develop healthy identities, society needs to accept the reality of multiple reference groups and not consider it as deficient or exotic. "The multiracial people of tomorrow may be discriminated against as the 'new minority,' be accepted as the new ambassadors of peace because they are able to bridge many groups, or represent the majority of people in the United States" (Iijima Hall, 1996, p. 410).

Though the amount and depth of study of other groups continues to lag behind that of White, non-Hispanic families, many groups that were noticeably absent from the literature on families have begun to appear. There has been considerable growth in the amount of work of Asian Indian families (Baptiste, 2005; Gupta & Pillai, 2002), and efforts are under way to provide insight into the family lives of various Southeast Asian ethnic groups (Kim, Conway-Turner, Sherif-Trask, & Woolfolk, 2005; Wong, 2002). In addition, work related to the impact of religion on family life has also begun to appear in family science journals (Ghazal Read, 2004; King, 2003; Marks, 2004) and texts (Mindel et al., 1998). In addition, some discussion has begun about the differences in religious groups within the American Indian population (Kawamoto & Cheshire, 1997). Benokraitis (2002) edited a textbook that moves beyond merely describing the characteristics of diverse families and instead explores the lives of diverse families in a variety of contexts, including work, gender roles, parenting, and caregiving.

Cultural Competence

Though space does not permit an in-depth treatment of this issue, there is the need for scholars and practitioners to acknowledge the impact of culture on their work, both with respect to race or ethnicity and as a broadly defined notion. It is equally important that this acknowledgment extend beyond an acceptance of difference in others to include an acceptance that the cultures of researchers and practitioners impact their perceptions and interpretations of data and life experiences. Acceptance of diversity on these two levels is a step toward the achievement of cultural competency. *Cultural competency* is defined as a "set of congruent behaviors, attitudes, and policies that come together in a system, agency, or among professionals and enables that system, agency, or those professionals to work effectively in cross–cultural situations" (Cross, Bazron, Dennis, & Isaacs, 1989, p. 13). As an emerging perspective in the study of culturally diverse families, this effort to achieve cultural competence would allow those who now represent the bulk of family science scholarship and decisions about the dissemination of scholarship to be more accepting of the work of scholars belonging to a wide variety of cultural groups. It would also allow scholars from the currently dominant group to produce work about cultural groups other than their own that is relevant and culturally coherent.

Conclusions

This chapter aimed at examining the historical trends that have guided the description and understanding of diverse families. Although much has changed from the time when family diversity was studied from a deficit or pathology paradigm, and from when different groups were studied in a homogenous way, the findings of the old research are still used as a basis for program and policy development. Even as we made a conscious decision to try to broaden our perspectives, we found ourselves using the panethnic names to depict family diversity as it relates to ethnic, racial, and cultural issues.

This chapter also illustrates the disparity in research available to understand family diversity. Even as scholarship about diverse families has become more prevalent, the research is still mostly from a deficit perspective and has treated diverse families as homogenous groups. The different reviews of journals portray a dismal picture of the availability of quality research. The textbooks are still relegating descriptions of African American families, Latino families, and Asian families to the chapter on family diversity. Some books offer inserts in their attempts to show a more inclusive perspective. This perpetuates the definition of family diversity as only an ethnic or racial issue and reinforces the topic as an add-on rather than as a topic with a legitimate place within the fabric of the textbook.

In order to broaden understanding of the diversity in families, we need to address issues related to variations in immigration experience, occupational level and skill, language, religion, cultural values and beliefs, education, disability, class, gender, sexual orientation, and age. We realize the complexity of integrating all of these areas into research; however, the systematic inclusion of these factors is essential to broaden our understanding of what family life looks and feels like for diverse families.

References

Allen, W. R. (1978). The search for applicable theories of Black family life. *Journal of Marriage and the Family, 40,* 117–129.

Anderson, S. A., & Sabatelli, R. M. (2003). Family interaction: A multigenerational developmental perspective. Boston: Allyn & Bacon.

Aulette, J. R. (2002). *Changing American families.* Boston: Allyn & Bacon.

Baca Zinn, M. (2000). Feminism and family studies for a new century. *The Annals of the American Academy of Political and Social Science, 571*(1), 42–56.

Baca Zinn, M., & Eitzen, D. S. (1988). Transforming the sociology of family: New directions for teaching and texts. *Teaching Sociology, 16,* 180–184.

Baca Zinn, M., & Eitzen, D. S. (2005). *Diversity in families* (7th ed). Boston: Allyn & Bacon.

Baca Zinn, M., & Wells, B. (2000). Diversity within Latino families: New lessons for family social science. In D. H. Demo, K. R. Allen, & M. A. Fine (Eds.), *Handbook of family diversity* (pp. 252–273). New York: Oxford University Press.

Baptiste, D. A. (2005). Family therapy with East Indian immigrant parents rearing children in the United States: Parental concerns, therapeutic issues and recommendations. *Contemporary Family Therapy: An International Journal, 27,* 345–366.

Barrera, I., & Corso, R. M. (2002). Cultural competence as skilled dialogue. *Topics in Early Childhood Special Education, 22,* 103–113.

Benokraitis, N. V. (2002). *Contemporary ethnic families in the United States: Characteristics, variations, and dynamics.* Upper Saddle River, NJ: Prentice Hall.

Berardo, F. M. (1990). Trends and directions in family research in the 1980s. *Journal of Marriage and the Family, 52,* 866–884.

Billingsley, A. (1968). *Black families in White America.* Englewood Cliffs, NJ: Prentice Hall.

Billingsley, A. (1992). *Climbing Jacob's ladder: The enduring legacy of African American families.* New York: Simon & Schuster.

Boyd-Franklin, N. (2003). *Black families in therapy: Understanding the African American experience.* New York: Guilford Press.

Carrasquillo, H. (1997). Puerto Rican families in America. In M. K. DeGenova (Ed.), *Families in cultural context: Strength and challenges in diversity* (pp. 155–172). Mountain View, CA: Mayfield.

Carter, B., & McGoldrick, M. (1999). *The expanded family life cycle: Individual, family and social perspectives.* Boston: Allyn & Bacon.

Coontz, S. (2000). *The way we never were: American families and the nostalgia trap*. New York: Basic Books.

Cross T., Bazron, B., Dennis, K., & Isaacs, M. (1989). *Towards a culturally competent system of care, Vol. I*. Washington, DC: Georgetown University Child Development Center, CASSP Technical Assistance Center.

Davidson, J. K., & Moore, N. B. (1996). *Marriage and family: Change and continuity*. Boston: Allyn & Bacon.

Dilworth-Anderson, P., & McAdoo, H. P. (1988). The study of ethnic minority families: Implications for practitioners and policymakers. *Family Relations, 37*, 265–267.

Dwyer, J. W., & Youngblade, L. M. (1997). Editorial. *Family Relations, 46*, 195.

Fang, S., McDowell, T., Goldfarb, K., & Gonzalez-Kruger, G. (in press). Content analysis of refereed family focused publications: Asian American families.

Frazier, E. F. (1939). *The Negro family in the United States*. Chicago: University of Chicago Press.

Frazier, E. F. (1957). *Black bourgeoisie: The rise of a new middle class in the United States*. Glencoe, IL: Free Press.

Gardiner, H. W., & Kosmitzki, C. (2005). *Lives across cultures*. Boston: Allyn & Bacon.

Geschwender, J. A., & Carroll-Seguin, R. (1990). Exploding the myth of African-American progress. *Signs, 15*, 285–299.

Ghazal Read, J. (2004). Family, religion and work among Arab American women. *Journal of Marriage and the Family, 66*, 1042–1050.

Goldfarb, K. P. (1998). Creating sanctuaries for Latino immigrant families: A case for the schools. *Journal for a Just and Caring Education, 4*, 454–466.

Gonzalez-Kruger, G., Umaña-Taylor, A., Goldfarb, K., & Villarrruel, F. (2003, November). *What do we REALLY know about Latino families? A content analysis of refereed publications*. Poster presentation presented at the National Council on Family Relations 65th Annual Conference, Vancouver, BC, Canada.

Graham, S. (1996). The real world. In M. P. P. Root (Ed.), *The multiracial experience: Racial borders as the new frontier* (pp. 37–48). Thousand Oaks, CA: Sage.

Grinberg, J., & Saavedra, E. (2000). The constitution of bilingual/ESL education as a disciplinary practice: Genealogical explorations. *Review of Educational Research, 7*(4), 419–441.

Gupta, R., & Pillai, V. K. (2002). Elder care giving in South Asian families: Implications for social service. *Journal of Comparative Family Studies, 33*, 565–576.

Hill, R. (1972). *The strengths of Black families*. New York: Emerson-Hall.

Hines, P. M., Preto, N. G., McGoldrick, M., Almeida, R., & Weltman, S. (1999). Culture and the family life cycle. In B. Carter & M. McGoldrick (Eds.), *The expanded family life cycle: Individual, family and social perspectives* (pp. 69–87). Boston: Allyn & Bacon.

Iijima Hall, C. (1996). A race odyssey. In M. P. P. Root (Ed.), *The multiracial experience: Racial borders as the new frontier* (pp. 395–410). Thousand Oaks, CA: Sage.

Ishii-Kuntz, M. (1997). Chinese American families. In M. K. DeGenova (Ed.), *Families in cultural context: Strength and challenges in diversity* (pp. 109–130). Mountain View, CA: Mayfield.

Ishii-Kuntz, M. (2000). Diversity within Asian American families. In D. H. Demo, K. R. Allen, & M. A. Fine (Eds.), *Handbook of family diversity* (pp. 274–292). New York: Oxford University.

Kawamoto, W. T., & Cheshire, T. C. (1997). American Indian families. In M. K. DeGenova (Ed.), *Families in cultural context: Strength and challenges in diversity* (pp. 15–34). Mountain View, CA: Mayfield.

Kim, S., Conway-Turner, K. Sherif-Trask, B., & Woolfolk, T. (2006). Reconstructing mothering among Korean immigrant working class women in the United States. *Journal of Comparative Family Studies, 37,* 43–58.

King, V. (2003). Influence of religion on fathers' relationships with their children. *Journal of Marriage and the Family, 65,* 382–395.

Lamanna, M. A., & Reidman, A. (2006). *Marriages and families: Making changes in a diverse society* (9th ed.). Belmont, CA: Thomson Wadsworth.

Lambert, S. (2005). Gay and lesbian families: What we know and where to go from here. *Family Journal, 13,* 43–51.

Mann, S. A., Grimes, M. D., Kemp, A. A., & Jenkins, P. J. (1997). Paradigm shifts in family sociology: Evidence from three decades of family textbooks. *Journal of Family Issues, 18,* 315–348.

Marks, L. D. (2004). Sacred practices in highly religious families: Christian, Jewish, Mormon, and Muslim perspectives. *Family Process, 43,* 217–231.

Mathis, A. (1978). Contrasting approaches to the study of Black families. *Journal of Marriage and the Family, 40,* 667–676.

McGoldrick, M., Giordano, J., & Garcia-Preto, N. (2005). *Ethnicity and family therapy* (3rd ed.). New York: Guilford Press.

McGoldrick, M., Giordano, J., & Pearce, J. K. (1996). *Ethnicity and family therapy* (2nd ed.) New York: Guilford Press.

Mindel, C. H., Haberstein, R. W., & Wright, R. (Eds.). (1998). *Ethnic families in America: Patterns and variations.* Upper Saddle River, NJ: Prentice Hall.

Moynihan, D. P. (1965). *The Negro family: The case for national action.* Washington, DC: U.S. Department of Labor.

Munro, B., & Munro, G. (2003). Definition of family. In J. J. Ponzetti (Ed.), *International encyclopedia of marriage and family* (2nd ed., pp. 549–555). New York: Macmillan Reference.

Parrillo, V. N. (1996). *Diversity in America.* Thousand Oaks, CA: Pine Forge Press.

Peters, M. F. (1974). The Black family—perpetuating the myths: An analysis of family sociology textbook treatment of Black families. *The Family Coordinator, 23,* 349–357.

Rodriguez, M. C., & Morrobel, D. (2004). A review of Latino youth development research and a call for an asset orientation. *Hispanic Journal of Behavioral Sciences, 26*(2), 107–127.

Rodriguez, M. C., Morrobel, D., & Villarruel, F. A. (2003). Research realities and a vision of success for Latino youth development. In F. A. Villarruel, D. F. Perkins, L. M. Borden, & J. G. Keith (Eds.), *Community youth development: Programs, policies, and practices* (pp. 47–78). Thousand Oaks, CA: Sage.

Scanzoni, J. (1971). *The Black family in modern society.* Boston: Allyn & Bacon.

Segal, U. A. (1998). The Asian Indian American family. In C. H. Mindel, R. W. Haberstein, & R. Wright (Eds.), *Ethnic families in America: Patterns and variations* (pp. 331–360). Upper Saddle River, NJ: Prentice Hall.

Skolnick, A. S., & Skolnick, J. H. (2005). *Family in transition.* Boston: Allyn & Bacon.

Sotomayor, M. (Ed.). (1991). *Empowering Hispanic families: A critical issue for the '90s.* Milwaukee, WI: Family Service America.

Stanfield, J. H., & Rutledge, M. D. (1993). *Race and ethnicity in research methods.* Newbury Park, CA: Sage.

Staples, R. (1971). Towards a sociology of the Black family: A theoretical and methodological assessment. *Journal of Marriage and the Family, 33,* 119–138.

Staples, R., & Mirande, A. (1980). Racial and cultural variations among American families: A decennial review of the literature on minority families. *Journal of Marriage and the Family, 42,* 887–903.

Stewart, P. (2004). Afrocentric approaches to working with African American populations. *Families in Society: The Journal of Contemporary Social Services, 85,* 221–228.

Sudarkasa, N. (1997). African American families and family values. In H. P. McAdoo (Ed.), *Black families* (pp. 9–40). Thousand Oaks, CA: Sage.

Sutton, C. T., & Broken Nose, M. A. (1996). American Indian families: An overview. In M. McGoldrick, J. Giordano, & J. K. Pearce (Eds.), *Ethnicity and family therapy* (pp. 31–45). New York: Guilford Press.

Tatum, B. D. (1999). *Assimilation blues: Black families in White communities: Who succeeds and why.* New York: Basic Books.

Taylor, R. L. (2000). Diversity within African American families. In D. H. Demo, K. R. Allen, & M. A. Fine (Eds.), *Handbook of family diversity* (pp. 232–251). New York: Oxford University Press.

Taylor, R. J., Chatters, L. M., Tucker, M. B., & Lewis, E. (1990). Developments in research on Black families: A decade review. *Journal of Marriage and the Family, 52,* 993–1014.

Taylor, R. J., Jackson, J. S., & Chatters, L. M. (1997). *Family life in Black America.* Thousand Oaks, CA: Sage.

Toliver, S. D. (1998). *Black families in corporate America.* Thousand Oaks, CA: Sage.

Wong, B. (2002). Family traditions and values: The bedrock of Chinese American business. In N. V. Benokraitis (Ed.), *Contemporary ethnic families in the United States: Characteristics, variations and dynamics* (pp. 121–216). Upper Saddle River, NJ: Prentice Hall.

2

A Nation of Diversity

Demographics of the United States of America and Their Implications for Families

Fabienne Doucet and Raeann R. Hamon

We are all migrants, moving between our ancestors' traditions, the worlds we inhabit, and the world we will leave to those who come after us. For most of us, finding out who we are means putting together a unique internal combination of cultural identities.

—McGoldrick & Giordano, 1996, p. 6

Today's United States is covered in Chinatowns and Little Italys, Miami houses both Little Haiti and Little Havana, and Los Angeles boasts Koreatown, Little Tokyo, and Little Armenia. Teenagers in the suburbs are as likely to party to rock and hip-hop as they are to dance to East Indian Bhangra music, and restaurant choices in small towns all over the country range from Mexican to Ethiopian. Religious diversity is also a characteristic of the U.S. population. According to the American Religious Identification

Survey (ARIS), in which researchers conducted telephone surveys with randomly selected households in the continental United States in 1990 and then again in 2001, the percentage of U.S. residents who define themselves as being a member of a Christian religion (i.e., Baptist, Catholic, Protestant) decreased from 86 percent in 1990 to 77 percent in 2001. Concurrently, those who regard themselves as a member of another religion (e.g., Muslim, Jewish, Hindu, Buddhist) or of no religious group (e.g., atheist, agnostic, no religion) increased from 3.3 percent to almost 4 percent and 8 percent to 14 percent, respectively (U.S. Census Bureau, 2004–2005).

Though cultural identity as fluid and ever changing is a long-standing American trait (McGoldrick & Giordano, 1996), in the past four decades, the United States has experienced unprecedented, sweeping changes in its racial and ethnic landscape—changes that are transforming urban, suburban, and rural settings throughout the nation. Most of these changes can be attributed to the impressive number of immigrants[1] reaching American shores, propelled by the Immigration Act of 1965 (Massey, 1995). Compared to earlier waves of immigration, which consisted primarily of persons of European descent, the majority of more recent immigrants hail from Latin America, Asia, and the Caribbean (Suárez-Orozco & Suárez-Orozco, 2001). The U.S.-born[2] population of people of color[3] likewise has continued to grow steadily, though with some exceptions. These extensive changes have important implications for "the American family," as native and foreign-born groups alike challenge our notions of what we know about families, what they hold dear, how they view the world, and how they relate to one another.

These changes are occurring within the context of other unprecedented shifts in the U.S. population. Our purpose in this chapter is to provide an overview of the demographic profile of native and foreign-born groups in the United States at the dawn of the twenty-first century, with a particular focus on the racial and ethnic characteristics of these populations, demonstrating how the increasing racial and ethnic diversity of the U.S. population is changing American families. We begin with a synopsis of general trends in demographic changes of the U.S. population as a backdrop for our discussion. We then highlight some characteristics of native and immigrant groups. With respect to the native population, we discuss demographic trends among people of color, trends in socioeconomic conditions (including education, unemployment, income, and poverty), and trends in the population of interracial and multiracial Americans. With respect to immigrant groups, we discuss racial and linguistic diversity, the ethos of reception, and socioeconomic conditions. We conclude the chapter with implications of these demographic changes for how family scientists study and understand families in general and families of color in particular.

We would like to point out that the current chapter's focus on the traditional major racial and ethnic group categories (i.e., Asian and Pacific Islander, Black and African American, Hispanic/Latino, Native/American Indian, Non-Hispanic White), is reflective of available demographic data provided by the U.S. Census and related sources.[4] This does not preclude our understanding of the amazing diversity that exists *within* these broad categories. For instance, the daily lived experiences of Korean Americans are likely quite different from those of Bangladeshi Americans, yet both groups are collapsed under the umbrella term "Asian American." Likewise, we recognize that "American Indian" cannot even begin to capture the widely different histories and experiences of groups as diverse as the Lumbee of North Carolina and the Washoe of Nevada. The sociopolitical, historical, and economic reasons for the construction of these categories are extensive, and a discussion of these is beyond the scope of the current chapter. We ask our readers to consider the data we present in this chapter as painting with a very broad brush a picture of this intensely complex society in which we live, while the other chapters in the book provide more detailed images of how this diversity is lived out in family life.

Population Characteristics

U.S.-Born Population Growth by Race and Ethnicity

In their comprehensive report on the growth of the "Minority"[5] population, He and Hobbs (1999) make several projections about expected changes in the U.S. population from 1995 to 2050, three of which we highlight here. First, close to 90 percent of the growth in the U.S. population between 1995 and 2050 will be accounted for by people of color, a group that will outnumber Whites sometime after 2050. Projections suggest that people of color will compose one-third of the U.S. population by 2015 and almost 50 percent of the population by 2050 (Schmidt, 2004).

Second, the diversity of the U.S. population will increase as the growth of all "Minority" groups steadily outpaces that of Whites. Asians and Pacific Islanders and Hispanics/Latinos are the fastest-growing Minority groups. By 2050, Asians are expected to compose almost 10 percent of the U.S. population, and by 2015, Hispanics/Latinos are expected to compose nearly 24 percent of the total U.S. population (He and Hobbs, 1999; Schmidt, 2004). In 2002, the Hispanic/Latino population outgrew the African American one, thus exceeding previous population predictions.

Third, He and Hobbs (1999) predict that by 2030, young children of color (aged five and under) will outnumber their non-Minority counterparts.

Higher fertility rates, particularly among Hispanics/Latinos, will account for the population growth among people of color. The fertility rate is an average of three children for Hispanic/Latina women, 2.2 for African American women, and 1.8 for Whites (Schmidt, 2004). Similarly, the population of color aged 0–14 will more than double between 1995 and 2050, even as the non-Minority youth population declines. In fact, largely due to higher fertility rates, every group of U.S.-born people of color will represent a greater share of U.S. youth, while Whites will constitute the majority of the nation's elderly (Schmidt, 2004).

U.S.-Born People of Color

According to the 2000 census, approximately 28 percent of the U.S-born population consists of people of color, a category that includes (in alphabetical order) American Indians or Alaskan Natives, Asians, Blacks and African Americans, Latinos, Native Hawaiians or other Pacific Islanders, the "Two or more races" population, and people who chose "Some other race" among the categories listed on the census. Of these, the Black and African American population composes the largest proportion of the U.S.-born, followed by the Hispanic/Latino population. Figure 2.1 displays the racial distribution of the U.S.-born population according to 2000 census figures (U.S. Census Bureau, 2000).

One of the greatest challenges with analyzing data on U.S.-born people of color is that often the sociodemographic characteristics of racial and ethnic groups as reported by the U.S. Census Bureau combine foreign-born and native populations. Furthermore, as will be seen in the section on the immigrant population below, when racial and ethnic subgroups of the foreign-born are compared with the native population, these comparisons do not compare racial and ethnic groups to one another (Ewing, 2003). For example, the Hispanic/Latino foreign-born population is compared to the native population as a whole, which consists mostly of White Americans, as opposed to comparing foreign-born Hispanic/Latinos to U.S.-born Hispanic/Latinos. To address this issue, and to shed light on actual disparities due to racial and ethnic discrimination rather than place of birth, the Lewis Mumford Center for Comparative Urban and Regional Research at the State University of New York at Albany conducted a study comparing U.S.-born and foreign-born Asians, Blacks, Hispanics/Latinos, and Whites (Logan, 2003). The data presented below on U.S.-born people of color come from this report. Unfortunately, the report does not cover all U.S.-born people of color but focuses instead on the three largest groups: Asians, Blacks, and Hispanics/Latinos.

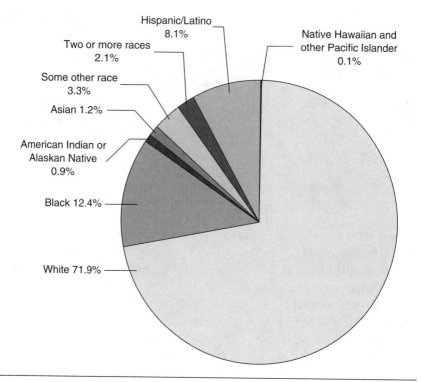

Figure 2.1   Racial Distribution of the U.S.-Born Population: 2000

SOURCE: Immigration Policy Center (Ewing, 2003).

The majority of the U.S.-born population, regardless of race, is concentrated in metropolitan areas. In 2000, 95.7 percent of Whites, 95.4 percent of Blacks, 59.1 percent of Hispanics/Latinos, and 32.4 percent of Asians lived in metropolitan areas. Compared to 1990 U.S. Census figures, all groups but Blacks were slightly less likely to live in metropolitan areas in 2000. In fact, the percentage of U.S.-born Blacks living in metropolitan areas increased slightly (by 0.4 percent). Another interesting set of findings regarding residential patterns of the U.S.-born reflect trends in neighborhood segregation. Logan (2003) found that Whites were more likely to be concentrated in neighborhoods where Whites were in the majority. Compared to Blacks and Hispanics/Latinos, Asians were the most likely to live in neighborhoods with high concentrations of Whites. It is also noteworthy that while the percentage of the population that was White decreased in predominantly White, predominantly Asian, and predominantly Hispanic/Latino neighborhoods, Black neighborhoods maintained a minimal White presence. These patterns with respect to metropolitan residence and neighborhood segregation, showing Blacks at a clear disadvantage when compared to Asians and Hispanics/Latinos, were consistent across almost all socioeconomic conditions as well.

Socioeconomic Conditions

Education

In today's high-stakes educational climate, in which school closures happen routinely based on test scores, it is imperative that we take into account the disparities in the "separate and unequal" schools attended by our populations of color (Neill, 2003). In the adult population, there are some clear differences in the educational attainment of racial and ethnic groups. According to data from the 2000 census, the U.S.-born Hispanic/Latino population had an average of 12.1 years of educational attainment (indicating slightly more than a high school education), the average for U.S.-born Blacks was 12.5 years, and for the Asian population it was 14.5 years, which exceeded the average 13.5 years of education for the White population (Ewing, 2003). Figure 2.2 shows these data in graphic form.

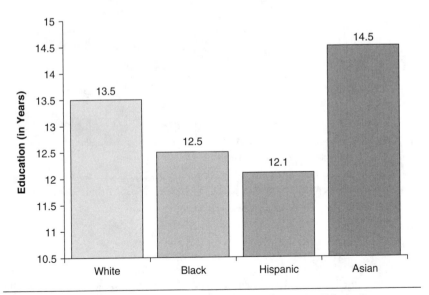

Figure 2.2   Educational Attainment of U.S.-Born by Major Ethnic Group: 2000

SOURCE: Immigration Policy Center (Ewing, 2003).

When considering the data on neighborhoods discussed above, and considering that school funding for inner-city, predominantly Black and Hispanic/Latino schools is increasingly sparse (Mathis, 2003), we should expect that these patterns will continue for younger generations unless policy makers attempt to intervene.

Unemployment Rates

Another sociodemographic marker of how our populations and families are faring is the percent of the labor force without jobs. As Figure 2.3 shows, there are several quite striking differences in unemployment rates across racial and ethnic U.S.-born groups.

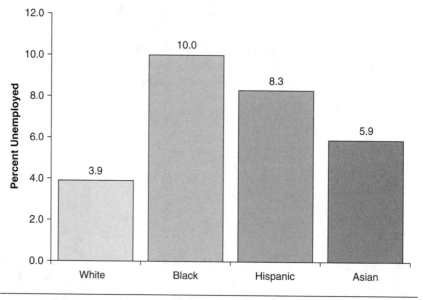

Figure 2.3   Unemployment Rates of U.S.-Born by Major Ethnic Group: 2000
SOURCE: Immigration Policy Center (Ewing, 2003).

Once again, the U.S.-born Black and Hispanic/Latino populations led with the highest unemployment rates in 2000, at 10 percent and 8.3 percent respectively. By contrast, the U.S.-born Asian population had an unemployment rate of 5.9 percent while the rate for U.S.-born Whites was 3.9 percent.

Income

The median household income is calculated by dividing in half the number of households that fall above and below a given amount. As Figure 2.4 shows, U.S.-born Asians had the highest median household income in 2000, far surpassing Whites, Blacks, and Hispanics/Latinos.

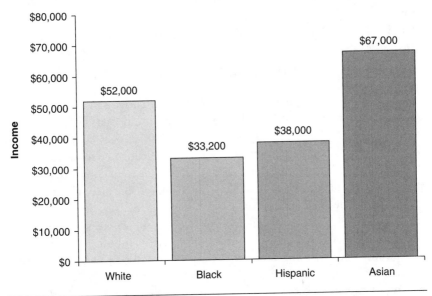

Figure 2.4   Median Household Income of U.S.-Born by Major Ethnic Group: 2000

SOURCE: Immigration Policy Center (Ewing, 2003).

While income figures were commensurate with educational attainment for Asians and Whites, Blacks actually had a significantly lower median household income than Hispanics/ Latinos even though with respect to educational attainment, Blacks were slightly ahead of Hispanics/Latinos.

Poverty

The poverty line is an important gauge of the expected quality of life for individuals and families. In 2006, the federal poverty line for a family of four was $20,000 (National Center for Children in Poverty, 2006). Yet some scholars have argued that families can barely afford to provide their children with such basic necessities as food, housing, and health care until they reach *double* the poverty level (Fuller, 2003). According to the most recently available data on poverty levels by race and ethnicity, Whites had the lowest poverty rate (8.1 percent) in 1999, followed by Asians (12.6 percent) and Native Hawaiians or other Pacific Islanders (17.7 percent). Poverty rates were higher among Hispanics/Latinos (22.6 percent), African Americans (24.9 percent), and American Indians and Alaskan Natives (25.7 percent), exceeding the national average of 22.6 percent. This suggests populations of color may find it difficult to maintain a quality of life they would consider acceptable.

Interracial and Multiracial Individuals and Families

The United States has become increasingly attentive to diversity as evidenced by the fact that although interracial and multiracial families always have been part of the U.S. population, the 2000 census was the first to allow respondents to choose more than one race category to describe their racial identities (Jones & Smith, 2001), providing a much more accurate picture of the racial diversity of the United States. Surprisingly, however, according to the 2000 census, only 1.9 percent of the U.S.-born population identified themselves as belonging to two or more races (U.S. Census Bureau, 2000). The figures reported here include both U.S.-born and foreign-born persons who identify as part of the "two or more races" population, a group composing 2.4 percent of the total U.S. population, because detailed data were not available for the U.S.-born group alone.

So what are some characteristics of the "two or more races" population? A report on the 2000 census by Jones and Smith (2001) outlines some of the major findings about this group. First, census data showed that the "two or more races" population was most likely to live in the West (40.0 percent) and the South (27.1 percent) of the United States, though the two cities with the largest concentrations of people of two or more races were New York (4.9 percent of the population) and Los Angeles (5.2 percent of the population). Second, the racial and ethnic groups least likely to report more than one race were Whites, followed by Blacks or African Americans, while the group most likely to report more than one race was Native Hawaiian and other Pacific Islander. Table 2.1 shows the percent of the population reporting two or more races, specified by race, for the 2000 census.

A third characteristic of this population was that approximately four-fifths of the persons who reported more than one race identified "White" as one of their races, close to half reported "some other race," and about one-fourth of all responses included "Black or African American," "American Indian and Alaskan Native," and "Asian" (see Figure 2.5).

Table 2.1   Percentage Reporting Two or More Races by Specified Race: 2000

Specified race	Alone or in combination[1]	Alone[2]	In combination[3]	% in combination[4]
White	216,930,975	211,460,626	5,470,349	2.5
Black or African American	36,419,434	34,658,190	1,761,244	4.8
American Indian and Alaskan Native	4,119,301	2,475,956	1,643,345	39.9
Asian	11,898,828	10,242,998	1,655,830	13.9
Native Hawaiian and other Pacific Islander	874,414	398,835	475,579	54.4
Some other race	18,521,486	15,359,073	3,162,413	17.1

SOURCE: Jones & Smith, 2001.

1. People who reported only one race, together with those who reported that same race plus one or more other races, are combined to create the race alone or in combination categories.
2. People who reported only one race create the race alone categories.
3. People who reported more than one of the six race categories create the race in combination categories.
4. The "percent in combination" is the proportion that the "in combination" population represented of the "alone or in combination" population. This is the equivalent of the percent of people reporting a specified race who reported two or more races.

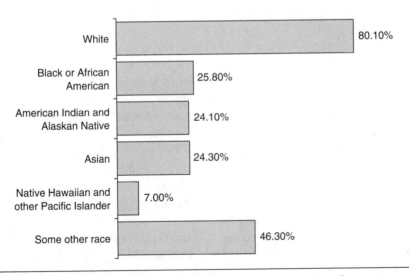

Figure 2.5   Race Reported as a Proportion of the Two or More Races Population: 2000

SOURCE: Jones & Smith, 2001.

Finally, there was a significant age difference among those reporting more than one race. Specifically, 42 percent of the people who reported more than one race were under 18, while 25 percent of the people who reported only one race were under18. As Tafoya, Johnson, and Hill (2004) pointed out, however, not all persons who are indeed biracial or multiracial report this information. Because census data are collected at the family level, these researchers investigated the extent to which parents of different races identify their children as having two or more races. Interestingly, they found that most couples of different races did not report their children as multiracial. However, some particular combinations of mixed-race couples are more likely to report their children as multiracial—parents of Asian/White and Black/White interracial children were much more likely than American Indian or Alaskan Native/White, non-Latino "Some other race"/White, and Latino "Some other race"/White to report their children as interracial. Increasingly, the reality is that many families have two or more cultural or ethnic identities represented within them, requiring "syncretism," or the "blending of cultural influences" (Falicov, 1995).

The Foreign-Born Population

> The story of the American people is a story of immigration and diversity. The United States has welcomed more immigrants than any other country—more than 50 million in all—and still admits as many as one million persons a year. (U.S. Society & Values, 1999, p. 7)

With the exception of American Indians, Mexican-origin people,[6] and the descendants of enslaved Africans, today's U.S. population is composed of migrants—people who make the decision to leave their countries of origin and come forge a new life on American shores (Schaeffer, 2002). They come to the United States for three primary reasons: economic, political, and familial (Suárez-Orozco & Suárez-Orozco, 2001). As the Suárez-Orozcos explain, changes in the global market have created strong pulls in the high-tech and service industries for immigrant labor, while simultaneously pushing people out of their countries due to the depressed economies in these less developed nations. Political instability, political persecution, and religious and ethnic discrimination have compelled others to emigrate from their home countries. For example, millions of Colombians, Haitians, Cubans, and Sudanese immigrants seek political refuge in the United States. Finally, since many families migrate in stages (as will be described later), family reunifications are an important factor in the large numbers of migration to this country. Once family members have established themselves in the new homeland, they are eager for spouses, children, and other relatives to join them.

At the time of the most recent report by the U.S. Census Bureau (Larsen, 2004), the foreign-born population of the United States constituted 11.7 percent of the total population. Though in sheer numbers the foreign-born population is larger than ever—an astonishing 33.5 million residents of the United States are foreign-born—at the height of the first large wave of immigration (1880–1920), the foreign-born constituted 14 percent of the U.S. population (Suárez-Orozco, 2000). What has changed dramatically is the world regions from which recent immigrants hail. Table 2.2 displays the change in region of birth among immigrants from 1880 to 2003. Immigrants in early 1900 originated in countries like Italy, Austria-Hungary, Russian Canada, and England), while the majority of today's foreign-born population is from Latin America (including the Caribbean), followed by Asia, Europe, and other regions, such as Africa, Australia, and Canada.

Table 2.2   Percentage of Foreign Born by Region of Origin[a]

	1880	1920	1950	1980	2000	2003
Europe	97%	93.6%	89.3%	49.6%	15.8%	13.7%
Asia	1.6%	1.7%	2.65	18%	26.4%	25%
Latin America	1.3%	4.2%	6.3%	31%	51.7%	53.3%
Other regions	0.2%	0.4%	1.8%	1.4%	6%	8%

SOURCES: Larsen, 2004; Malone, Baluja, Costanzo, & Davis, 2003; Suárez-Orozco, 2000.

a. According to the U.S. Census Bureau, the numbers do not all add to 100% due to rounding.

With respect to specific countries of origin, at the time of the 2000 census, the top 10 countries of birth for immigrants to the United States were Mexico, China, the Philippines, India, Vietnam, Cuba, Korea, Canada, El Salvador, and Germany (Malone, Baluja, Costanzo, & Davis, 2003). It is important to note that this list represents the approximate numbers of immigrants from each country *living* in the United States at the time of the 2000 census. The numbers of immigrants *admitted* to the United States vary from year to year, so that in 2003, one of the top 10 countries from which immigrants to the United States were admitted was Russia (U.S. Department of Homeland Security, 2004).

Just as the majority of immigrants come from particular regions of the world, so do they tend to settle in particular regions of the United States. Immigrants are typically drawn to magnet areas due to a "strong reunification tradition in U.S. immigration laws" and the practical necessity for these new residents to reside in communities where others share their language and cultural background and where they can gain entry into job networks (U.S. Society & Values, 1999). According to Pyke (2004), "New immigrant groups, who do not have the benefit of longstanding ethnic enclaves with firmly established social networks to assist in successful adaptation, must create from scratch the meaning of their ethnicity" (p. 254). Many of these individuals and families must grapple with a racial minority status and forms of racism for the first time in their lives.

Since the 1990s, an interesting shift has occurred in the regions to which immigrants have been drawn. As U.S. demographer William Frey (2002) pointed out, though the traditional immigrant magnets (i.e., California, Texas, New York, Florida, Illinois, and New Jersey) continue to attract the majority of immigrants, other states have experienced unprecedented growth in their immigrant populations. Nevada, for example, had a 123 percent increase in its Latino population between 1990 and 2000, Arkansas had a 148 percent increase, North Carolina a 110 percent increase, and Nebraska sustained a 96 percent increase (Schmidley, 2001). Table 2.3 displays the regions of the United States where immigrants were living in 2000, divided by immigrants' world region of birth.

Contemporary immigrant families are structurally diverse, depending upon such variables as criteria for admission to the host country and economic and political conditions and family patterns in both the home and new countries. These heterogeneous family forms are represented in transnational families (when one member enters the host country ahead of the rest, usually for the purpose of finding housing and work), parachute children (when children aged 8 to 17 are sent to the United States to live with others, without their parents), chain migration (when family members are reunited over time in the host country, causing families to experience bicultural households), nuclear families (when an immigrant family arrives in total), extended families (when more than one generation of parents and children live together), and coresident groups (those formed out of necessity) (Pyke, 2004). Consequently, family members who immigrate to the United States at different times experience their own unique challenges. As Pyke describes,

> When family reunification is complete, the years of separation contribute to bicultural households, with some family members having had more time to adapt to life in the United States The result can be a family of related strangers

Table 2.3 Percentage of Foreign-Born Population by World Region of Birth and Region of Residence in the United States 2000

Area	Total foreign-born population[a]	Europe	Asia	Africa	Oceania	Northern America[b]	Latin America Total	Mexico	Other Latin America
Northeast	23.2%	38.3%	22.2%	31.2%	10.3%	22.7%	18.9%	3.0%	40.0%
Midwest	11.3%	18.6%	12.8%	15.0%	7.8%	16.0%	7.8%	10.9%	3.8%
South	27.7%	20.2%	19.9%	34.9%	16.0%	26.9%	33.7%	29.6%	39.2%
West	37.8%	22.9%	45.1%	18.9%	65.9%	34.4%	39.5%	56.5%	17.1%

SOURCE: Malone et al., 2003.

a. Does not include the foreign-born population "born at sea."
b. The region Northern America includes Canada, Bermuda, Greenland, and St. Pierre and Miquelon.

who have very different values, needs, and perspectives, and who may not even speak a shared language—particularly when children, who adapt more quickly, are among those who arrived first. (p. 256)

Family scholars and practitioners need to take into account the range of family types and family strains when working with immigrant families.

One of the oldest and most common misconceptions about immigrant groups is that they never will truly become "American." As Mindel, Habenstein, and Wright (1998) pointed out, complaints about the cultural differences of newcomers date from as early as the colonial period. As in the past, recent scholarly work on the new immigrants of today convincingly demonstrates that this fear is unfounded (Portes & Zhou, 1993; Rumbaut, 1999; Suárez-Orozco & Suárez-Orozco, 2001) as immigrants do become absorbed into the complex fabric of U.S. society. A publication by Farkas, Duffett, and Johnson (2003) describes what America's immigrants have to say about life in the United States. The majority of the participants in this random sample expressed commitment to the United States and considered it their permanent home. They also identified themselves as American, while cherishing their own heritages and maintaining a strong bond with their native countries. The longer immigrants had been in this country, the more connected they seemed to be to the United States. Overall, immigrants were thankful and appreciative of their adopted nation, though this gratitude was moderated by the struggles and sacrifices they have also experienced in the new country.

It is the case, however, that the process of assimilation is not linear or unidimensional (Suárez-Orozco, 2002). As Portes and Zhou (1993) argued, "segmented assimilation" is the best way to describe the numerous ways today's immigrants become part of U.S. society, some integrating into mainstream culture, others becoming part of the underclass, and still others becoming successful through ethnic solidarity and the preservation of their own cultures. Thus, although it is the case that immigrant groups have many experiences in common as they make the transition to a new homeland, it is true also that there is a tremendous amount of diversity among immigrant groups.

Racial and Linguistic Diversity

While immigrants from Europe in the early 1920s struggled to transcend social class boundaries, immigrants today often have to contend with prejudice due to skin color (Rumbaut, 1994), which is arguably the most powerful characteristic for social stratification and discrimination in the United States (Appiah & Gutmann, 1998). Figure 2.6 displays the percent distribution of race and Hispanic/Latino origin for the foreign-born population. According to these data, the majority of immigrants identified themselves as Asian in the 2000 census (close to 70 percent). Among those who identified as Hispanic/Latino, 40 percent were foreign-born.

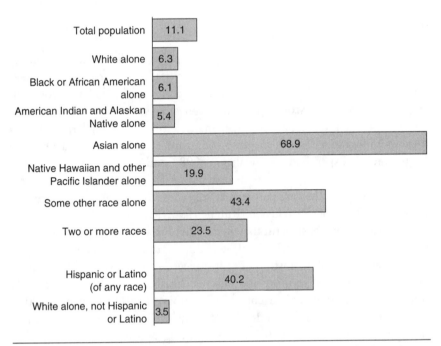

Figure 2.6   Percent Foreign-Born for the Population by Race and Hispanic Origin: 2000

SOURCE: Malone et al., 2003.

In terms of language, Spanish is spoken by the largest proportion of new immigrants (Suárez-Orozco & Páez, 2002). However, there is a great deal of linguistic diversity among immigrant groups as well. For example, in New York City public schools, there are more than 100 different languages represented, and more than 90 are found in Los Angeles Unified School District (Suárez-Orozco & Suárez-Orozco, 2001). Even in smaller school districts, it is not unusual to find 30 different languages and dialects spoken (Suárez-Orozco, 2000). According to 2000 census data, the top 10 languages spoken at home in the United States (after English) were Spanish, French, Chinese (which includes what are actually several separate languages), German, Tagalog, Vietnamese, Italian, Korean, Russian, and Polish. With more languages, there is a greater chance for misunderstanding and conflict. Words and nonverbal expressions of communication—like eye contact, hand gestures, and touch—can vary as well. In light of such diversity, policy makers, educators, family life specialists, and other human service providers need to be aware of the cultural and linguistic needs of their clients.

The Ethos of Reception

The general social climate, or ethos of reception, plays a critical role in the adaptation of immigrants to the U.S. context (Suárez-Orozco & Suárez-Orozco, 2001). While intolerance for newcomers is an all too common response all over the world, discrimination against immigrants of color is widespread and intense, particularly in many settings receiving large numbers of new immigrants. This is the case in Europe (Suárez-Orozco, 1996), the United States (Espenshade & Belanger, 1998), and in Japan (Tsuda, 2003). As today's immigrants are more diverse than ever in terms of ethnicity, skin color, and religion, they are particularly subject to the pervasive social trauma of prejudice and social exclusion (Rubin, 1994; Tatum, 1997).

Exclusion can be structural, when individuals are excluded from the opportunity system, or attitudinal, when immigrants are vulnerable to disparagement and public hostility. For instance, Arab Americans always have been at the center of scrutiny and mistrust (Ibish, 2001), but this has only intensified since the tragic events of September 11, 2001 (Muzher, 2001). Americans' general lack of knowledge about and understanding of Islam has fueled this discrimination further, putting Muslim Americans in the uncomfortable position of having to defend their religious beliefs, which are erroneously believed to promote violence (Ibish, 2001).

The structural barriers and the social ethos of intolerance and racism encountered by many immigrants of color intensify the stresses of immigration. Philosopher Charles Taylor argues that

> our identity is partly shaped by recognition or its absence, often by the misrecognition of others, and so a person or group of people can suffer real damage, real distortion, if the people or society around them mirror back to them a confining or demeaning or contemptible picture of themselves. (1994, p. 25)

Socioeconomic Conditions

Immigrant groups also differ in regard to their socioeconomic conditions in the host society. Also, according to recent data, there are marked differences between the foreign-born and native populations in socioeconomic characteristics.

Education

An interesting paradox exists among the children of immigrants today. They are simultaneously among the most likely to attend Ivy League universities and become incredibly successful and among the most likely to drop out of school, engage in illegal activities, and become incarcerated (Fuligini, 1998; Suárez-Orozco & Suárez-Orozco, 2001), a phenomenon Howard Gardner refers to as the "Princeton or Prison/Yale or Jail" syndrome (Suárez-Orozco & Gardner, 2003).

Looking across the adult population of immigrant and native groups, we find that the foreign-born were just as likely to report having earned a bachelor's degree in 2003 as their native counterparts (27.3 percent versus 27.2 percent, respectively). However, immigrants were overrepresented among those having less than a ninth-grade education (21.5 percent), whereas only 4.1 percent of the native population were in this category (Larsen, 2004).

Attempting to account for the socioeconomic effects of ethnicity and minority status, Ewing (2003) offers comparative data of immigrants and natives within the same ethnic group. His analysis suggests that when comparing native and immigrant Whites, Blacks, Hispanics, and Asians, only immigrant Blacks have more education than native Blacks. Educational attainment of native Whites, Hispanics, and Asians exceeds that of the immigrants in these ethnic groups.

Occupation and Unemployment Rates

On the whole, immigrant workers were more likely to be employed in service occupations than were native workers, with 23.3 percent of immigrants in such positions compared to 14.9 percent of U.S. natives (Larsen, 2004). Examples of service occupations include health care support (e.g., nurse's aide), food preparation and service, and buildings and grounds maintenance (Fronczek & Johnson, 2003). Conversely, native workers were more likely to be employed in management or specialty occupations than were immigrant workers (36.2 percent compared to 26.9 percent), though this pattern was not consistent across gender. Foreign-born women were more likely to be employed in the service sector, whereas their male counterparts held more management and professional occupations (Larsen, 2004). Looking across immigrant groups, Asian immigrants were far more likely to be employed in management and professional occupations (47 percent) than were Latin American immigrants (7.9 percent).

The foreign-born population also was slightly more likely to be unemployed than the native population (7.5 percent versus 6.2 percent, respectively). Looking across gender, unemployment rate differences were not statistically different between native men (6.9 percent) and foreign-born men (7.2 percent), but statistically significant differences did emerge between native women (5.5 percent) and foreign-born women (7.9 percent) (Larsen, 2004). With further examination of native versus immigrant ethnic groups, Ewing (2003) discovered that unemployment rates of natives in all four ethnic groups exceeded that of foreign-born individuals.

Income

Disparities emerged for income as well, both between the native and foreign-born and within the foreign-born groups. According to Larsen (2004), in 2002, a greater proportion of foreign-born households (24.6 percent) reported a total income below $20,000 than did native households (22.3 percent). Households with a Caribbean-born householder were the most likely to report an income less than $20,000. Contrasting this trend, households with an Asian-born householder were more likely to report a total income of $50,000 or more (53.8 percent) than were native households (44.0 percent). Households with an Asian-born householder also were far more likely than those with householders from other regions to report incomes of $50,000 or more. Ewing's (2003) analyses revealed that the median income for native Whites, Hispanics, and Asians exceeded that of their immigrant counterparts. However, native Blacks experienced lower median household incomes than their immigrant peers.

Poverty

Income figures alone do not predict the poverty level, however. Although the patterns shown above among native and foreign-born groups was consistent for percentages of families living below the poverty level—that is, only 11.5 percent of the native population was living in poverty compared to 16.6 percent of the foreign-born population—the groups most likely to live below the poverty level were from Latin America and Central America (Larsen, 2004). This is because the poverty level is calculated by household size, and Latin Americans and Central Americans had larger households than other immigrant groups. Ewing's (2003) comparisons are helpful here again. Immigrant Whites, Hispanics, and Asians had slightly higher poverty rates than did their native counterparts. In contrast, immigrant Blacks had an 8.5 percent lower poverty rate than native Blacks.

Conclusion

The remaining chapters of this book will more thoroughly highlight the implications of family diversity on the field of family science. We discuss here the socioeconomic implications of the demographic changes highlighted in this chapter. While there is a great deal of diversity in the education and skill level of those immigrating to the United States today (Pyke, 2004), the new immigrants are more likely to be poor than those from earlier waves of immigration (U.S. Society & Values, 1999). The financial strain on these families and pressure on the social programs designed to assist them will become apparent. The paucity of economic resources is likely a contributing factor to long-standing disparities in the health status of U.S. ethnic minority groups. More attention needs to be given to research that identifies how to explain and address the greater incidence of illness and health of African Americans, Latino/Hispanic Americans, American Indians, Asian Americans, Alaskan Natives, and Pacific Islanders when compared to the U.S. population as a whole. So too, there is potential for a new source of racial tension as the predominantly White older generation retires and a younger, largely minority population is required to provide financial support to an older, less racially and ethnically diverse population (Sweeney, 2004). As economic resources continue to be strained, we can expect family researchers and practitioners to confront questions relative to access to and distribution of services. Family professionals should remain cognizant of their own level of hospitality to those from immigrating groups.

Family science educators need to adapt their classrooms to an increasingly diverse student body, and students will be required to become culturally competent in preparation for their professional roles. Future family researchers, family practitioners, family and consumer sciences teachers (Adams, Sewell, & Hall, 2004), family policy makers and advocates, and family therapists (McGoldrick & Giordano, 1996) need to discard their monocular vision of families and assume more pluralistic cultural perspectives. Greater cultural awareness and sensitivity will enrich our work as we engage in an increasingly global environment.

Notes

1. We use the terms *immigrant* and *foreign-born* interchangeably to refer to individuals who were not born as U.S. citizens, in keeping with the definition outlined by the U.S. Census Bureau (Larsen, 2004).

2. *U.S.-born,* or *native,* in keeping with the U.S. Census definition, refers to persons "who were born in one of the following areas—the United States, Puerto Rico, Guam, American Samoa, the U.S. Virgin Islands, or the Northern Mariana Islands—or were born abroad of at least one parent who was a U.S. citizen" (Larsen, 2004, p. 1).

3. *People of color* refers to non-White groups that have been native to the United States for more than one generation, including African Americans, Asian Americans, Hispanic/Latino Americans, and American Indians.

4. For detailed descriptions of U.S. Census definitions for the terms listed here, please visit http://www.census.gov.

5. In He and Hobbs's (1999) report, the term *Minority* is "used to represent the combined population of people who are Black, American Indian, Eskimo, Aleut, Asian, Pacific Islander, or of Hispanic origin (who may be of any race). Equivalently, the Minority population comprises all people other than non-Hispanic Whites (who are termed the 'non-Minority' population when compared to the combined Minority population group)" (p. 1). As the following section will make clear, use of the term *Minority* to refer to these groups will need reconsideration.

6. Mexican-origin people inhabited the states we know today as Arizona, California, Colorado, New Mexico, Texas, Nevada, and Utah (as well as portions of Kansas, Oklahoma, and Wyoming) for centuries before these states became part of the United States through conquest during the Mexican-American War of the nineteenth century (Alicea, 1994).

References

Adams, E., Sewell, D. T., & Hall, H. C. (2004). Cultural pluralism and diversity: Issues important to family and consumer sciences education. *Journal of Family and Consumer Sciences Education, 22*(1), 17–28.

Alicea, M. (1994). The Latino immigration experience: The case of Mexicanos, Puertorriqueños, and Cubanos. In N. Kanellos & C. Esteva-Fabrigat (Eds.), *Handbook of Hispanic cultures in the United States* (pp. 15–36). Houston, TX: Arte Público Press.

Appiah, K. A., & Gutmann, A. (1998). *Color conscious: The political morality of race.* Princeton, NJ: Princeton University Press.

Espenshade, T., & Belanger, M. (1998). Immigration and public opinion. In M. M. Suárez-Orozco (Ed.), *Crossings: Mexican immigration in interdisciplinary perspective* (pp. 363–403). Cambridge, MA: David Rockefeller Center for Latin American Studies.

Ewing, W. A. (2003). *Minority newcomers: Fair comparisons of immigrants and the native born.* Washington, DC: Immigration Policy Center, American Immigration Law Foundation. Retrieved June 4, 2005, from http://www.ailf.org/ipc/policy_reports_2003_MinorityNewcomers.asp#note3

Falicov, C. J. (1995). Training to think culturally: A multidimensional comparative framework. *Family Process, 34,* 378–388.

Farkas, S., Duffett, A., & Johnson, J. (2003). *Now that I'm here: What America's immigrants have to say about life in the U.S. today.* A report from Public Agenda. Retrieved July 7, 2005, from http://www.publicagenda.org

Frey, W. H. (2002). U.S. Census shows different paths for domestic and foreign-born migrants. *Population Today, 30*(6), 1, 4–5.

Fronczek, P., & Johnson, P. (2003). *Occupations: 2000.* Washington, DC: U.S. Census Bureau.

Fuligini, A. (1998). The adjustment of children from immigrant families. *Current Directions in Psychological Science, 7*(4), 99–103.

Fuller, M. L. (2003). Poverty: The enemy of children and families. In G. Olsen & M. L. Fuller (Eds.), *Home-school relations: Working successfully with parents and families* (pp. 273–289). Boston: Pearson Education.

He, W., & Hobbs, F. (1999). *Minority population growth: 1995 to 2050. The emerging minority marketplace.* Minority Business Development Agency, Washington, DC: U.S. Department of Commerce. Retrieved June 4, 2005, from http://www.mbda.gov/documents/mbdacolor.pdf

Ibish, H. (2001). "They are absolutely obsessed with us": Anti-Arab bias in American discourse and policy. In C. Stokes, T. Melendez, & G. Rhodes-Reed (Eds.), *Race in 21st century America* (pp. 40–54). East Lansing: Michigan State University Press.

Jones, N. A., & Smith, A. S. (2001). *The two or more races population: 2000.* Washington, DC: U.S. Census Bureau.

Larsen, L. J. (2004). *The foreign born population in the United States: 2003.* Current Population Reports, P20–551. Washington, DC: U.S. Census Bureau.

Logan, J. R. (2003). *America's newcomers.* Albany: Lewis Mumford Center for Comparative Urban and Regional Research, State University of New York at Albany. Retrieved June 4, 2005, from http://mumford1.dyndns.org/cen2000/NewComersReport/NewComer01.htm

Malone, N., Baluja, K. F., Costanzo, J. M., & Davis, C. J. (2003). *The foreign-born population: 2000.* Washington, DC: U.S. Census Bureau.

Massey, D. S. (1995). The new immigration and ethnicity in the United States. *Population and Development Review, 21*(3), 631–652.

Mathis, W. J. (2003). No Child Left Behind: Costs and benefits. *Phi Delta Kappan, 84*(9), 679–686.

McGoldrick, M. J., & Giordano, J. (1996). Overview: Ethnicity and family therapy. In M. J. McGoldrick, J. Giordano, & J. K. Pearce (Eds.), *Ethnicity and family therapy* (2nd ed., pp. 1–19). New York: Guilford.

Mindel, C. H., Habenstein, R. W., & Wright, R., Jr. (1998). Diversity among America's ethnic minorities. In C. H. Mindel, R. W. Habenstein, & R. Wright, Jr. (Eds.), *Ethnic families in America: Patterns and variations* (4th ed.). Upper Saddle River, NJ: Prentice Hall.

Muzher, S. (2001). *It's not easy being an Arab-American: One person's experience.* Retrieved August 30, 2004, from http://www.mediamonitors.net/sherri22.html

National Center for Children in Poverty. (2006). *Basic facts about low-income children: Birth to age 18.* Retrieved April 2, 2006, from http://www.nccp.org/pub_lic06.html

Neill, M. (2003). Leaving children behind: How No Child Left Behind will fail our children. *Phi Delta Kappan, 85*(3), 225–228.

Portes, A., & Zhou, M. (1993). The new second generation: Segmented assimilation and its variants. *The Annals of the American Academy of Political and Social Science, 530,* 74–96.

Pyke, K. (2004). Immigrant families in the U.S. In J. L. Scott, J. Treas, & R. Martin (Eds.), *The Blackwell companion to the sociology of families* (pp. 253–269). Malden, MA: Blackwell.

Rubin, L. B. (1994). Is this a white country, or what? In *Families on the fault line: America's working class speaks about the family, the economy, race, and ethnicity* (pp. 172–196). New York: HarperCollins.

Rumbaut, R. G. (1994). The crucible within: Ethnic identity, self-esteem, and segmented assimilation among children of immigrants. *International Migration Review, 28,* 748–794.

Rumbaut, R. G. (1999). Assimilation and its discontents: Ironies and paradoxes. In C. Hirschman, J. DeWind, & P. Kasinitz (Eds.), *The handbook of international migration: The American experience* (pp. 172–195). New York: Russell Sage Foundation.

Schaeffer, R. T. (2002). *Sociology: A brief introduction.* Boston: McGraw-Hill.

Schmidley, D. (2001). *Profile of the foreign-born population in the United States: 2000.* Series P23-206. Washington, DC: U.S. Census Bureau.

Schmidt, A. L. (2004). *Executive summary: A population perspective of the United States.* Retrieved September 16, 2005, from http://www.prcdc.org/summaries/uspopperspec/uspopperspec.html

Suárez-Orozco, C. (2000). Meeting the challenge: Schooling immigrant youth. *NABE News, 24,* 6–9, 35.

Suárez-Orozco, C., & Suárez-Orozco, M. (2001). *Children of immigration.* Cambridge, MA: Harvard University Press.

Suárez-Orozco, M. (1996). Unwelcome mats. *Harvard Magazine, 98,* 32–35.

Suárez-Orozco, M. M. (2002). Everything you ever wanted to know about assimilation but were afraid to ask. In R. A. Shweder, M. Minnow, & H. R. Markus (Eds.), *Engaging cultural differences: The multicultural challenge in liberal democracies* (pp. 19–42). New York: Russell Sage Foundation.

Suárez-Orozco, M. M., & Gardner, H. (2003). Educating Billy Wang for the world of tomorrow. *Education Week, 23*(8), 34, 44.

Suárez-Orozco, M. M., & Páez, M. (2002). Introduction: The research agenda. In M. M. Suárez-Orozco & M. Páez (Eds.), *Latinos: Remaking America* (pp. 1–37). Berkeley: University of California Press.

Sweeney, K. (2004). What growing diversity will mean for America [Electronic version]. *Public Relations Tactics, 11*(8), 16–17.

Tafoya, S. M., Johnson, H., & Hill, L. E. (2004). *Who chooses to choose two? Multiracial identifcation and Census 2000.* New York: Russell Sage Foundation and Population Reference Bureau.

Tatum, B. (1997). *"Why are all the Black kids sitting together in the cafeteria?" and other conversations about race*. New York: Basic Books.

Taylor, C. (1994). *Multiculturalism: Examining the politics of recognition*. Princeton, NJ: Princeton University Press.

Tsuda, T. (2003). *Strangers in the ethnic homeland: Japanese Brazilian return migration in transnational perspective*. New York: Columbia University Press.

U.S. Census Bureau. (2000). *Census 2000 Summary File 3*. Washington, DC: Author.

U.S. Census Bureau. (2004–2005). *Statistical abstract of the United States: 2004–2005* (p. 55). Retrieved April 21, 2005, from http://www.census.gov/prod/2004pubs/04statab/pop.pdf

U.S. Department of Homeland Security. (2004). *Yearbook of immigration statistics, 2003*. Washington, DC: U.S. Government Printing Office.

U.S. Society & Values. (1999, June). *Changing America: The United States population in transition*. Retrieved July 28, 2006, from http://usinfo.state.gov/journals/itsv/0699/ijse/ijse0699.pdf

3

Theoretical and Methodological Approaches to the Study of Culturally Diverse Families

Bahira Sherif Trask and Ramona Marotz-Baden

Social sciences are experiencing a shift in the perception of cultural issues. Scholars are debating what it means to be a diverse society and which scientific methods of inquiry are most appropriate. Varying and oft-conflicting views about family issues coexist with unexamined "truths." In no aspect of family science is this more evident than in research on culturally diverse families. Heterogeneity is celebrated as the foundation of American society, and yet those whose lives seem to differ from the supposed norm are viewed as deviant or are marginalized. We recognize diversity, and yet we are puzzled by how to study, describe, and interpret differences.

In part, some of these methodological and analytical issues stem from the fact that as a relatively young field, family science has drawn primarily from the theories and methodologies of other social sciences (Hollinger, 2002). However, the many conflicting views about family life are not easily captured by other discipline-specific discourses that do not view the family unit as the fundamental unit of analysis.

Some theoretical disputes in family science can be attributed to current disagreement around conceptualizations of what a family unit really is. Is family defined through biology, social affiliation, or ideological persuasion? Definitional disputes leave the field seeking answers by often examining family issues rather than the families themselves. While this is one way of understanding families, it is imperative that families are also examined as units unto themselves, as they constitute a vital aspect of societies.

As Geertz (1973) and others (e.g., Daly, 2003; Siegfried, 1994) suggest, social science research is shaped by the society that produces it. Larger social systems influence every aspect of research, from which questions we ask to the particular issues that we merit of value enough to explore. Like the disciplines from which it derives its roots, family science has not been able to grapple adequately with issues facing contemporary families, especially when it comes to issues of cultural diversity. With the ever-changing demographics of the United States and increasing global migrations, it is imperative to refocus on the roles families play in societies. Family scientists can contribute to the resolution of a myriad of societal problems by making greater attempts to connect their research with global issues.

As the United States becomes increasingly diverse, society will change. While the United States was founded by diverse groups, historically, social, political, and cultural norms served to reject the notion of diversity. Complete assimilation and conformity were prized and deemed necessary to achieve success. As attitudes toward cultural pluralism have modified, diversity is increasingly seen as a hallmark. This implies that we are creating a society in which "all families will interface between cultures and customs" (Szapocznik & Kurtines, 1993, p. 406), although the history of immigration in the United States suggests that various forms of diversity have always been a distinguishing feature of the country (e.g., Mindel & Habenstein, 1976; Sowell, 1981).

Currently there is a striking disconnect between the demographic reality of the United States and the populations family scientists study. As mentioned in previous chapters, while there is superficial acknowledgment of the country's changing composition and the potential implications of these changes, most scholars do not include diverse samples in their work. This is ironic given that individuals who work either with policy makers or in professions that deal directly with families and children, such as human services and education, are impacted by diversity. In conducting a review of research published in prominent social science journals over the past 10 years, McLoyd, Cauce, Takeuchi, and Wilson (2000) discovered that most studies do not reflect the demographic makeup of society. In particular, quantitative research usually focuses on White middle-class families as the norm. On a few occasions, research with White middle-class families is juxtaposed with work on African American or another group's families but without necessarily controlling for social class. The lack of social class comparisons is dangerous, because it reinforces common stereotypes and prejudices that are, at times, based on knowledge or hearsay about a few individuals or families who are often dealing with serious problems in their lives (McLoyd et al., 2000). There is also little longitudinal research on culturally diverse families; most studies are cross-sectional or short-term. The few longitudinal studies that exist focus primarily on high-risk families.

Family as a Unit of Analysis

Some have described the 1950s as the "golden age" of family; families were considered more stable, with lower divorce rates, fewer single-parent families, and smaller numbers of children born out of wedlock (Mintz & Kellogg, 1988). During the postwar economic boom, there was a renewed interest in family. "Psychologists, educators, and journalists frequently repeated the idea that marriage was necessary for personal well-being. Individuals who deviated from this norm were inevitably described as unhappy or emotionally disturbed" (Mintz & Kellogg, p. 181). Coontz (1992, 1997) also noted that families were thought to fit one mold, and those that did not were perceived as dysfunctional. The ideal nuclear family was conceptualized as composed of a father who worked outside of the home, a homemaker mother, and several children. In part, this notion resulted from a sociological bias that based interpretations of societal phenomena on statistical norms. These norms focused on averages that emerged from a bell-shaped curve, the standard distribution, with the middle results labeled as normal and the ends as deviant (Walsh, 1982).

Indeed, the United States witnessed an increase in the percentage of two-parent families during the decades of the 1950s, 1960s, and 1970s (Seward, 1978). Masnick and Bane (1980) found that it wasn't until the late 1970s that the number of nuclear families broken by divorce exceeded the number disrupted by death. As the prevalence of divorce and of mothers with children under age 18 entering the workforce increased, American families (defined by the U.S. Census Bureau as two or more people living together related by blood, marriage, or adoption) began to deviate from the 1950s and 1960s concept of the typical family. Sociological analyses of families, however, continued to reflect the structural view of families that emerged in the period of the 1950s to the 1970s.

Deviations from the ideal middle-class nuclear family form produced outcries that the family was decaying (e.g., Brandwein, Brown, & Fox, 1974; Glasser & Navarre, 1965, Goldstein, Freud, & Solnit, 1973). In

"Family Form or Family Process? Reconsidering the Deficit Family Model Approach," Marotz-Baden, Adams, Bueche, Munro, and Munro (1979) questioned this assumption and concluded that process rather than family structure determined family members' well-being. Process, according to these researchers, should emphasize individual and family role behavior within a historical, social, and demographic context. For more than a decade, however, their conclusions were contentious. Many researchers maintained the perspective that family structure was key to assessing developmental outcome rather than adopting the view that interaction dynamics are major contributors to developmental outcomes. Talcott Parsons and William Goode, the most well-known sociologists at that time, helped perpetuate this view. Their work still exerts significant influence today, often hidden behind research questions that mask the inherent bias of researchers (Smith, 1993). The significance of this work extends far beyond the borders of the United States, as American publications reach every part of the globe, perpetuating a distinct brand of family life and correspondingly appropriate behaviors (Ambert, 1994).

Fundamental to the theoretical basis of family science was the notion that families were units that mediated between individuals and the larger society. This belief was primarily derived from structural function theory, which posited that all vital social institutions must work toward preserving both the well-being of individuals and their respective societies. From this perspective, families worked to perform essential functions (such as personal growth and development) for the benefit of individuals and society. This view also proposed that the universal function of families was to meet the need for human survival through reproduction and socialization of children (Reiss, 1965).

Talcott Parsons suggested that nuclear (or conjugal) families are small enough to be mobile in industrialized societies, and they also lack obligations to kin that would tie them down and make them less accessible to employers. Parsons emphasized the primacy of the conjugal tie between husband and wife, suggesting that this is the central family relationship in the Western world (Parsons, 1943). In contrast, the relationship between parents and children was deemphasized, leading to the lack of solid kinship groups. From the Parsonian perspective, families in contemporary industrial societies have two functions: the socialization of children and "personality stabilization" of adults. Other functions of the family, especially the economic productivity of families, were lost over time as these functions were taken over by other societal institutions (e.g., public schools provided education, churches offered religious training, and stores supplied processed food and relatively inexpensive ready-made clothing). Parsons also advocated that a breadwinner/homemaker couple represented a critical differentiation of sex roles, as otherwise competition between spouses for occupational status would detrimentally impact the solidarity of the marital relationship (Parsons, 1949). In his work he described the man's role as the "instrumental leader" of the family and the woman's role as the "expressive leader." Sex roles arose, according to Parsons, from the "natural" biological bond between mothers and their children. While today most social scientists question this view, it still permeates work-family connections.

Goode (1963) argued that the family is a force in bringing about change and, thus, should also be considered as an independent variable in understanding social dynamics. He viewed the family as a changing institution and system, and he focused, in particular, on the congruence of fit between family structure and industrialization-urbanization. Scholars believed that families would adapt in response to societal changes.

A large body of work concentrating on the goodness of fit between family types and society emerged as a result of such theorizing. For example, structural functionalists understood nuclear families to fit the needs of industrial societies, which require a high level of mobility from their members.

The post–World War II period was characterized by massive cultural changes including migration to suburbs, increases in marriage and birth rates, and a decline in divorce. These social changes were accompanied by new developments in the family field (Doherty, Boss, La Rossa, Schumm, & Steinmetz, 1993). In the immediate postwar period, family development theory arose from the necessity of understanding soldiers' experiences and the consequent necessary adjustments to family life. Researchers moved from conceptualizing the family as a "closed system of interacting personalities" to viewing the family as "a semi-closed system" working in conjunction with other systems in society (Hill & Rodgers, 1964, p. 178, as cited in Doherty et al., 1993). Simultaneously, family systems theory became increasingly popular and provided the family field with intervention concepts in the mold of family therapy.

While Parson's views shaped much of what we know of family life, structural function theorists have come under criticism, because family life as they described it was not an accurate depiction of individual experiences even for that time. Family life has always been diverse due to death, remarriage, poverty, immigration, and cultural issues. Historical work has documented that nuclear families did not arise as a response to the industrial revolution but were instead an intrinsic aspect of society in earlier agricultural times. This research unraveled the myth that preindustrial societies were dominated by extended families composed of coresident generations and characterized by family harmony and community life (Goode, 1963) and replaced it with new understandings that moved away from the perspective of families as static units in time. Instead, studies demonstrate that industrialization brought an increase in coresidence with extended kin due to newly arrived migrants sharing housing in urban centers (Goode, 1963; Hareven, 1977; Laslett & Wall, 1972).

Historical research on the family introduced a new distinction as well: Family could be differentiated from household. This distinction was crucial for contemporary work on culturally diverse families, because it illustrated that domestic groups (households) could contain nonrelatives as well as relatives (Seward, 1978). Furthermore, families were not restricted to households, because extended family ties could stretch far beyond the household unit (Goody, 1972; Hareven, 1974, 2000). These conceptualizations of families and households moved the study of families to an investigation of the family's interactions with other institutions in society, such as employment, education, and religion as well as with processes such as urbanization and migration (Hareven, 2000).

Perhaps the most critical juncture for the study of culturally diverse families in family science has come about through feminist analysis. As social and political upheavals reformed American society from the late 1960s through the 1970s, these changes began to influence academia as well. By the mid-1970s, the theoretical convergence that marked so much of the research and writing on families came to an end. While there were still those who favored the structural functional model of an ideal harmonious family model, evidence to the contrary was emerging from several venues. Historical and anthropological research revealed that societies exhibited a multiplicity of family forms. Even traditional sociological family research indicated that the actual experiences of families did not conform to one ideal type. The setting was ripe for radically new understandings of family life, and some of these came from feminist analysis.

Feminism and Its Influence on the Study of Families

In the mainstream social scientific studies of families, the family was conceptualized as a unit working in cooperation as a unified interest group. As a voice of an emerging feminist perspective, Heidi Hartmann (1981) introduced the notion of family as "a location where people with different activities and interests in these processes often come into conflict with one another" (p. 368). Family members were not only part of a family structure but also members of gender categories. As such, allocation of work in families was unequal, as women bore a larger burden under an umbrella of a shared division of labor (Hartmann, 1981). Familial division of labor was interpreted as oppression, reflecting the larger patriarchal system that advantaged men by allocating social power to them in every arena of society, including the most intimate sphere. Hartman, working from a Marxist-feminist perspective, highlighted accomplishing equal outcomes for men and women in social relationships. Her work, based on Marx's writings, viewed monogamous marriage as subjugation of one sex by the other and mistakenly thought abolishing capitalism and monogamous marriage in favor of socialism would end sexual and class inequalities (Smelser, 1975). Marxist-oriented feminists advocated that the family was the site of women's oppression and that the cohesive system of fixed sex roles benefited men while suppressing experiences of women. By deconstructing this notion and the experience of the family, these feminists introduced new ideas about what families are and how they should be defined. They emphasized multiple configurations, meanings, and relationships and the concept that fixed structural models fundamentally deviated from reality (Osmond & Thorne, 1993). Feminist analysis promoted the centrality of women's experiences, the social construction of gender, the importance of sociocultural context, the reality of multiple family forms, and a commitment to social change in family studies (Osmond & Thorne, 1993).

As these themes revolutionized the study of families, new issues emerged. By the 1980s, gender and inequality had emerged as core issues in understanding families. Feminism came under attack especially by scholars of color in the United States and researchers from non-Western societies. They argued that family had different meanings depending on cultural context and that the use of gender as a universalizing category subsumed and obscured the struggles of women in multiple family experiences. Instead, they suggested that for some women, especially those from persecuted groups, family life provided a haven and a solidifying sense of relationships not found in the outside world. Their work revealed that these women joined with the men in their families and communities to forge political struggles against racial and class discrimination (Baca Zinn, 2000). Mainstream socialist feminists identified the family as the source of female oppression; however, this new research revealed that families could also be the arena where racial and class solidarity was formed and expressed. For women and men of color, gender issues were often less important than social and political concerns. Gay and lesbian feminists noted heterosexuality dominated the study of families (Baca Zinn, 2000). Experiences of marginalized groups evoked questions about universal generalizations being made about the experiences of individuals. Context and sociohistorical time moved to the forefront in family analyses, laying the foundation for our current concerns and understandings with respect to the experiences of culturally diverse families.

The Contributions of Multiracial Feminism

Perhaps the single most valuable contribution to the theoretical study of culturally diverse families has come from multiracial feminism. The basic premise of Marxist multiracial feminism is that social location matters and that various privileges and disadvantages are allocated to individuals based on their position in the social hierarchy of racially stratified, class-based society (Baca Zinn, 2000; Baca Zinn & Dill, 1996). This approach criticizes pluralistic approaches to diversity that present differences between groups as typologies composed of an exotic mixture of cultural, gender, and personal characteristics. Instead, it emphasizes power differentiations in these various constellations. Difference is not to be perceived as differing from the norm but rather as differential access to power, status, and resources. Multiracial feminism recognizes that race comes with choices and opportunities and that experiences of people of color have often been obscured.

However, even aspects of this literature are inherently flawed. For example, Baca Zinn and Dill (1996) write that "historically, the categories of African American, Latin American, Asian American and Native American were constructed as both racially and culturally distinct. Each group has a distinctive culture, shares a common heritage, and has developed a common identity within a larger society that subordinates them" (p. 325). However, by employing purely racial terms, large groups of individuals with multiple experiences are again subsumed under headings that do not reveal the multiplicity of their experiences. While race is without a doubt a major identifying marker in American society, complexities of *defining* race are not clarified using this approach. Are Black, Spanish-speaking Dominicans living in the United States African American? What about individuals who recently immigrated from sub-Saharan Africa and have completely different historical and cultural experiences? Emphasizing race over all other categories obscures the complexity of the multicultural mix that is a fundamental aspect of our society.

The inadequacy of race as a meaningful category of classification is evidenced, in particular, by emerging literature on Hispanics (Bean & Tienda, 1987). This work illustrates that attempts to identify the cultural markers of various groups is extremely problematic. For example, Oropesa and Landale (2004) point out that in research on culturally diverse families, ethnicity is often used as a "crude identifier of groups that are assumed to form a communicative system" (p. 908). Even though this is common practice in work on cultural diversity, it is very problematic because much intragroup diversity is masked under an implied overarching cultural hegemony. Using terms such as *Hispanic* or *African American* does not reveal the enormous differences between subgroups, classes, educational levels, and genders.

Even within one supposedly clearly defined ethnic group such as "Mexican Americans," individuals may describe themselves as Mexican American, Chicano, or Mexican. While each of these terms is associated with individuals of Mexican descent, the terms also indicate varying cultural identities. For example, *Mexican American* refers to being American, and use of the term *Mexican* acknowledges Mexicanness (Oropesa & Landale, 2004). The term *Chicano* currently implies some form of oppositional resistance to the more assimilationist term *Mexican American*. This debate reveals just how complicated labeling may be and how important it is to represent the multiple views of the members of a particular group.

Multicultural feminism attempted to address some of the complex issues around classification and identification by introducing a "matrix of domination" (Collins, 1990). The underlying assumption is that various social systems interact with one another, sometimes in unseen ways. Interaction of race, ethnicity, class, gender, and sexuality determine individual, family, and group experiences. Thus, individuals of the same race or ethnicity may have strikingly different lives depending on their location in the class system (Gordon, 1964). Differences associated with social positioning are central to understanding families, as they can affect every aspect of family life including marital relations, parenting, and family structure. For example, Gordon found that parents would rather have their children marry someone within the same social class than marry someone from their own ethnic group from a lower social class. Thus a productive approach to studying culturally diverse families includes the importance of cultural variation, sociohistorical context, and access to power. As Baca Zinn (2000) aptly writes, "Diversity is not an intrinsic property of different groups but the product of power relations that structure the experience of all families, albeit in different ways" (p. 48).

Positivistic and Postpositivistic Approaches

Until relatively recently, we assumed that the scientific method would yield an understanding of family relationships and that this knowledge would ultimately be used to strengthen families and society (White, 2005). We also assumed that positivistic research was value free, even when the research was on a sensitive topic such as family life. Positivistic thought traces its origins to one of the fathers of social science, Auguste Comte (1798–1857), who argued that the principles applied in science should be adopted by the social sciences. According to Comte, observation was only valid if it was accompanied by data and scientific principles. Comte's ideas set the stage for the foundation of most social scientific research including work by Durkheim, Burgess, Merton, Parsons, and Hill. Characteristic of this research was a preoccupation with, and imitation of, methodological techniques used in the physical sciences (White, 2005). For more than half a century, the positivistic tradition remained entrenched in much of the social sciences, and it has figured prominently in the study of families.

Debate about the validity of positivistic approaches began in the social sciences at the end of the 1960s. In part spurred by feminist analysis and the advent of critical ethnography, some social scientists began to question the concept of a value-free objectivity, particularly for gender and diversity issues. The discipline as a whole, however, stayed away from this debate as evidenced by the continued dominance of quantitative positivist research in the major family-related journals (McLoyd et al., 2000).

Interestingly, controversy about the production and interpretation of knowledge in the social sciences derives its origins from the physical sciences. Kuhn (1962) launched the debate by arguing that science is influenced by political upheavals instead of scientific discoveries and that scientific advancement is subject to human vagaries that are intertwined with individual egos, political advancement, and other human situations. Thus, he asserted, positivistic thought, like other types of thought, is the product of a specific time and place. A logical extension of his argument is to question whether it is possible to produce value-free objective knowledge and whether a viable science of human behavior is even possible to achieve. Fundamental to this debate is the question of whether the complexity of human behavior and its meanings can actually be measured by quantitative means (White, 2005). According to this line of thinking, positivistic measurement also prevents us from taking into account the agency of individuals. Humans modify their behavior based on personal inclination and circumstances, a process not captured through quantitative measures. What this means is that quantitative measures of human behavior do not have either accurate descriptive or explanatory powers with respect to individuals within a group; humans are unable to predict another individual's actions, although they may describe group behavior.

While family science has avoided discourse about the philosophical aspects of knowledge production, other social scientists fiercely debate this topic. Critical ethnography, with its emphasis on reflexivity and power relations, its establishment of rapport in the field, and its debate about methodology and production of knowledge, has moved to the forefront of many social science discussions. The realization that knowledge is produced in a historical and social context by *individuals* has come to dominate the conversation about process and product, and the conversation has become political, personal, and experiential. Increasingly, the researcher, as producer and writer, is understood as creating meaning and interpretation out of his or her ongoing experiences (Collins, 1990, p. 206). This realization has also highlighted the crucial issue of rapport in the field: Who is the researcher, who is being researched, how is a relationship to be established, and what are the power issues involved? The traditional methodological assumption that the researcher should remain distant from the research participants and site in order to maintain objectivity has increasingly been replaced by a recognition that the ethnographer's self impacts every aspect of the research process from conception to final interpretation (Coffey, 1999, p. 6).

Postpositivistic thought contributed to thinking about actions of individuals and groups as reflecting their values. Value orientations influence every aspect of human existence as well as how groups and individuals interact with one another (Dilworth-Anderson, Burton, & Turner, 1993). This link is critical for understanding relationships between researchers and the people they study. It is also important for deciding how to conceptualize, study, and interpret diverse families. Every aspect of family life, from gender relations to parenting practices to aging, is subject to the values and interpretation of the researcher. This extends from the most basic aspect of research—which questions are asked—to where this research is presented. Even topics researchers choose to examine reflect significant issues of a specific sociohistorical time. Research on culturally diverse families is even more complex. Who the researcher is, what his or her relationship is to the population studied, and how research results might be used or applied are all parts of this myriad of complexity. Important questions include the following: Can only insiders study their own groups? (This is an issue that has long been disputed in anthropology.) What is the role of outsider interpretation of data? How do power hierarchies related to gender, class, race, and ethnicity play out in terms of access to research populations?

At this point, family scientists must find a more comfortable relationship in balancing positivistic and postpositivistic approaches. Often these approaches and their methodologies are presented as being mutually exclusive, while in reality, the study of families would benefit from the combination of both. For example, quantitative work, the hallmark of positivist orientations, can inform us about the composition of families. Qualitative inquiry, which is today associated almost exclusively with postpositivist thinking, can reveal patterns of interactions among family members. It is especially important to realize that measures created using the typical White family as the norm may have very little relevance for understanding relationships within and between culturally diverse families. Postpositivist, qualitative approaches can develop new ways of conceptualizing heterogeneity that may then be investigated with more traditional quantitative measures.

Implications of Broader Culturally Based Theoretical Approaches for Family Sciences

Culturally diverse families present new opportunities for theory development in family science. Much of the traditional theorizing in family science has attempted to look at families as if "they are suspended in time, space, and culture" (Daly, 2003, p. 774). Positivist approaches attempt to explain family phenomena as though they represent fixed family patterns, immutable over time. Yet, as Daly so aptly points out, families are constantly changing. Culturally diverse families provide a window into the dynamics of some of these changes. By focusing on these families, we may be able to develop methodologies and insights that help us understand all families. In part, culturally diverse families can be better understood by focusing on the contextual aspects of their lives. Instead of targeting their supposedly typical characteristics, it is the circumstances of their lives that will assist us in developing frameworks for understanding cultural pluralism (Szapocznik & Kurtines, 1993). By focusing on the matrix of choices families have, on the meanings they draw on and create from the world around them, and on how they cope with societal hierarchies and power differentiation, we will gain greater insight into the interrelationship between families and their lived experiences. This will allow us, as family scientists, to create programs and interventions to better meet the needs of families and their members.

Several theoretical directions allow us to pursue this line of thought. Ecological perspectives, systems theory, symbolic interaction, and life course theories provide dynamic frameworks that incorporate context, agency, and voice into social scientific analysis. However, building on social theories stemming primarily from nineteenth-century thought is insufficient for understanding twenty-first-century phenomena. Incorporating historical context and ethical or moral considerations into research will provide greater insight into the dynamism inherent in experiences of families.

New Directions

While much is written about societal diversification, Judith Stacey (1996) points out that gay and lesbian couples with children are "one of the only new, truly original, and decidedly controversial genres of family formation and structure to have emerged in the West during many centuries" (p. 110). Transnational and immigrant families also provide an area that is ripe for study (Schmalzbauer, 2004). Research examining role sharing, labor distribution, parenting practices, and extended and fictive kin relationships in these families may increase our understanding of family interaction in families who have at least some members residing in the United States. We understand very little about the complex network of relationships that span continents, cultures, and generations.

One in 10 Americans alive today is foreign-born—this implies that an increasingly larger group of people interact regularly, either physically through travel or through telephones and computers, with members of their families living abroad. This constant interaction leads to a form of cultural sharing and, at times, a form of cultural preservation, unprecedented before the advent of global communication capabilities and the ease of movement available now. Members of these families are often separated from one another for long periods, yet they manage to retain their ties and to preserve a feeling of unity in the name of family. Individuals belonging to transnational families provide a new glimpse into issues of identity and self-identification. Their identities and affiliations are no longer a given through state membership. Instead, they must consciously choose how they identify themselves, with whom or what they feel allegiance, and whose customs, values, and mores they adapt. Studies of these individuals and their families will reveal much that is not currently understood about the role of ethnicity, race, and group membership in people's lives. It may give us a broader insight into the myriad ways in which families construct a place for themselves in society and how society itself is affected by the constantly shifting nature of family life (Goode, 1963).

A primary issue in the debate around the incorporation of heterogeneity centers on whether "the new emphasis on family diversity preclude[s] a unified family analysis" (Baca Zinn, 2000, p. 50) or if too much emphasis on diversity will, ultimately, fragment the family field and obscure those commonalities that families share (Doherty et al., 1993). We would argue that this is not the case. Instead, we agree with Cheal (1991) that pluralism in thought and analysis is the new marker of studies of families. Multiple meanings in social life and in social theory imply that multiple realities coexist (Cheal, 1991). No longer do established, hegemonic ideas represent a core of accumulated knowledge that must be built upon or destroyed. Instead, from the margins, we are hearing a new, previously neglected, informative discourse. Cheal (1991) refers to this as "moving from polarization to pluralization" (p. 158). He claims there is no more "unified" body of knowledge or accepted truths and that the "most important ideas in social theory today are those which have the capacity to generate new ideas and hence more scientific activity" (p. 159). Incorporating the heterogeneity of our country and the larger global society into our studies will provide clearer insight into social phenomena previously inadequately studied or understood. Attempting to hold onto old ideas such as a unified concept of family will not give us the analytical tools needed to understand the needs and roles of families today.

Instead, we need to incorporate social change into analyses. This in turn will lead to new conceptual assumptions about families. These new assumptions will most likely be more culturally sensitive and challenge established ways of thinking (Dilworth-Anderson et al., 1993). They will highlight the importance of value orientation in conducting research and the positive features of family functioning among groups deemed as different or marginal. These studies will also provide insight into the tremendous variability that exists within and between groups due to sociohistorical circumstances, economic issues, and context. Further, family science can benefit on a theoretical and empirical level by engaging in a dialogue on these issues with anthropologists, sociologists, and other social scientists pursuing similar goals.

On another level, we should focus on how both culturally diverse and mainstream families interact with macrolevel processes. It is important to understand not just what is happening in families but also how these internal processes are reflected in the larger culture. As Hareven (2000) points out, how a family initiates and adapts to changes and how it interprets the impact of larger structural changes into its own operations are two of the most promising areas of research. Underlying this perspective is the understanding that families are active agents in the dynamic interplay between societal institutions and societal change. Families do not just react in response to societal stimuli. Instead, families are active players that plan, initiate, and at times reject change. It is these interactions we must capture to better understand social processes and the dynamic nature of families in society.

References

Ambert, A. (1994). An international perspective on parenting: Social change and social constructs. *Journal of Marriage and the Family, 56,* 529–543.

Baca Zinn, M. (2000). Feminism and family studies for a new century. *Annals of the American Academy of Political Science, 571,* 42–56.

Baca Zinn, M., & Dill, B. (1996). Theorizing difference from multiracial feminism. *Feminist Studies, 22,* 321–331.

Bean, F. D., & Tienda, M. (1987). *The Hispanic population of the United States.* New York: Russell Sage Foundation.

Brandwein, R., Brown, C., & Fox, E. (1974). Women and children last: The social situation of divorced mothers and their families. *Journal of Marriage and the Family, 36,* 113–121.

Cheal, D. (1991). *Family and the state of theory.* Toronto, ON: University of Toronto Press.

Coffey, A. (1999). *The ethnographic self: Fieldwork and the representation of identity*. London: Sage.

Collins, P. (1990). *Black feminist thought: Knowledge, consciousness and the politics of empowerment*. New York: Routledge.

Coontz, S. (1992). *The way we never were: American families and the nostalgia trap*. New York: Basic Books.

Coontz, S. (1997). *The way we really are: Coming to terms with America's changing families*. New York: Basic Books.

Daly, K. (2003). Family theory versus the theories families live by. *Journal of Marriage and Family, 65*, 771–784.

Dilworth-Anderson, P., Burton, L., & Turner, W. L. (1993). The importance of values in the study of culturally diverse families. *Family Relations, 43*, 243–248.

Doherty, W., Boss, P., La Rossa, R., Schumm, W., & Steinmetz, S. (1993). Family theories and methods: A contextual approach. In W. Doherty, P. Boss, R. La Rossa, W. Schumm, & S. Steinmetz (Eds.), *Sourcebook of family theories* (pp. 3–30). New York: Plenum Press.

Geertz, C. (1973). *The interpretation of cultures: Selected essays*. New York: Basic Books.

Glasser, P., & Navarre, E. (1965). The problem of families in the AFDC program. *Children, 12*, 151–157.

Goldstein, J., Freud, A., & Solnit, A. (1973). *Beyond the best interests of the child*. New York: Free Press.

Goode, W. (1963). *World revolutions and family patterns*. New York: Free Press.

Goody, J. (1972). Evolution of the family. In P. Laslett & R. Wall (Eds.), *Household and family in past time: Comparative studies in the size and structure of the domestic group over the last three centuries in England, France, Serbia, Japan, and colonial North America* (pp. 103–124). Cambridge, UK: Cambridge University Press.

Gordon, M. (1964). *Assimilation in American life: The role of race, religion, and national origin*. New York: Oxford University Press.

Hareven, T. (1974). The family as process: The historical study of the family cycle. *Journal of Social History, 7*, 322–329.

Hareven, T. (1977). Family time and historical time. *Daedalus, 106*, 57–70.

Hareven, T. (2000). The history of the family and the complexity of social change. In T. Hareven (Ed.), *Families, history, and social change* (pp. 3–30). Boulder, CO: Westview Press.

Hartman, H. (1981). The family as the locus of gender, class and political struggle. *Signs, 6*, 366–394.

Hollinger, M. (2002). Family science: Historical roots, theoretical foundations, and disciplinary identity. *Journal of Teaching in Marriage and Family, 2(3)*, 299–328.

Kuhn, T. (1962). *The structure of scientific revolutions*. Chicago: University of Chicago Press.

Laslett, P., & Wall, R. (1972). Introduction: The history of the family. In P. Laslett & R. Wall (Eds.), *Household and family in past time: Comparative studies in the size and structure of the domestic group over the last three centuries in England,*

France, Serbia, Japan, and colonial North America (pp. 1–73). Cambridge, UK: Cambridge University Press.

Marotz-Baden, R., Adams, G., Bueche, N., Munro, B., & Munro, G. (1979). Family form or family process? Reconsidering the deficit family model approach. *The Family Coordinator, 28*(1), 5–14.

Masnick, G., & Bane, M. J. (1980). *The nation's families.* Boston: Auburn House.

McLoyd, V., Cauce, A., Takeuchi, D., & Wilson, L. (2000). Marital processes and parental socialization in families of color: A decade review of research. *Journal of Marriage and the Family, 62,* 1070–1093.

Mindel, C., & Habenstein, R. (Eds.). (1976). *Ethnic families in America: Patterns and variation.* New York: Elsevier.

Mintz, S., & Kellogg, S. (1988). *Domestic revolutions: A social history of American family life.* New York: Free Press.

Oropesa, R., & Landale, N. (2004). The future of marriage and Hispanics. *Journal of Marriage and Family, 66,* 901–920.

Osmond, M., & Thorne, B. (1993). Feminist theories: The social construction of gender. In W. Doherty, P. Boss, R. La Rossa, W. Schumm, & S. Steinmetz (Eds.), *Sourcebook of family theories* (pp. 591–623). New York: Plenum Press.

Parsons, T. (1943). The kinship system of the contemporary United States. *American Anthropologist, 45,* 22–38.

Parsons, T. (1949). The social structure of the family. In R. Anshen (Ed.), *The family: Its function and destiny* (pp. 173–201). New York: Harper.

Reiss, I. (1965). The universality of the family: A conceptual analysis. *Journal of Marriage and the Family, 27,* 343–353.

Schmalzbauer, L. (2004). Searching for wages and mothering from afar: The case of Honduran transnational families. *Journal of Marriage and Family, 66,* 1317–1331.

Seward, R. (1978). *The American family: A demographic history.* Beverly Hills, CA: Sage.

Siegfried, J. (1994). Commonsense language and the limits of theory construction in psychology. In J. Siegfried (Ed.), *The status of common sense in psychology* (pp. 3–34). Norwood, NJ: Ablex.

Smelser, N. (1975). *Karl Marx on society and social change. With selections by Friedrich Engels.* Chicago: University of Chicago Press.

Smith, D. (1993). The standard North American family: SNAF as an ideological code. *Journal of Family Issues, 14,* 50–65.

Sowell, T. (1981). *Ethnic America.* New York: Basic Books.

Stacey, J. (1996). *In the name of the family: Rethinking family values in the postmodern age.* Boston: Beacon Press.

Szapocznik, J., & Kurtines, W. (1993). Family psychology and cultural diversity: Opportunities for theory, research and application. *American Psychologist, 48,* 400–407.

Walsh, F. (1982). Conceptualizations of normal family functioning. In F. Walsh (Ed.), *Normal family processes* (pp. 3–42). New York: Guilford.

White, J. (2005). *Advancing family theories.* Thousand Oaks, CA: Sage.

PART II

Family Life in Culturally Diverse Families

4

Gender and Class in Culturally Diverse Families

Katherine R. Allen and Ben K. Beitin

Jamie and Tracey: Townhouses and Trailer Parks

Jamie and Tracey are roommates at Northern University. They share a townhouse with two other women close to campus. Jamie is an African American female who comes from a working-class family in which her father is a construction worker and her mother is a secretary. Jamie also has two brothers. Jamie's parents, Jeff and Celia, did not encourage her to go to college, although they required her brothers to be in college if they wanted to live in their parents' house. Jeff and Celia believe that a woman's place is in the home, as Celia had been while raising Jamie and her brothers. Jeff and Celia have high school educations. Tracey is a European American female. Both her parents, Bob and Diane, are lawyers and come from Protestant backgrounds. The family is upper middle class with considerable wealth. They demanded she go to college because they believed this was the way Tracey could find an appropriate husband.

Living in the townhouse with three other women, Jamie could not concentrate and get her work done, because it was so crowded and noisy. She got into an argument with Tracey, because Tracey's boyfriend, Prescott, was selling cocaine out of their townhouse. At first, Jamie tried to ignore what was going on, but she started to resent how casually Tracey treated the whole thing. Jamie was sure she would be shamed by her family if the police got involved. Tracey told Jamie she was just being paranoid. Prescott found out that Jamie was not happy and threatened her by using racial slurs. Jamie works two jobs to put herself through school, unlike Tracey, whose parents pay her way. With all the stress, she just needed some peace and quiet and didn't feel like she fit in with her roommates' self-centered ways.

The only rental she could find on short notice was in a trailer park at the edge of town. It was inexpensive compared to what student apartments cost. Jamie is glad to be on her own. She made friends with Maria, the woman who lives next door. Maria has two kids for whom Jamie sometimes babysits when she has time. Jamie worries about Maria's drinking, and she just found out Maria has lung cancer. The other night, the trailer park was alive with sirens and blaring lights when the police were called. Maria's boyfriend threatened her with a knife after one of their fights. Maria's mother, Gladys, who lives with her, called the cops.

Jamie ran into Tracey, her old roommate, when Tracey stopped by the dry cleaners where Jamie works to pick up her laundry. Jamie wasn't surprised when Tracey told her about Prescott's arrest for selling cocaine. He has a court hearing in a few weeks. Tracey hopes the judge will be lenient, given that Prescott has no prior record. Tracey said she is glad her father is a lawyer because he is helping with the case. On her way out the door, Tracey winked at Jamie and told her to lighten up, have some fun, and not work so hard.

Before we begin our discussion of gender and class in culturally diverse families, consider the following questions:

1. Who is the person in the story with whom you most identify? In what ways?

2. What stereotypes do you notice about gender, class, and race in this story?

3. What are the intergenerational messages communicated about gender in this story?

4. How are gender, class, and race influencing the different characters?

5. In what ways have your gender, class, and racial backgrounds influenced your experiences as a student, employee, and roommate?

6. If you were a professional in the family field meeting with Jamie and Tracey to help them resolve their issues, how would you incorporate the intersecting tensions of gender, class, and race into the conversation?

Studying Gender and Class in Family Science: A Feminist Perspective

The approach we use to examine gender and class in family science in this chapter is informed by a feminist perspective. A feminist perspective is grounded in the real life of regular people, attends to social context, and acknowledges multiple and often contradictory perspectives. There are many feminist perspectives and considerable disagreement among feminist scholars about whether a unique feminist methodology even exists (see Chafetz, 2004, and Reinharz, 1992). Key to feminist ideas, however, are the desire to conduct research *for,* rather than *about,* women (Westcott, 1979) and the critical idea that by talking about previously silenced experiences, women have agency and are empowered (Smith, 1987). *Agency* in this context refers to a woman's existence as "a thinking, feeling social agent who is able to reflect on the prevailing cultural discourse and on the options available to her" (De Reus, Few, & Blume, 2005, p. 449). A feminist approach is not exclusively about women's lives, however, because it theorizes the power relations that attempt to construct "male" and "female" as otherwise independent categories. One cannot understand women without also considering their experiences in relation to men (Calasanti, 2004). A feminist approach includes the conscious aim to transform knowledge and social life for the better (Allen, 2000).

Research on domestic labor, such as housework and kinkeeping, has been the most influential in the family field (Thompson & Walker, 1995). Feminists made visible the organizational structure and meaning of housework as "women's work" as an expression of both love and subordination (Ferree, 1990), thereby improving on economic models that cannot explain why men and women often "collaborate to maintain a system that objectively imposes unequal burdens on women" (p. 877). Feminist scholars have generated critical theory concepts for women's reproductive work, such as "invisible labor" in and for families (Daniels, 1987). Women construct daily life through their emotional and domestic labor of feeding the family (DeVault, 1991). Feminist researchers have worked hard to document, publish, and publicize this work in the academic world, which is another form of invisible labor; the majority of people with advanced degrees are males, and scientific knowledge still has a sexist bias (Delamont, 2003).

Feminist perspectives have also been the first to document the demographics of intersectionality; that is, the ways in which sexism, racism, classism, and other forms of domination structure and oppress individual and family life (Collins, 1998). For example, the poorest members of society are most likely to be children (Seccombe, 2000). Our poorest older adults are most likely to be women. Caregivers of the old are also women: Wives, daughters, and daughters-in-law disproportionately are the family members who provide care to infirm older family members (Walker, 1999). These are but a few of the countless ways in which lives are structured and shaped by gender and class over the life course.

Social Stratification, Intersectionality, and Inequality

In the brief story about Jamie and Tracey that opens the chapter, we introduce issues of gender and class, mindful of their simultaneous intersections with race, sexual orientation, age, nationality, physical and mental ability, and other forms of social stratification. Both of these young women live in the same community, go to the same university, and for a while share the same dwelling. Both maintain connections to their families of origin and are influenced by parental guidance and pressure to conform to parental messages.

Though Jamie and Tracey have many similarities, they are also worlds apart. Their lives are characterized by varying degrees of inequality that are linked with the different levels of wealth, power, and prestige that they experience depending on their own and their family's placement in the social stratification system (Collins, 1990; Grusky, 2001). Although they share the same *social location* of gender, it is a superficial similarity in that gender intersects in complex ways with class, race, age, sexual orientation, and other structural stratifications to shape individual and family life. For example, Tracey's boyfriend is in trouble for selling cocaine, not its crack version that is found in poorer neighborhoods. Her worry about Prescott's legal fate is lessened because he is being helped by her attorney father, who brings critical resources connected to his knowledgeable and high-status profession. Thus, social stratification is the way in which society differentially rewards and oppresses individuals and groups based on the ascribed qualities or statuses a person is born with and the achieved qualities or statuses a person acquires over the life course.

Systems of Oppression and Privilege

Those differential rewards are *privileges,* or unearned advantages, that accrue to people on the basis of qualities that are more valued in society, such as White skin, male gender, higher social class, heterosexual orientation, first-world citizenship, athletic capability, and physical beauty. People, like Tracey and Prescott, who have those privileges, are less likely to recognize that they have them (as Tracey demonstrated when she winked at Jamie and suggested she not work so hard), because people on the margins of society are more often in a position of experiencing what W. E. B. Du Bois (1903/1996) defined as "double consciousness." This important idea means that people who are being oppressed by those with more power, that is, people who are on the outside of privilege, have an opportunity to develop a deeper form of knowledge—both of their own experience of oppression and of those who are oppressing them. Jamie experiences Tracey's disregard for her feelings as oppressive and possibly shameful; she recognizes the risk to her educational success of living in a hostile environment and makes a decision to leave. Collins (1990) refers to this kind of critical reflection on experience as "learning from the outsider-within" specifically as it relates to Black women's development of a distinctive Afrocentric women's culture. In the political economy of the early to mid-twentieth century, most of the paid jobs available to Black women were as domestic employees in White homes. Black women were both insiders to White families as cooks and maids, care-givers and nurturers of children, and confidants to the White women who employed them, and at the same time they "knew that they could never belong to their white 'families,' that they were economically exploited work-ers and thus would remain outsiders" (p. 11).

The social stratification system generates inequalities that are associated with gender, class, race, and other ways of marking difference among indi-viduals and families. Gender oppression is called sexism; class oppression is classism; racial oppression is racism. These oppressions are rooted in stereotypes—beliefs in the inherent superiority of one gender, class, or race over another and are based on irrational fears and prejudices (Lorde, 1984). Privilege is also morally corrupting and retards emotional and civic growth, as bell hooks (1995) explains in her analysis of how White supremacy, with its moral code of "the right to dominance" (p. 31), is frightening. In the matrix of domination, privilege and oppression are defined in relation to one another (Collins, 1990, p. 225). For people in positions of privilege, it is important to develop an informed reflexive consciousness about one's own social locations (Allen, 2000). As Black feminist thought teaches, "revolution begins with the self, in the self" (Collins, 1990, p. 229). Tracey's inability to decenter from her own privilege and consider how her choices impact those around her is a significant barrier in creating and sustaining authentic relationships with others, such as Jamie.

Intersectionality: Simultaneous Dislocations

Social structures are not additive, as in, "just add women and stir," but mutually influence and construct one another (Collins, 1998; Smith, 1987). Intersectionality is experienced at both personal and political levels, because it involves the negotiation of one's social location (identity) and a standpoint from which to enact social change (activism) (Collins, 1998; De Reus et al., 2005). Cuadraz and Uttal (1999) explain that when conducting in-depth interviews with Chicana women, for example, the sources of women's troubles are not simply a matter of either racism, classism, or sexism. Instead, intersectionality means that individuals are experiencing *simultaneous dislocations* that are shaping and colliding within a particular sociohistorical context. It is not enough to say a respondent is "a woman," or "working class," or "Hispana," because within each category, and across each person's life course, there is tremendous variability. Jamie experiences the slur by Prescott simultaneously as an African American being oppressed by a White person, as a woman in a position of possible aggression by a man, and as a person with fewer economic resources.

Intersectionality is a conceptualization that allows researchers and social actors to get beyond essentializing ideas such as the category of "woman," as if there was a single type of *woman* that can be applied to all *women*. From a social constructionist perspective, knowledge is partial and constantly changing. Identity is relational, as well, and is not seen as the stable property of the individual, but as an accomplishment of a social relationship (Gergen, 1999). Serious dialogue is needed to transform the intense feelings that often accompany the awareness of oppression and privilege. Instead of categories of fixed identities, when we envision the self emerging through dialogue, we can conceptualize new ways of relating to and affirming others, which in turn helps us to cocreate new worlds. Engaging in *difficult dialogue* can be transformative, because it allows us to imagine new identities for ourselves and to learn to take the role of the other, especially when it feels like we are worlds apart as Jamie and Tracey might have felt.

Engaging in difficult dialogues, whether we are confronting internal contradictions or dealing with people who seem to be in completely different places than we are, is necessary in a world marked by difference. Examples include Tillmann-Healy's (1996) description of her love-hate relationship with her body as she explores the compulsive pattern of bulimia, and Odeh's (2003) paradoxical relationship to being veiled as a Muslim feminist. Both women dialogue with various aspects of themselves, and they also imagine conversations with others, real or projected, revealing how complex and fragmented identity and social locations are.

In another example, Gergen (1999) describes the Public Conversation Project, which brought together prolife and prochoice activists to share their personal life experiences rather than their stuck political positions on abortion in the presence of each other. This relational project showed how dialogue can be transformative in stalemated public controversies when family therapists apply their skills to warring factions in the abortion conflict. In the process of telling their stories and having the opportunity to listen and ask some questions about which they were genuinely curious, both prolife and prochoice activists, equally passionate about and entrenched in their respective positions, came to a more complex understanding of the abortion struggle and backed away from demonizing members on the other side once again. They reported developing a significantly rehumanized view of the people with whom they continued to have fundamental political and value differences. The key to transformative dialogue is asking new questions, listening well, and being open to recognizing some common ground.

Individualization and Twenty-First-Century Family Life

Now consider Rachel, a Jewish woman who, at age 21, marries in a traditional ceremony. Five years later, she finds herself questioning her identity as a heterosexually married woman. Eventually, she and her husband divorce. She starts to explore an emerging lesbian sexuality. She returns to graduate school, living on a student stipend. Along the path of her spiritual journey, she begins to participate in Quaker services, now less comfortable in the religious services of her family of origin. Several of her identities have shifted, and the intersections of sexual orientation, social class, marital status, and religion have altered. Until demographic, social, and cultural cohorts changed recently, these identity alterations might have been unthinkable. Yet, in today's culture of the postfamilial family, which operates in a community of elective, as opposed to necessary, affinities, Rachel's identities are part of the contemporary social landscape of *individualization* (Beck & Beck-Gernsheim, 2002).

Individualization is part of the process of modernization that happens in advanced industrialized societies (Cheal, 2002), where individuals are increasingly liberated from traditional commitments. Along with their personal emancipation, however, comes an increased loss of stability and a greater chance of being disappointed in relationships, careers, and other personal investments. Many contemporary individuals do not know what to do with their emancipation and are headed into trouble with overindulgence in sexually addictive relationships and behaviors that take advantage of the power they have over others as a result of their race, class, and gender. In contrast, a feminist approach advocates *mutuality* rather than unequal power relations as a possibility for revitalizing nondestructive interpersonal gendered, class, and sexual relationships in individual and communal life in complex societies (Giddens, 1992).

Studying Social Class in Family Life

Social Classes in Industrial Society

Social class has proven difficult for researchers to both conceptualize and measure (Grusky, 2001). Family life educators have steered clear of it almost entirely, with notable exceptions (see Hughes & Perry-Jenkins, 1996).

Social class has been theorized from two perspectives. First, a structural approach refers to the macrostructural framework that includes sociohistorical contexts (e.g., the baby boom generation, the Great Depression, 9/11), the structure of economic opportunities, and global organization and immigration patterns (Baca Zinn & Wells, 2000). This dynamic view posits that broad-based social and economic structures produce and require a wide range of family forms that are needed to keep the global economic system functioning. For example, East Asian and South American families typically send male members of the family to the United States to work, and these workers send money home, thereby creating binational family systems. As well, Cubans who immigrated to the United States in 1959 came at the invitation of the host government, and their immigration and assimilation experiences have contrasted greatly to those of other Latino/Hispanic groups due to the conditions of their arrival and their higher class status.

In contrast, a cultural approach to social class views class differences as the result of different, and thus deficient, cultural values. Structural factors tend to be ignored in a cultural values approach. For example, in analyzing Mexican-origin families, earlier research has positioned Mexican family traditionalism as the chief cause of Mexican subordination in the United States, thereby stereotypically and falsely portraying Mexican Americans "in simplistic terms of rigid male dominance and pathological clannishness" (Baca Zinn & Wells, 2000, p. 253). A cultural values approach does not view Mexican families in their own sociohistorical context but instead compares them to the mythical standard of White North American families (Smith, 1993), and finds them "other."

The major components of the social-class system include institutional processes that specify certain types of behaviors as valuable and desirable (e.g., owning land, running a business, being head of a household, having good manners, getting a formal education), rules of allocation that distribute these goods across occupations in the division of labor (e.g., surgeon, pilot, teacher, janitor, housewife), and mobility mechanisms (e.g., going to an elite prep school, being a first-generation immigrant; dropping out of high school in the ninth grade) that link individuals to occupations and create unequal control over valued resources (Grusky, 2001).

Gender and social-class relations in the Western world typically unfold in the context of an industrialized society (Grusky, 2001). Hughes and Perry-Jenkins (1996, p. 177) summarize six categories of social classes, and estimate the percentage of the U.S. population that roughly corresponds to each:

1. Capitalist class (e.g., investors, heirs, top executives): 1 percent

2. Upper middle class (e.g., university-trained professionals, managers): 14 percent

3. Middle class (e.g., white-collar, lower-level professionals, managers, skilled blue-collar workers): 30 percent

4. Working class (e.g., semiskilled blue-collar and low-level white-collar workers): 30 percent

5. Working poor (e.g., laborers, service workers): 20 percent

6. Underclass (e.g., unemployed or erratically employed): 5 percent

Occupational positions and the rewards attached to them are relatively stable, but the people who occupy them are constantly in flux, because people are always dying, retiring, or being replaced. In the United States, it is evident that the American class structure is moving in the direction of even greater inequality (Hughes & Perry-Jenkins, 1996) with the permanence of the underclass and poverty (Seccombe, 2000). Other industrialized nations have poverty rates that are one-half or one-quarter of those in the United States. In 1999, the U.S. Census Bureau reported that nearly 19 percent of children under the age of 18 lived below the poverty line; a disproportionate number of children who live in deep poverty are more likely to be impacted by race, gender, family structure, and parental education variations (Seccombe, 2000). Although the persistence and degree of poverty in the United States is strong, it is not stagnant. People move in and out of poverty, and public policies designed to ameliorate poverty change as well.

The Structural Embeddedness of Inequality

Inequality is produced by two types of matching processes. The jobs, occupations, and social roles in society are first matched to rewards packages of unequal value, and individual members of society are then allocated to the corresponding positions and rewarded (Grusky, 2001). The rewards packages are designed for those most valued in society: members of the dominant group, who are male, White, upper middle class, educated, Christian, heterosexual, married, fathers, healthy, and attractive (Goffman, 1963). They represent the mythical norm that members of nondominant groups, who are on the outside of power, know as "not me" (Lorde, 1984, p. 116).

It takes generations for members of nondominant group—those other than White, Anglo-European, heterosexual males—to accumulate wealth and prestige in the United States, as Zweigenhaft and Domhoff (1998) found in their analysis of the movement of women, ethnic minorities (Jews, African Americans, Asian Americans, Hispanics, and Native Americans) and gay men and lesbians into prestigious positions in government and corporate America, including federal cabinet posts, the U.S. Congress, and industry and university administration. Only those of Jewish origin, who compose 2 percent of the U.S. population, have come close to being fully integrated into the U.S. power elite, and they still face social and religious barriers. The other minority groups in Zweigenhaft and Domhoff's study still confront major structural barriers, which have been referred to, for women, as "the glass ceiling" and "a wall of tradition and stereotype" that separates women from the top executive level (Morrison, White, & Van Velsor, 1992).

Methodological Issues in Conceptualizing Class

Research on family diversity within cultural groups is still sparse (Hughes & Perry-Jenkins, 1996). This issue has long been recognized in the way that the vast diversity of Asian Americans are often collapsed into a single group, as if Japanese, Chinese, Korean, Filipino, and the more than 28 other subgroups who compose the overall group of people from the Pacific Rim can be categorized as a uniform whole on the assumption of common ethnic origins in Asia, similar physical appearance, and similar cultural values. Instead, as Ishii-Kuntz (2000) explains, the "classification of a multitude of groups under the single rubric of Asian American masks important differences among and within groups" (p. 274).

Recently, as well, American Indian tribal nations have reestablished sovereignty and returned to traditional practices and language usages, opening new possibilities and challenges for family researchers. As Letiecq and Bailey (2004) observe, tribal languages may differ as much linguistically from one another as English does from Japanese; gaining access and understanding are but two of the logistical issues researchers face in doing research on the reservation.

Sampling issues are also apparent when considering that there are often few comparison groups in research examining class. Researchers often use gender and class as control variables when analyzing data (Cuadraz & Uttal, 1999). Feminist researchers criticize the use of these categories to define group membership, especially since it separates and categorizes women of different classes and races. Even when samples are compared, class and gender are difficult to break down. For example, Woo (1985) sampled White and Asian American women and found no differences in family income levels. After a breakdown of the data, it was evident that Asian American women reported more people in their households contributing to income, and they also had more education for jobs at the same level. This information would not show up in a simple analysis of what women reported as their family income.

Social Class, Family Life, and Childrearing Values

Social class and family life are intricately connected. Kohn's (1977) investigations of parents' occupational positions and approaches to self-direction and conformity in children best illustrates the intersection of family and class. Social class is most effectively conceptualized as a *continuum* of positions, with no sharp demarcations (Hughes & Perry-Jenkins, 1996). Kohn measured class by two indicators: education and occupational position. Note that other researchers use three indicators: education, occupation, and income. Perry-Jenkins and Folk (1994) observe that in certain family situations, such as dual-earner households, it is imperative to separate income from occupation in order to assess the combined effects of both partners' class levels, especially if a middle-class spouse is married to a working-class spouse.

Grounded in Kohn's theoretical perspective on class, Lareau (2003) conducted an ethnographic study of middle- and working-class children in Black and White families. Participant observers typically spent three-hour daily shifts with each of 12 families, videotaping and tape recording interactions, conversations, and in-depth interviews, and collecting detailed field notes in three primary areas: the organization of daily life, the use of language, and the interactions between families and institutions. Among the findings were the intense stress levels in the households, including yelling, screaming, and in some cases physical violence. At the same time, all families were engaged in the daily effort to improve their quality of life. Concerning class divisions, working-class and poor homes provided children with greater personal freedom for self-directed childhood experiences, with little cultivation of adult behaviors. This led to missed opportunities for these less advantaged children to develop the expanded sense of self that predicts success in adulthood. Middle-class homes were much more hectic, and children's lives were more fully organized and overscheduled. This led to a kind of parental micromanaging but perhaps better equipped children with the opportunities to acquire advanced skills for dealing with career and personal relationships in adulthood.

Intersections of Gender and Class in Family Studies: New Directions

Family scholars are challenged by the increasing structural and cultural diversity of our society. Three critical and exciting areas of contemporary research are new immigrant families, changing meanings of marriage, and the dynamic nature of social class over the family life course.

Gender and Class Variations Among New Immigrant Families

The traditional gender roles of many new immigrant families are challenged by opportunities for economic and educational advancement. The United States offers women a chance to break tradition and enter the workforce. Zhou and Bankston (2001) examined the effects of these economic opportunities for Vietnamese immigrant families. They found that Vietnamese American girls want to further their education not to break gender roles but to become socially mobile. Fathers of these girls were supportive, since they believed it would benefit the family monetarily. Baker (2004) studied Mexican American women who immigrated to the United States to work. These women recognized that a woman who worked was breaking the traditional gender-role behaviors of her culture, but they also believed that by having appropriate goals—reuniting with their families and working for their children's future—they were maintaining their gender-role ideology.

A larger percentage of Arab American women are educated than those in the Middle East, and they have higher employment rates as well (Marshall & Read, 2003). The influence of education and acculturation into American society has given women more power to challenge traditional gender dynamics. As a woman achieves educational and economic advantages, she has more power to challenge male authority. Women lower in educational and economic power may find solace in traditional male authority or feel powerless to change their circumstances.

In the example of recently immigrated Arab American men and women, gender and class intersect with culture, acculturation, and political context, as Beitin and Allen found in their research on couple resilience in the wake of responses to terrorism (2005). Some Arab American women are constrained by centuries of patriarchy and oppression in environments where men believe it is acceptable to physically abuse wives when they are not conforming to traditional roles (Haj-Yahia, 2000). A husband's position as head of the family gives him considerable power. These gendered expectations are instilled from birth, and sons and daughters are treated differently.

Social Class and the New Meanings of Marriage

Over the last century, marriage has become deinstitutionalized (Cherlin, 2004). That is, marriage has become disentangled from trends in cohabitation, sexual relations, and parenting. The model for achieving intimacy that was considered standard for the middle-class nuclear family in American society at the mid-twentieth century—first marriage and then parenthood—and that has become idealized and encoded (Smith, 1993) is not now practiced by most adults. Although this model is idealized and valued by members of the poorer classes, they do not typically have the economic stability to support lifelong marriage; cohabitation and informal unions are substituted as a practical reality. Members of the upper classes have always had the economic means to flout convention as they desired, since marriage has been, historically, an economic arrangement (Cherlin, 2004).

Heterosexuals accomplished this world historical transformation of marriage (Coontz, 2004). At this time of gay men and lesbians struggling for legal recognition of their unions and having achieved it in countries such as Canada, the United States still lags behind. The real revolution in marriage was in its transformation from an institution of economics to one based on love (Coontz, 2004). People in modern societies are requiring a therapeutic quality to their relationships (Giddens, 1992). Ironically, as Coontz observes, just as gay men and lesbians are struggling for the legal rights to protect their vulnerable family ties, intimate relationships between men and women are more about being friends and lovers and less about legal property rights.

Gender and Class Differences Within Families

Many older adults are better off than their adult children and young adult grandchildren, signaling a new form of class differences within families. Grandparents are helping their children pay for their grandchildren's college tuitions, private schools, and summer camps and are providing other subsidies for their children's standard of living. Aid exchange traveled up the generations 30 years ago, with the younger generation expected to provide care for the older generation. With recent economic setbacks, the younger generation has not been able to accumulate wealth (Lewin, 2005). In many families, grandparents have emerged as an important source of economic and emotional support and stability (Bengtson, Biblarz, & Roberts, 2002).

Changes in later adulthood are related to the elongation of the period of youth, leading scholars to suggest a new "young young adulthood" between adolescence and young adulthood (Furstenberg, 2000). Many young adults who once left the parental nest are moving back home. This is after a period of time that they have gone off to college and are finding that they cannot support themselves at the standard of living in which their wealthier parents raised them (Aquilino, 1997). Even within the same families, pluralism is increasing, as predicted by individualization theory (Beck & Beck-Gernsheim, 2002). In his quantitative research on young adults and their parents, Aquilino (1994) observed that we're looking at a future of older men who are potentially socially isolated, given their history of marital instability in their younger years.

Conclusions and Directions for Future Research and Practice

In conclusion, we return to Jamie and Tracey. What would they be thinking if they sat down together and read this chapter? What if they read it out loud together, and said the words "sexism, classism, racism" to each other? How have their families informed their beliefs about gender, class, and race? What have they learned about systems of oppression, privilege, inequality, and double consciousness? How do gender and social class intersect in predictable and unpredictable ways? How do women and men manage to have agency, when so much seems stacked against the individual's ability to take positive action on behalf of social change? In what ways do you, as a reader, feel empowered to act on behalf of self and other, armed with the knowledge that it is important to reflect on how oppression and privilege intersect in your own life?

Implications for future research and practice are exciting, because we are concerned with individuals in their most intimate relational contexts— families, households, and intergenerational commitments. From a social constructionist perspective, *transformative dialogue* holds great promise for therapeutic, educational, and political practice, as we cocreate new worlds of meaning and understanding (Gergen, 1999). This perspective provides a way of thinking that allows us to *be curious* about others, without necessarily having to give up our own fundamental values. In asking our questions, we open ourselves to new possibilities and new windows of understanding about self and other. What are the unresolved issues in your own life? What questions would you like to ask someone who seems different from you?

From a feminist perspective, intersectionality and the perspective of simultaneous dislocation is a liberating idea for theory and method in terms of not making people choose only one social location on which to focus. How can I choose my gender over my class or race, as if one were the most exclusive unit of analysis? Similarly, how can we understand how and why women *and* men collude in maintaining women's double burden of work in housework and in the paid labor force if we do not simultaneously consider the multiple layers of advantage and disadvantage that are socially structured and mutually constructed in intimate relationships? These are but a few of the exciting research directions and avenues for change to explore in family science when considering a gender and class lens for culturally diverse families.

References

Allen, K. R. (2000). A conscious and inclusive family studies. *Journal of Marriage and the Family, 62*, 4–17.

Aquilino, W. S. (1994). Impact of childhood family disruption on young adults' relationships with parents. *Journal of Marriage and the Family, 56*, 295–313.

Aquilino, W. S. (1997). From adolescent to young adult: A prospective study of parent-child relations during the transition to adulthood. *Journal of Marriage and the Family, 59*, 670–686.

Baca Zinn, M., & Wells, B. (2000). Diversity within Latino families: New lessons for family social science. In D. H. Demo, K. R. Allen, & M. A. Fine (Eds.), *Handbook of family diversity* (pp. 252–273). New York: Oxford University Press.

Baker, P. (2004). "It is the only way I can survive": Gender paradox among recent Mexicana immigrants to Iowa. *Sociological Perspectives, 47*, 393–408.

Beck, U., & Beck-Gernsheim, E. (2002). *Individualization: Institutionalized individualism and its social and political consequences*. London: Sage.

Beitin, B. K., & Allen, K. R. (2005). Resilience in Arab American couples after September 11, 2001: A systems perspective. *Journal of Marital and Family Therapy, 31*, 251–267.

Bengtson, V. L., Biblarz, T. J., & Roberts, R. E. L. (2002). *How families still matter: A longitudinal study of youth in two generations*. Cambridge, UK: Cambridge University Press.

Calasanti, T. (2004). Feminist gerontology and old men. *Journal of Gerontology: Social Sciences, 59B*, S305–S314.

Chafetz, J. S. (2004). Bridging feminist theory and research methodology. *Journal of Family Issues, 25*, 963–977.

Cheal, D. (2002). *Sociology of family life*. London: Palgrave.

Cherlin, A. J. (2004). The deinstitutionalization of American marriage. *Journal of Marriage and Family, 66*, 848–861.

Collins, P. H. (1990). *Black feminist thought: Knowledge, consciousness, and the politics of empowerment*. Boston: Unwin Hyman.

Collins, P. H. (1998). *Fighting words: Black women and the search for justice*. Minneapolis: University of Minnesota Press.

Coontz, S. (2004). The world historical transformation of marriage. *Journal of Marriage and Family, 66*, 974–979.

Cuadraz, G. H., & Uttal, L. (1999). Intersectionality and in-depth interviews: Methodological strategies for analyzing race, class, and gender. *Race, Gender and Class, 6,* 156–186.

Daniels, A. K. (1987). Invisible work. *Social Problems, 34,* 403–415.

Delamont, S. (2003). *Feminist sociology.* London: Sage.

De Reus, L. A., Few, A. L., & Blume, L. B. (2005). Multicultural and critical race feminisms: Theorizing families in the third wave. In V. L. Bengtson, A. C. Acock, K. R. Allen, P. Dilworth-Anderson, & D. M. Klein (Eds.), *Sourcebook of family theory and research* (pp. 447–468). Thousand Oaks, CA: Sage.

DeVault, M. (1991). *Feeding the family: The social organization of caring as gendered work.* Chicago: University of Chicago Press.

Du Bois, W. E. B. (1996). *The souls of black folk.* New York: Penguin. (Original work published 1903)

Ferree, M. M. (1990). Feminism and family research. *Journal of Marriage and the Family, 52,* 866–884.

Furstenberg, F. F. (2000). The sociology of adolescence and youth in the 1990s: A critical commentary. *Journal of Marriage and the Family, 62,* 896–910.

Gergen, K. J. (1999). *An invitation to social construction.* London: Sage.

Giddens, A. (1992). *The transformation of intimacy: Sexuality, love and eroticism in modern societies.* Palo Alto, CA: Stanford University Press.

Goffman, E. (1963). *Stigma: Notes on the management of spoiled identity.* New York: Simon & Schuster.

Grusky, D. B. (2001). The past, present, and future of social inequality. In D. B. Grusky (Ed.), *Social stratification: Class, race, and gender in sociological perspective* (pp. 3–51). Boulder, CO: Westview Press.

Haj-Yahia, M. (2000). Wife abuse and battering in the sociocultural context of Arab society. *Family Process, 39,* 237–255.

hooks, b. (1995). *Killing rage: Ending racism.* New York: Henry Holt.

Hughes, R., Jr., & Perry-Jenkins, M. (1996). Social class issues in family life education. *Family Relations, 45,* 175–182.

Ishii-Kuntz, M. (2000). Diversity within Asian American families. In D. H. Demo, K. R. Allen, & M. A. Fine (Eds.), *Handbook of family diversity* (pp. 274–292). New York: Oxford University Press.

Kohn, M. (1977). *Class and conformity: A study in values* (2nd ed.). Chicago: University of Chicago Press.

Lareau, A. (2003). *Unequal childhoods: Class, race, and family life.* Berkeley: University of California Press.

Letiecq, B. L., & Bailey, S. J. (2004). Evaluating from the outside: Conducting cross-cultural evaluation research on an American Indian reservation. *Evaluation Review, 28,* 342–357.

Lewin, T. (2005, July 14). Financially set grandparents help keep families afloat, too. *New York Times,* pp. A1, A22.

Lorde, A. (1984). *Sister outsider: Essays and speeches.* Freedom, CA: Crossing Press.

Marshall S., & Read, J. (2003). Identity politics among Arab American women. *Social Science Quarterly, 84,* 875–891.

Morrison, A. M., White, R. P., Van Velsor, E., & The Center for Creative Leadership. (1992). *Breaking the glass ceiling: Can women reach the top of America's largest corporations?* (updated ed.). Reading, MA: Addison-Wesley.

Odeh, L. A. (2003). Post-colonial feminism and the veil: Thinking the difference. In M. Gergen & K. J. Gergen (Eds.), *Social construction: A reader* (pp. 216–225). London: Sage.

Perry-Jenkins, M., & Folk, K. (1994). Class, couples and conflict: Effects of the division of labor on assessments of marriage in dual-earner families. *Journal of Marriage and the Family, 56,* 165–180.

Reinharz, S. (1992). *Feminist methods in social research.* New York: Oxford University Press.

Seccombe, K. (2000). Families in poverty in the 1990s: Trends, causes, consequences and lessons learned. *Journal of Marriage and the Family, 62,* 1094–1113.

Smith, D. E. (1987). *The everyday world as problematic: A feminist sociology.* Boston: Northeastern University Press.

Smith, D. E. (1993). The standard North American family: SNAF as an ideological code. *Journal of Family Issues, 14,* 50–65.

Thompson, L., & Walker, A. J. (1995). The place of feminism in family studies. *Journal of Marriage and the Family, 57,* 847–865.

Tillmann-Healy, L. M. (1996). A secret life in a culture of thinness: Reflections on body, food, and bulimia. In C. Ellis & A. P. Bochner (Eds.), *Composing ethnography: Alternative forms of qualitative writing* (pp. 76–108). Walnut Creek, CA: AltaMira Press.

Walker, A. J. (1999). Gender and family relationships. In M. Sussman, S. K. Steinmetz, & G. W. Peterson (Eds.), *Handbook of marriage and the family* (2nd ed., pp. 439–474). New York: Plenum.

Westcott, M. (1979). Feminist criticism of the social sciences. *Harvard Educational Review, 49,* 422–430.

Woo, D. (1985). The socioeconomic status of Asian American women in the labor force. *Sociological Perspectives, 28,* 307–338.

Zhou, M., & Bankston, C. L. (2001). Family pressure and the educational experience of the daughters of Vietnamese refugees. *International Migration, 39*(4), 133–151.

Zweigenhaft, R. L., & Domhoff, G. W. (1998). *Diversity in the power elite: Have women and minorities reached the top?* New Haven, CT: Yale University Press.

5

Trends in Marriage and Cohabitation

Bahira Sherif Trask and Julie M. Koivunen

As the United States becomes increasingly diverse, individuals of varying backgrounds are interacting and negotiating issues that even 30 years ago most people assumed to be clear-cut. In the family arena, one of the most complicated and controversial topics today is marriage. There is little general agreement about who should be permitted to marry (heterosexuals versus homosexuals), the steps leading up to marriage (sexuality, cohabitation, and out-of-wedlock births), and expectations once married (children, gender roles, work versus family, and divorce).

While marriage and its conceptualization have become much more contentious, it remains a significant institution in the United States. Although some observe a retreat from marriage in the United States, demographics indicate that marriage has not lost its powerful ideological significance (Cherlin, 2004). The United States leads the rest of the industrialized world in terms of marriage rates and, according to the U.S. Census Bureau, approximately 90 percent of Americans will eventually marry. What has changed, however, is that individuals are waiting longer to marry, they may cohabit at some point, and they may divorce with greater ease.

Recent research indicates that across races, ethnicities, and sexual orientations, the ideal of marriage remains significant to a majority of both men and women but that members of some racial and ethnic groups may not always have access to appropriate marital partners (Crowder & Tolnay, 2000). Nonetheless, the attributes of marriage are changing. Historically, marriage signified the formation of a new household unit, the initiation of a sexual relationship, and the birth of children. With the increasing social acceptance of premarital sex, cohabitation, childbirth outside of marriage, and same-sex partnerships, the fundamental aspects of this institution have been separated and, for some, redefined.

The problems of what marriage is and of how individuals of different races, ethnicities, sexual orientations, and educational and class backgrounds perceive and practice marriage is more complex than is often acknowledged. Anthropologists have long documented that some form of a marital relationship, a public acknowledgment of a couple's relationship, exists in all societies. As such, marriage takes on multiple forms. But this cross-cultural knowledge is rarely acknowledged in the family literature. Studies and discussions about marriage center on the definition and legal aspects of marriage and often ignore that marriage is a societal institution that is dynamic and subject to change over time. Furthermore, the heterogeneity of the U.S. population coupled with significant regional differences suggests that individuals of different ages and backgrounds may have quite varied perceptions of marriage. Who we believe to be appropriate and inappropriate partners and what we believe to be acceptable or unacceptable behaviors with respect to the marital process are the products of multiple factors including our families, culture, religion, media, social contacts, and various other pervasive factors such as technology and globalization. Furthermore, our own outlook may change as a result of personal experiences and the ever-shifting nature of our culture. This explains, at least in part, why as a society we are surrounded by a complex and variable array of attitudes and values with respect to the definition, meaning, and utility of marriage.

The Issue of Sample Populations

Up to this point, there is scant research examining the links between cultural diversity and marriage. The problem central to the study of all aspects of culturally diverse families is also inherent in the marriage literature. The major focus of marital research has focused on White European American families with some recent contrasting work on African Americans. The findings have then been generalized to the rest of the U.S. population (Bean, Crane, & Lewis, 2002; McLoyd, Cauce, Takeuchi, & Wilson, 2000).

Despite the changing demographics of our society and the awareness in the scholarly community of the implications of these changes, there is a significant dearth of work on marriage among various Hispanic, Asian, and Indian American families (McLoyd et al., 2000). Other culturally diverse peoples such as Armenians, Arabs, Turks, and Eastern Europeans are subsumed under the census heading "White non-Hispanic," and are, thus, often not specifically accounted for in marital research. Scholarship on marriage often glosses over class and ethnic differences by concentrating on racial categories instead of delineating the specific population that may be under study. For example, we also know very little about the relationship between religion and marriage. The reliance on racial typologies serves to subsume these complex fundamental differences that could give us a very different picture of how marriage is conceptualized and practiced in different groups.

This lack of differentiation leads to generalizations, even about White families, and misses the many meanings and practices of marriage that coexist in our society. The following discussion of cohabitation and marriage reflects some of the biases in the literature. This chapter concentrates on issues of demographics, cohabitation, marital quality, same-sex relationships, power, communication, and divorce. A more nuanced discussion of gender roles and the division of household labor is found in the following chapter on the relationship between work and family.

Demographics

The bulk of research on the relationship between cultural diversity and marriage has focused on trends in structural changes of families among various racial groups. Of particular interest has been the overall decline in the rate of marriage and later age at first marriage accompanied by the phenomenon of higher proportions of unwed mothers, higher percentages of mother-only or father-only families, and higher numbers of families living in poverty (McLoyd et al., 2000).

The census breakdown by racial and ethnic group indicates an uneven distribution with respect to marriage trends. In 2001, approximately 62 percent of non-Hispanic Whites and Asians, 60 percent of Hispanics, and 42 percent of African Americans were married (U.S. Census Bureau, 2001). Statistics for the same year indicate that 8 percent of Black men and 7 percent of Black women aged 55 and older had never married, in contrast to White men at 4 percent and White women also at 4 percent. Among Asians, approximately 2 percent of men and 6 percent of women were unmarried, while Latinos were at 5 percent for men and 7 percent for women.

Much of the research on marriage and cultural diversity has focused on trends among African American families. Since 1970, these patterns include the decline in two-parent families from 68 percent in 1970 to 42 percent in 2000, the doubling of divorce rates, and a rise in the proportion of children being brought up in single-parent households (Teachman, Tedrow, & Crowder, 2000). In terms of age of marriage, African Americans tend to marry later and have higher rates of divorce than Whites (Sweeney & Phillips, 2004). Furthermore, parental status does not play a role: The marriage gap between Whites and Blacks remains equally strong whether or not a Black woman has children.

Recent scholarship points primarily to demographic and economic explanations for these trends. Currently there are a disproportionate number of African American women available in relation to men, especially during the marital age bracket of 20–49 years, the time when women are most likely to marry. Based on an economic explanation, Black women are not marrying because there is a lack of eligible partners; that is, those who have an education and a job. Changes in the labor market have created unfavorable employment conditions that prohibit men from becoming economic providers and, thus, make them less eligible on the marriage market (Ooms, 2002). It is important to note that African Americans are not against marriage, and in fact hold strong marital ideals. Instead, differences in marital patterns are determined primarily by economic differences among various groups. Among African Americans, marital patterns closely correlate to class. Middle-class and upper-class families are much more likely to be headed by a married, usually dual-income, husband-wife team (Hirschl, Altobelli, & Rank, 2003; White & Rogers, 2000).

Notable in the marital literature is that family demographers have given considerable attention to differences in marriage rates between Black and White women but not to the race gap between Black and White men (Raley, 2002). Yet, the gap with respect to being unmarried is considerably smaller for Black men at 16 percent than for Black women at 26.9 percent (Raley, 2002, p. 774). Possible explanations include that men still have an easier time finding marriage partners due to power differentials that exist in our society with respect to gender differences and marriageability.

Statistically, some similar trends are found among Latinos: There has been a significant increase in female-headed families, to about 31.2 percent of all Latino families in 1998; they are less likely to be married than Whites or Asians; a single parent is more likely to be the head of the household; and they are more likely to become parents at younger ages. These trends, however, are not consistent among Latino subgroups. Instead, we find a great deal of variation across class and national origin. For example, female-headed households are twice as common among Puerto Rican Americans as they are among Mexican and Cuban Americans. Interestingly, Cuban women tend to be older than their other Hispanic counterparts when having children and have the lowest fertility rates (U.S. Census Bureau, 2001).

Another change in the Hispanic population is the projected future composition of this group. Presently, about 40 percent is foreign-born due to patterns of increasing immigration (Suro & Passel, 2003). However, over the next few years, fertility will begin to supersede immigration as the basis for Hispanic population growth. This trend indicates that it will become increasingly important to study generational differences as well as attitudes toward marriage and the process of assimilation, such as intermarriage, across generational lines.

When it comes to Asian American families, it is equally difficult to discuss general trends. While the average Asian American household contains 3.3 members (in contrast to White households that average 2.5 members and Hispanic households at 3.5), there is much variation depending on group. For example, on average, Vietnamese households are estimated at 4.0, while other Southeast Asian households such as those of Cambodians, Hmong, and Laotians contain approximately 5.1 persons. These figures stand in contrast to figures for Japanese Americans who have an average of only 2.5 members per household (McLoyd et al., 2000). Larger household size among Asian Americans is correlated with the presence of extended family members such as grandparents, cousins, aunts, and uncles. These individuals play important roles in these families but are often ignored in both research and policy decisions, since they do not fit a Eurocentric notion of who constitutes the core family.

Other distinguishing features of Asian American families are that the women in them tend to be foreign-born, have a higher average educational level than women in families of other groups, and are the least likely to have a child outside of marriage. These trends are likely to be interrelated and may explain the low incidence of out-of-wedlock births among Asian Americans. However, as Southeast Asian women are having more children than either Chinese or Japanese Americans, the demographic picture of Asian Americans will change. Notable also is that South Asian Indian Americans, while playing an increasingly significant role in certain facets of U.S. culture, are subsumed under the Asian category, even though their religious affiliations are usually Hindu and Muslim, which indicates that, at times, they may exhibit different cultural patterns in marital and family customs.

Indian American families are probably the most understudied group by family scientists. Currently about 62 percent of families are maintained by married couples, 30 percent by women with no husband living in the household, and 2 percent by men with no wife present. Almost 24 percent of children, similar to those in Black and Asian households, live in extended families (Fields, 2003). Beyond these census figures, we know virtually nothing about the dynamics of marriages among the various Indian American groups.

Theoretical Approaches Used to Understand Cohabitation and Marriage

Much of the research on marriage is dominated either explicitly or implicitly by a structuralist perspective and concepts of social exchange. Structuralism, which gained its greatest momentum in the 1960s, advocates that role distribution, and specifically clearly defined gender roles, is a fundamental aspect of marriage. While this perspective has dropped out of favor in recent years, implicit assumptions about appropriate roles and tasks continue to pervade much of the marriage literature.

Social Exchange Theory

Recently, cohabitation and marriage have been studied much more extensively from a social exchange perspective. The central component of this approach assumes that human behavior is fundamentally self-interested and that interactions with others are sought primarily to maximize rewards and minimize costs. From this perspective, cohabiting and marital relationships are based on levels of attraction, the availability of alternative relationships, and dependence between the partners (Sabatelli & Ripoll, 2004). Social and cultural elements influence both the types of resources that partners bring to their relationship and also what is seen as a fair or advantageous exchange. Relationships become unstable when the exchange becomes uneven; that is, when one or both partners feel that they are not maximizing their rewards and they are not as dependent on one another (Carroll, Knapp, & Holman, 2005).

Feminist Theories or Frameworks

In the field of marriage research, new directions have been proposed primarily through feminist theorizing. Feminist analysis has served to reveal aspects of marriage that remained hidden with more traditional positivist approaches (Thompson, 1993). For example, feminists advocate that traditional marriages with a homemaker wife and breadwinner husband serve to reinforce the patriarchal order; prevent women from being acknowledged for their contributions to the family, the community, and the larger society; and often have negative consequences for women with respect to financial, emotional, and physical factors (Blaisure & Allen, 1995).

Feminist approaches have also allowed researchers to pursue the question of why certain forms of social organization continue to dominate and why mainstream practices may not represent the voices of all members of our society. Through feminist analysis, we now know that there is a great deal of variation in cohabiting and marital behaviors between and within groups. We also now recognize that we are only at the beginning of understanding the impact of these differences on the larger society and for individual couples.

Cohabitation

Since the 1970s there has been a great deal of scholarly debate about the role of cohabitation with respect to marriage. Is cohabitation a stage in the courtship process leading to marriage, or is it a separate institution functioning as an alternative to marriage? However, while similar on the surface, cohabitation and marriage are not the same phenomenon. Cohabitation is a shared union between two individuals based on private feelings. Marriage is a public institution governed by overt rules and laws about the rights and responsibilities of its members. Framing the debate as a unified concept diverts attention from the multitude of cohabiting experiences that can encompass same-sex couples, young college-age students, middle-aged individuals with children, and older adults. Furthermore, cohabitation may range from a short-term arrangement to a long-term union with all the shared economic and parenting responsibilities that are present in marriage.

Based on a racial breakdown, African Americans and Indian Americans are most likely to cohabit with rates at about 17 percent for each group. The lowest rates of cohabitation are found among Asian Americans at about 5 percent while Whites are at about 8.2 percent and Latinos at 12.2 percent (Simmons & O'Connell, 2003). These statistics, however, mask a multitude of interrelated complicated issues with respect to why different groups exhibit such dramatically varied behaviors.

Patterns of Cohabitation

Current research indicates that three-quarters of cohabiting women expect to marry their partners (Manning & Smock, 2002); however, only about one-third of those living together marry within a three-year time period (Bumpass, 1995). Research also indicates that patterns of cohabitation and marriage differ among different groups. For example, Whites who cohabit are much more likely to marry than are Blacks. Two-thirds of White cohabiting women eventually marry their partners, while only 10 percent of cohabiting Black women do (Manning & Smock, 1995). Furthermore, should a pregnancy result, Whites are much more likely to marry than are Blacks (Manning, 1993). Interestingly, employment plays a role in marriage decisions too. For example, if both individuals in a Black couple are working, they are more likely to marry. The same is not true in White couples, specifically if the woman is not working (Manning & Smock, 1995).

These findings suggest that cohabitation has different meanings among Whites and Blacks; among Whites it is often a transitional step to marriage, while among some Blacks it functions as a substitute for marriage. Similar findings have been found among certain Hispanic groups. For example, Puerto Rican women tend to view cohabitation as a substitute for marriage. These findings, however, need to be contextualized. Research indicates that many Black and Latino women, in particular, place a high value on marriage and feel that cohabitation is morally wrong. This would indicate that there are other factors than race and ethnicity at work in the decision to cohabitate. While often ignored, the economic situation of couples contributes immensely to the choice of cohabitation over marriage. Economic opportunities for men and skewed sex ratios in populations where there are more women than men seem to contribute to the phenomenon of higher cohabitation rates among certain racial and ethnic groups.

Research on this topic for other ethnic and cultural groups is virtually nonexistent. Since so many Asian cultures do not favor cohabitation, it would be instructive to examine if there are class variations among these groups as well.

Gender Roles and Marital Quality in Marriage

Most research on gender roles, marital quality, and marital processes among culturally diverse marriages has been on White and Black families. We are only now beginning to see some interest in marriage scholarship on Latinos, and research on Asian Americans remains scarce at best. In fact, as McLoyd et al. (2000) point out, statistical differences between Asian Americans and other groups are often explained through cultural interpretations that have not been verified through systematic empirical observations.

Division of Labor

One of the most popular discussions in terms of gender and the family involves the division of labor in the home. Research on racial differences in gender roles reveals differences between African American and White men with respect to their participation in household work. For example, John and Shelton (1997) report that African American men spend an average of 21.7 hours per week engaged in housework, while White men spend an average of 17.8 hours per week participating in household labor. This finding is supported by other authors who report that Black men participate more frequently in childcare and household work than do White men (Blee & Tickamyer, 1995). The increase in Black men's participation may be attributed to the belief of African American women that their employment outside the home is part of their familial obligation, and thus the men are expected to participate evenly in household tasks as well (Piotrkowski & Hughes, 1993). Different life experiences in White and Black families may account for differences in gender roles and gender attitudes as well as the more equitable participation in household labor in African American marriages.

Marital Dynamics and Communication

There have been various studies that have documented the differences in gender roles and housework participation in different cultures. In one study, Lim (1997) examined working Korean women's experiences in attempting to decrease the unequal division of labor in the home. The author suggests that "a sense of unfairness develops when they feel their lives relatively more burdened than their husbands'. With a sense of injustice, wives attempt to change the unequal division of family work by demand or appeal to their husbands" (p. 41). Despite the tendency for more traditional gender roles in Korean culture, the women respectfully challenged gender inequality within the home through expressing their opinions and a growing sense of entitlement.

In another study that addresses cultural differences in marital dynamics, Hampson, Beavers, and Hulgus (1990) discuss different interactional patterns in White, Black, and Mexican American families. They argue that their findings are "consistent with and supportive of the hypothesis that any differences found between ethnic groups are likely to be differences in style of structure or interaction rather than differences in competence or health" (p. 316). They report in their study that Black families expressed fewer feelings and thoughts in a verbally direct or clear manner and were higher in sanctioning the expression of positive over negative feelings as compared to

White or Mexican American families. Also, Mexican American families were more likely than White or Black families to allow the most expression of dependency needs and to emphasize emotional bonding between family members (Hampson et al., 1990).

The authors believe their findings may be useful for a greater understanding of marital and familial dynamics among those from different ethnic backgrounds. Further, their data "encourage the view that for families of all ethnic backgrounds, subtle ethnic and social class differences exist, and imposing one's own ethnically influenced standards regarding clarity of expression, autonomy, egalitarianism, and even sex-role standards may limit efficacy" and be detrimental to a greater understanding of these different cultures (Hampson et al., 1990, p. 318).

Marital Quality Over Time

Over the past 25 years, research on marriage has been dominated by an emphasis on marital quality and observable patterns of interactions between couples. Much of this research has concentrated on identifying causes of marital conflict in order to help stabilize marriages (Gottman & Notarius, 2000). Marital quality is conceptualized as being composed of two primary factors— marital stability and marital satisfaction. These two components have been studied since the early 1940s, initially through self reporting on large-scale surveys and more recently through clinical observation (Carroll et al., 2005). It is important to note that the early studies on marital quality focused exclusively on White middle-class heterosexual samples, thus skewing interpretations of marital behavior among diverse groups.

In describing contemporary marriages, spousal satisfaction and relationship stability have remained the key factors in analyses (Karney & Bradbury, 1995). While observational research on marriages has yielded fascinating descriptions of marital interactions and marital problems, the marriage field is plagued by a lack of information about the underlying factors that influence marital processes and outcomes among various groups.

Marital Quality and the Transition to Parenthood

While changing societal trends in employment, gender equality, and income levels affect marital quality over time, other factors that relate to marital dynamics and interactions also may affect levels of marital satisfaction. For example, a study by Crohan (1996) explored the changes in marital quality and conflict that occur during the transition to parenthood for both White and African American couples. The results of the study indicate similar trends: Among White and African American couples, participants who had become parents by the third year had higher levels of tension in their marriages.

In regard to marital quality and couple interaction, the researcher found similar levels of conflict resolution among African American and White participants, but found that for women, destructive conflict behavior correlated with less happiness in the marriage (Crohan, 1996). The findings of the study indicate that more research is needed to gain a clearer understanding of the intersection of the transition to parenthood, marital stressors, and race and gender issues.

In a study on African American and European women's experiences of marital well-being, Goodwin (2003) studied a sample of 247 women and explored factors that influenced their relationships such as individual, interpersonal, economic, and social resources. She found that for both groups of women, equity and trust, which were considered interpersonal resources, and emotional health, an individual resource, predicted marital well-being. However, she found that among the African American women, their physical health and the closeness of their relationships to their in-laws also predicted an increase of marital well-being, whereas this was not the case for the White women in the sample. The author states, "Given the importance of strong family ties for support and guidance among African Americans, it is not surprising that in-law relations could affect marital functioning" (Goodwin, 2003, p. 558).

In their review of longitudinal studies on marriage and marital quality, Karney and Bradbury (1995) reviewed the 115 studies that have been published that address the issue of marital quality over time. Of the 68 independent samples in these studies, they found that only 8 percent draw from African American populations, and only 17 percent of the research includes a sample that is representative of the national population of those who are married. They found that 75 percent of the samples used in these studies consist primarily of those who are White and middle class. Again, this raises a question about the nature of the knowledge we *really* have about marital quality and satisfaction among culturally diverse families.

Power and Communication

The institution of marriage, characterized as a rigid institution defined by patriarchal norms, is undergoing a significant transformation. In particular, issues of power in marriage are being transformed through the greater level of education of women and the large numbers of women in the labor force around the world. In the household, power tends to take on multiple forms and can change and mutate over time. Sparse studies on power in the marriages of culturally diverse individuals indicate that old stereotypes are often falsely perpetuated due to inaccurate cultural explanations. Thus, for example, the portrayal of Hispanic families that are characterized by an all-powerful husband and a submissive wife have been reevaluated and found not to be representative of the current situation (Gutmann, 1996). Similarly, research on Muslim families relies on religious depictions of family life instead of indicating that there is a great deal of intragroup diversity (Sherif-Trask, 2004). We know little about the effects of immigration on marriage and power, but scant research indicates that migration requires flexibility in roles and decision-making in order for the couple to be successful in its new environment (Hondagneu-Sotelo, 1994, as discussed in Oropesa & Landale, 2004).

Power, and how it is realized in the gap between a culture's ideals and an individual's behavior, has been a focus in particular in the study of Chicano families. For example, Baca Zinn (1982) found important differences in the concept of *entre dicho y hecho* (between what is said and what is done). Interviews with Chicana women indicate that verbally they may support patriarchal ideologies; however, they do not abide by those rules in their daily lives. Instead, especially when women are employed in the labor force, they are likely to challenge their partners, make their own decisions, and in general defy their husbands (Baca Zinn, 1982; Williams, 1990).

Same-Sex Relationships

Currently, little is known about culturally diverse lesbian or gay couples. Scant research indicates that they are likely to experience prejudice and discrimination from two fronts simultaneously: heterosexuals and other gay and lesbian couples (Kurdek, 2004). Regionality plays a role in the development and maintenance of all gay and lesbian relationships, since some areas of the country, such as large urban places and the Northeast and West Coasts, are more accommodating of people with varying lifestyles. It is logical to assume that in these areas, diverse couples are also more likely to find communities of others with whom they share cultural, linguistic, or educational commonalities.

Culturally diverse, same-sex relationships are characterized by many of the same definitional and typological issues that plague a discussion of all culturally diverse families. In the case of same-sex relationships, the issue of boundary definition is wrought with even more complex dimensions pertaining to inherent prejudices with respect to sexuality. It is important to note that while distinctions such as heterosexuality, homosexuality, and lesbianism are politically and socially important, they are socially constructed constructs. From a social constructionist perspective, "Sexuality is situational and changeable, modified by day-to-day circumstances throughout the life course" (Blumstein & Schwartz, 1990, as quoted in Aulette, 2002, p. 173). How people identify themselves, the types of relationships they may have engaged in, and the question of whether they would like to be part of a same-sex relationship are just some of the variables.

Current debates about the legality of same-sex marriages indicate that certain segments of U.S. society are very uncomfortable with redefining marriage in any manner that is not strictly religious and restricts marriage to heterosexual partners. However, the legality of same-sex marriages in Canada, the Netherlands, and Germany indicates that Western societies are becoming more open to redefinitions of marriage even on a legal level. The public debates on this subject in the United States indicate that attitudes are changing, albeit slowly.

Interracial Marriage

As Oropesa and Landale (2004) point out, "The extent of intermarriage between racial/ethnic groups is a reflection of the social distance between them" (p. 911). Significantly, rates of intermarriage in the United States have increased, but not dramatically, in the past 30 years. In 1970, approximately 300,000 couples were identified as interracial. By 1990, this figure had jumped to 1.5 million and by 2000, to 3 million. This translates to approximately 1 percent of couples being interracial in 1970 and 5 percent in 2000 (Lee & Edmonston, 2005). The rise in interracial marriages can be attributed to both a growth in population and changing social mores that are more open to marriages across social lines. It is important to point out that until 1967, many states had antimiscegenation laws forbidding Whites from marrying either Blacks or Asians. The low number of interracial marriages especially among older demographic groups reflects these laws.

Currently, African Americans are the least likely to marry outside of their group. In 2000, approximately 7 percent of marriages among Blacks involved a Black spouse and an individual of a different race. Interestingly, African American women are the least likely to be in an interracial marriage and are about one-third as likely as African American men to marry someone from another race. Asians exhibit the opposite pattern: One-fifth of all married Asian women are married to someone of another race or ethnicity; this is more than double the rate among Asian men. According to census statistics, American Indians, Hawaiians, and individuals of mixed race have the highest interracial marriage rates (Lee & Edmonston, 2005). Data from the 2000 census indicate that the most common interracial marriages are between a person of "some other race" (usually refers to Hispanic) and a White spouse, a Black husband and a White wife, and a White husband and an American Indian wife. In sum, Asian women married to White husbands, along with these three other types of couples, represented 70 percent of all interracial couples in 2000.

Census data also indicate that it is more common for U.S.-born Asians and Hispanics to become involved in interracial marriages than for foreign-born individuals. For example, foreign-born Hispanic wives (87 percent) and foreign-born Hispanic husbands tend to be married to Hispanic spouses (92 percent). Furthermore, foreign-born individuals tend to marry someone from their county of origin. Among U.S. immigrants, of Mexicans born in their home country, 75 percent are married to other Mexicans; 69 percent of El Salvadorans and Dominicans are married to individuals from their native societies, and 79 percent of women born in Cuba are married to other Cubans. Similar figures exist for native-born Hispanics, with 65 percent of women and 78 percent of men having Hispanic spouses (Oropesa & Landale, 2004).

Intermarriage is dependent on a variety of factors including the availability of potential spouses, regionality, location, age, and education. For example, the higher the educational level of the partners, the greater is the potential for intermarriage. However, a study by Rosenblatt, Karis, and Powell (1995) revealed that interracial couples still face a great deal of obstacles. For example, individuals revealed that other people, including their own families, often treated them poorly upon learning of their interracial relationship. Others experienced prejudice and discrimination from church members, coworkers, and even the police, while a few cited the benefits of having married outside of their group.

There is much that is unknown about intermarriages. For example, we do not understand why the rates of intermarriage have been so slow to shift or how interracial and interethnic coupling affects marital processes, the retention of cultural traditions, assimilation, and the rearing of children. Trends such as cohabitation and out-of-wedlock fertility among culturally diverse families are also understudied and misunderstood. This is unfortunate, since these are growing trends not just in the White population but throughout American society, and greater insight would allow us to understand more about the dynamics of group formation and ethnic identity.

Divorce

While the divorce rate increased in the period between 1940 and 1998, this trend has slowed and leveled off in recent years. In a recent survey, Teachman et al. (2000) found that demographic trends in divorce are similar for Hispanic, African American, and White women. Statistics indicate that there was a sharp increase in the proportion of those aged 40–44 who were divorced from a first spouse between 1975 and 1990. For Hispanic women, the increase within this age group rose from less than 20 percent in 1980 to 27 percent in 1990. Among African Americans, the increase in those divorced rose from just under 30 percent in 1975 to 45 percent in 1990. Among Whites, there was an increase from 20 percent to 32 percent during the years of 1975 to 1985, and a slight increase from 32 percent to 35 percent from 1985 to 1990 (Teachman et al., 2000). A recent study by Schwartz and Finley (2005) sought to determine the role of ethnicity in moderating the consequences of divorce and how children perceive levels of parental involvement. The study included a diverse sample of participants—56 percent Hispanic, 24 percent White, 10 percent Black, 7 percent Asian, and 4 percent mixed ethnicity. The authors found that in examining father involvement upon parental divorce, participants noted lower levels of nurturant fathering among all ethnic groups in the study compared to those in intact families.

Immigration and Divorce Rates

In comparison to all other groups, Asian Americans are least likely to divorce; their divorce rates—meaning the percentage of the population that is divorced at any given time—are estimated at 4 percent for men and 4.7 percent for women, in contrast with rates for the general population of 8 percent for men and 10.3 percent for women. These statistics are somewhat deceptive, however. A decreased incidence of divorce is closely correlated with being foreign-born and having immigrated to the United States. Individuals who are born in the United States, whatever their country of origin, are much more likely to be divorced than those who are not native-born. These observations point to the significant role that cultural norms play in helping influence behavior. As divorce remains a stigmatized condition in many societies, this provides a plausible explanation for the relatively low incidence of divorce among immigrants. Furthermore, limited research indicates that often, unhappy couples will stay together for the sake of making the immigration experience work for the good of the whole family. By the second generation, other values, such as those attached to more individualistic actions, begin to pervade and influence marital and family behaviors.

Cultural Competence

Research on marriage and culturally diverse families reveals that it is extremely important not to draw implications and assumptions from group membership. Simplistic typologies that attempt to draw on general descriptions of groups explicitly and implicitly stereotype individuals without much attention to the problems that this may create. It is not useful, for example, to imply that all Latino or Muslim Middle Eastern families are patriarchal in nature. Some may be, but this will vary depending on country of origin, age of the family members at arrival in the United States, educational level, wealth, etc. For family service providers, teachers, and mental health administrators and other individuals who work with diverse groups, it is important to realize that there is as much intragroup variation as there is intergroup variation. The popular practice of employing typologies of cultures and characteristics of individual groups only serves to obscure the heterogeneous nature of the various segments of American society. Cultural competence becomes a more useful concept when individual differences within specific social contexts are acknowledged (Berg & Miller, 1992).

Recommendations for Future Research

A useful productive perspective for understanding cohabitation and marriage is an ecological systems framework. This allows researchers to account for the influence of historical, cultural, and environmental conditions in which phenomena occur. Relationships are defined and experienced based in great part on social placement and sociohistorical time. Contextual factors influence patterns of attraction and the structure, organization, and experience of relationships.

In studies of culturally diverse families, it is important to acknowledge that assimilation and acculturation are not a one-way process with immigrant groups being absorbed into the middle-class mainstream. Instead, assimilation is a dynamic two-way process whereby the larger culture is also affected by the new trends and values that are brought to it. We currently know very little about the relationship between assimilation, acculturation, and marital processes among underrepresented groups and immigrants in particular. To what extent have any of the cultural norms of these groups affected mainstream conceptions about marriage, cohabitation, and relationships in general? Also, the interplay between marriage and class is an understudied topic. We know that economics influence stressors in marriage. However, we do not have information about how middle-class, upper-middle-class, and wealthy diverse families conceive of cohabitation and marriage throughout the life cycle. There exists an implicit assumption in the literature that most culturally diverse families are poor and uneducated. However, the enormous variations between groups and within groups indicates that we must acknowledge that individuals at different points on the socioeconomic ladder may perceive and live out their relationships and marriages differently. We know that this is true for African Americans, with middle- and upper-class African American families closely resembling similarly situated White families. We do not have the same type of information for other groups in our society.

We also know very little about how religion intersects with group identity and marital issues. Are the marriages of Korean Christians in the United States similar to those of Korean Buddhists? What about secular Muslims from North Africa or Southeast Asia versus conservative Muslims from Iran? What about the issues of generational differences when it comes to cohabitation and to same-sex and heterosexual marriage? Are young Mexican Americans just as likely to marry young and have children as their parents? Recent information indicates that even for Mexicans, who have traditionally had one of the highest fertility rates in the United States, young women are choosing to limit the number of children born in marriage due to the costs associated with childrearing. This is altering projected demographic growth profiles for Mexicans.

In order for us to gain a better understanding of the relationship between marriage and cultural diversity, it is imperative that social scientists and, specifically, marriage researchers begin to ask new questions, examine intragroup variation, and account for context and socioeconomic positioning. This will provide the path to new understandings about the role of cultural diversity in the marital process.

References

Aulette, J. (2002). *Changing American families*. Boston: Allyn & Bacon.

Baca Zinn, M. (1982). Qualitative methods in family research: A look inside Chicano families. *California Sociologist, 5*(2), 58–79.

Bean, R. A., Crane, D. R., & Lewis, T. L. (2002). Basic research and implications for practice in family science: A content analysis and status report for U.S. ethnic groups. *Family Relations, 51*, 15–21.

Berg, I. K., & Miller, S. D. (1992). Working with Asian American clients: One person at a time. *Families in Society: The Journal of Contemporary Human Services, 17*, 356–363.

Blaisure, K. R., & Allen, K. R. (1995). Feminists and the ideology and practice of marital equality. *Journal of Marriage and the Family, 57*, 5–19.

Blee, K. M., & Tickamyer, A. R. (1995). Racial differences in men's attitudes about women's gender roles. *Journal of Marriage and the Family, 57,* 21–30.

Blumstein, P., & Schwartz, P. (1990). Intimate relationships and the creation of sexuality. In D. McWhirter, S. Sanders, & J. Reinisch (Eds.), *Homosexuality/ heterosexuality: Concepts of sexual orientation* (pp. 96–109). New York: Oxford University Press.

Bumpass, L. L. (1995). *The declining significance of marriage: Changing family life in the United States.* National Survey of Families and Households Working Paper No. 66. Madison: University of Wisconsin, Center for Demography and Ecology.

Carroll, J., Knapp, S., & Holman, T. (2005). Theorizing about marriage. In V. Bengtson, A. Acock, K. Allen, P. Dilworth-Anderson, & D. Klein (Eds.), *Sourcebook of family theory and research* (pp. 263–277). Thousand Oaks, CA: Sage.

Cherlin, A. J. (2004). *Public and private families: An introduction* (4th ed.). New York: McGraw-Hill.

Crohan, S. E. (1996). Marital quality and conflict across the transition to parenthood in African American and White couples. *Journal of Marriage and Family, 58,* 933–944.

Crowder, K. D. & Tolnay, S. E. (2000). A new marriage squeeze for Black women: The role of racial intermarriage by Black men. *Journal of Marriage and Family, 62,* 792–807.

Fields, J. (2003). *Children's living arrangements and characteristics: March 2002.* Current Population Reports, P20–547. Washington, DC: U.S. Census Bureau.

Goodwin, P. Y. (2003). African American and European women's marital well being. *Journal of Marriage and Family, 65,* 550–560.

Gottman, J. M., & Notarius, C. I. (2000). Decade review: Observing marital interaction. *Journal of Marriage and the Family, 62,* 927–947.

Gutmann, M. C. (1996). *The meanings of Macho: Being a man in Mexico City.* Berkeley: University of California Press.

Hampson, R. B., Beavers, W. R., & Hulgus, Y. (1990). Cross-ethnic family differences: Interactional assessment of White, Black, and Mexican-American families. *Journal of Marital and Family Therapy, 16,* 307–319.

Hirschl, T. A., Altobelli, J., & Rank, M. R. (2003). Does marriage increase the odds of affluence? Exploring the life course probabilities. *Journal of Marriage and Family, 65,* 927–938.

Hondagneu-Sotelo, P. (1994). *Gendered transitions: Mexican experiences of immigration.* Berkeley: University of California Press.

John, D., & Shelton, B. A. (1997). The production of gender among Black and White women and men: The case of household labor. *Sex Roles, 36,* 171–192.

Karney, B. R., & Bradbury, T. N. (1995). The longitudinal course of marital quality and stability: A review of theory, method and research. *Psychological Bulletin, 118,* 3–34.

Kurdek, L. (2004). Gay men and lesbians: The family context. In M. Coleman & L. Ganong (Eds.), *Handbook of contemporary families: Considering the past, contemplating the future* (pp. 96–115). Thousand Oaks, CA: Sage.

Lee, S. M., & Edmonston, B. (2005). New marriages, new families: U.S. racial and Hispanic intermarriage. *Population Bulletin, 60*(2), 3–36.

Lim, I. S. (1997). Korean immigrant women's challenge to gender inequality at home: The interplay of economic resources, gender, and family. *Gender and Society, 11,* 31–51.

Manning, W. D. (1993). Marriage and cohabitation following premarital conception. *Journal of Marriage and Family, 55,* 839–850.

Manning, W. D., & Smock, P. J. (1995). Why marry? Race and the transition to marriage among cohabitors. *Demography, 32,* 509–520.

Manning, W. D., & Smock, P. J. (2002). First comes cohabitation and then comes marriage? *Journal of Family Issues, 23,* 1065–1087.

McLoyd, V. C., Cauce, A. M., Takeuchi, D., & Wilson, L. (2000). Marital processes and parental socialization in families of color: A decade review of research. *Journal of Marriage and Family, 62,* 1070–1093.

Ooms, T. (2002). Strengthening couples and marriage in low-income communities. In A. J. Hawkins, L. D. Wardle, & D. O. Coolidge (Eds.), *Revitalizing the institution of marriage for the twenty-first century* (pp. 79–100). Westport, CT: Praeger.

Oropesa, R. S., & Landale, N. S. (2004). The future of marriage and Hispanics. *Journal of Marriage and Family, 66,* 901–920.

Piotrkowski, C. S., & Hughes, D. (1993). Dual earner families in context: Managing family and work systems. In F. Walsh (Ed.), *Normal family processes* (pp. 185–207). New York: Guilford Press.

Raley, R. K. (2002). The effects of the differential undercount on survey estimates of race differences in marriage. *Journal of Marriage and Family, 64,* 774–779.

Rosenblatt, P., Karis, T., & Powell, R. (1995). *Multi-racial couples: Black and White voices.* Thousand Oaks, CA: Sage.

Sabatelli, R., & Ripoll, K. (2004). Variation in marriage over time: An ecological/exchange perspective. In M. Coleman & L. Ganong (Eds.), *Handbook of contemporary families: Considering the past, contemplating the future* (pp. 79–95). Thousand Oaks, CA: Sage.

Schwartz, S. J., & Finley, G. E. (2005). Fathering in intact and divorced families: Ethnic differences in retrospective reports. *Journal of Marriage and Family, 67,* 207–215.

Sherif-Trask, B. (2004). Muslim families in the United States. In M. Coleman & L. Ganong (Eds.), *Handbook of contemporary families: Considering the past, contemplating the future* (pp. 394–408). Thousand Oaks, CA: Sage.

Simmons, T., & O'Connell, M. (2003). *Married couple and unmarried-partner households: 2000.* Retrieved May 23, 2005, from http://landview.census.gov/prod/2003pubs/censr-5.pdf

Suro, R., & Passel, J. (2003). *The rise of the second generation: Changing patterns in Hispanic population growth.* Washington, DC: Pew Hispanic Center.

Sweeney, M. M., & Phillips, J. A. (2004). Understanding racial differences in marital disruption: Recent trends and explanations. *Journal of Marriage and Family, 66,* 639–650.

Teachman, J. D., Tedrow, L. M., & Crowder, K. D. (2000). The changing demography of America's families. *Journal of Marriage and Family, 62,* 1234–1246.

Thompson, L. (1993). Conceptualizing gender in marriage: The case of marital care. *Journal of Marriage and Family, 55,* 557–569.

U.S. Census Bureau. (2001). *Statistical abstract of the United States: 2001.* Washington, DC: U.S. Government Printing Office.

White, L., & Rogers, S. J. (2000). Economic circumstances and family outcomes: A review of the 1990s. *Journal of Marriage and Family, 62,* 1035–1051.

Williams, N. (1990). Role making among married Mexican American women: Issues of class and ethnicity. In C. Carlson (Ed.), *Perspectives on the family: History, class and feminism* (pp. 186–204). Belmont, CA: Wadsworth.

6

Women, Work, and Families

Locating Experiences in Social Contexts

Seongeun Kim and Tara Woolfolk

I s an absent mother always a bad one? Picture a woman leaving her children at home, seeking employment elsewhere. Has she abandoned them, or made a great sacrifice? And who comes to mind? Envision the woman is from Mexico and left to earn money in the United States because her family lacked other viable options. What is your opinion of her? Imagine instead that this is an American White woman whose job "away" is not economically essential but provides an opportunity for a lucrative career. Does this change what you think of her?

Picture a teen working many hours after school in her family's business. When her parents are too busy, the extended family helps care for the teen. What does this teen look like? What about her family and their business? Would it shock you if she were a White, middle-class American instead of an immigrant American? Does the idea of such a middle-class teen confront our assumption that American children deserve a responsibility-free, play-oriented childhood? Is it strange to think a mainstream family would voluntarily include an extended kin network in childrearing? Is the nuclear family still expected to enact childrearing in America, no matter what?

This chapter addresses some issues regarding contemporary racial and ethnic families in the continental United States, including people of African descent born in America, Asian Americans, and Central and South Americans. We hope to encourage readers to think critically about how to best conceptualize and understand diversity, work, and families. This topic is complicated and far-reaching; no one chapter can cover it exhaustively. Thus, per this book's theme, our primarily focus is on scholarship from disciplines that support the reconceptualization of work and diverse families. This chapter contains four sections:

1. Brief review of the scholarly literature on work and family in the United States, focusing primarily on ethnically marginalized families

2. Exploration of two important ideological frameworks used to discuss work and family:
   a. Feminist social construction of work and motherhood
   b. Children as active agents in the social process

3. Analysis of selected research findings in three areas:
   a. Impact of women working *outside* of the home on gender relations *in* the home
   b. Mothering practices of women who work outside the home
   c. Children's roles in the work and family arenas

4. Implications for family science and future research

A Brief Overview of Research on Work and Family Among Culturally Diverse Families

Analysis of culturally diverse women's experiences began with the recognition that the mainstream American feminist movement in the 1960s and 1970s did not address the concerns of women outside the White middle class (Baca Zinn & Dill, 1998; Glenn, 1985, 1994). Seminal scholars of women and families argued that a preexisting theory on gender, referencing the dynamics of mainstream families, stressed men's patriarchal power over women, women's struggles to gain independence, or "gender conflict . . . and the division of reproductive labor" (Glenn, 1985, p. 86). They contended that this framework needed to include a broader range of women's experiences (Baca Zinn, 1994; Baca Zinn & Dill, 1998; Glenn, 1985). Early attempts to do this introduced double (race and gender) or triple (plus class) oppression models of culturally diverse women (Glenn, 1985). They intended to identify which category was foremost in women's experiences (Collins, 2001), or to assess the cumulative oppressions of combined categorical membership.

Unfortunately, these approaches lacked the ability to capture the complexity of multiple marginality and the ways social statuses interact dynamically within one's life. This has pushed scholars to develop a model that analyzes work and family experiences in the interacting contexts of race, class, and gender. From this perspective, race, class, and gender are viewed as "primary organizing principles of a society which locates and positions groups within that society's opportunity structures" (Baca Zinn & Dill, 1998, pp. 322–323). Human experiences are understood in terms of where people are placed or ranked in their social and historical contexts (Weber, 1998). The resulting power relationships are the cornerstones of marginalization (Weber, 1998). This idea highlights social processes and structures through which social inequalities are produced and how individuals and families experience systems of race, class, and gender differently depending upon their social locations (Baca Zinn & Dill, 1998; Collins, 1994, 2001).

One cannot capture the dynamics of a heterosexual, two-parent African American household using the assumptions utilized for their White counterparts, for several reasons. Both the man and woman of an African American household experience ethnic marginalization. Therefore, they cannot define power in a way that is limited to assuming that man is the primary oppressor of woman. They must also account for the oppression of Blacks by structural elements of American society, which disadvantage them and limit opportunities. This means their family dynamic must balance efforts to endure external oppression while also dealing with male-female dynamics. Most feminist scholars argue that African American couples do this by forming a male-female alliance to cope with racial and ethnic marginalization (Collins, 1994). Further, they acknowledge that the male-female dynamic becomes exponentially more complicated when one also considers racial marginalization. Not only does the male-female hierarchy remain; it exists inside a system ranking one's social value and privilege according to race, class, and gender in concert. This has often been argued as a challenge for Black families, in that Black men are perceived as more of a threat to the mainstream power structure than are Black women. This effectively places Black women in the social location of being "greater than," "less than," and "ally to" their male partners, all at once.

The influx of immigrants from Asia, the Caribbean, Mexico, and Central and South America, particularly after 1965, also generated scholarship on gender, labor, immigration, and families, and this scholarship enhanced the understandings of multiple marginality of culturally diverse families. At first, the focus was only on male immigrants (Hondagneu-Sotelo, 2003; Pessar, 2003). The initial effort to capture women's immigration experiences and address male bias was made by adding women as a variable for comparison. Subsequent scholarly efforts emphasized studying women's immigration experiences separately.

However, the problem with the first-stage studies lies, as Pessar (2003) argued, in the decontextualization of work and immigration experiences of women. Neither women's labor nor its influence on family relations was discussed in the larger social contexts.

More-recent scholarship has explored men's and women's labor and family experiences within the contexts of immigration policies, changing sociopolitical conditions, and global industrial restructuring (Espiritu, 1997, 2003; Lowe, 1997; Pessar, 2003). It focuses primarily on the engendered nature of the migration process, such as "how men and women experience migration differently, how they create and recreate patriarchal ideologies across transnational migration circuits, and how patriarchy is affirmed, reconfigured, or both as a consequence of migration" (Pessar, 2003, p. 36).

Thus, contemporary scholarship on work and family experiences among culturally diverse families in the United States has shifted the central focus of the discourse on gender. It has moved from the concept of gender as dichotomous, a simple variable with which to measure male-female differences that resulted in marginalization or exclusion of women's experiences, particularly those of culturally diverse women. Instead, in recent scholarship, gender is recognized as a contextualizing force through which we can better understand the sociopolitical matrix of race, class, gender, and immigration. It allows us to understand that gender has more than an additive effect and to avoid fitting women's experiences into preestablished frameworks.

Theoretical Underpinnings

Social Construction of Work and Motherhood

The idea of a feminist social construction of work and motherhood emerged after it challenged the previous predominant idea, based on the biological construction of gender. This position argues for innate differences between women and men and sees women's role in reproduction as a basis of oppression and subordination to men (Firestone, 1970). It also asserts women's orientation to nurturance, and men's orientation to independence (Chodorow, 1989). Several assumptions operate in this model. First, it views the public/political economy and private/nonpolitical households as fundamentally separate. This leads to further contrasting of work against family (Collins, 1994). Further, gender roles are seen as inseparable from the same private/public dichotomy: Men are assumed to be patriarchal family breadwinners and women to be family caregivers.

However, feminist scholarship on African Americans, Asian Americans, Native Americans, and Hispanic Americans argues consistently that these simplistic dichotomies leave out the realities and experiences of culturally diverse women and families, because they are situated in such different social and political systems (Collins, 1994; Dill, 1988; Glenn, 1985, 1994; Romero, 1997). The exemplary arrangement of breadwinner father and homemaker mother is specific to certain historical periods and predominantly found in middle- and upper-class families that can afford to live on a single income. In the United States, this arrangement was particularly visible during the 1950s (Hood, 1986; Kunz & Parson, 1997).

The historic split between work and family has not been found in culturally diverse families. Culturally diverse women were virtually always doing paid work because their husbands or male partners—also marginalized—could not earn enough alone to support a family. These women could not afford to be stay-at-home mothers (Collins, 2001; Dill, 1988, 1994; Espiritu, 1997; Glenn, 1985, 1994). For example, Chan (1991) discussed the nineteenth-century use of Asian men as coolie labor, restricted to low-level agriculture and service work, whereas men in the White labor force had options to work "in the growing metallurgical, chemical, and electrical industries" (as cited in Espiritu, 1997, p. 29). In this context, Asian wives in America have become important sources of labor (Espiritu, 1997), ensuring economic survival of their families. Similarly, Black women continued to engage primarily in agricultural and domestic work for generations after the era of American slavery officially ended. Correspondingly, due to limited choices, many Chinese women frequently worked in family businesses or in the domestic work sector (Espiritu, 1997; Glenn, 1985).

Although the same argument can also be applied in general to working-class families in the United States, Glenn (1985) argued that White working-class families' lives are still different. They have not been subjugated to the "institutional attacks such as forced separation directed at Blacks, Chicano and Chinese families" (p. 105).

Because work outside the home has been integral to the lives of women of color, clear boundaries between work and home were rarely found in their families (Collins, 1994, 2001; Dill, 1988, 1994; Espiritu, 1997; Glenn, 1985, 1994; Romero, 1997). For example, among the nineteenth-century Chinese in California, many families' living places were attached to their shops (Glenn, 1985). Also, contemporary working-class Korean immigrant women's paid labor is an integral part of their work as mothers (Kim, Conway-Turner, Sherif-Trask, & Woolfolk, 2006). As Espiritu (1997) argues, women's work outside of the home is an "extension of . . . domestic responsibilities as all family members . . . pool their resources to ensure economic subsistence" (p. 10).

In sum, feminist theory on the construction of work and motherhood makes us aware of this reality: The fact that most women mother their children does not mean that mothering is universal or identical across families. In brief, the contribution of a feminist theoretical construction of work and motherhood is that mothering is recognized as neither universal nor identical across families simply because most women mother their children. Nurturing children among culturally diverse women in a context where husbands' wages are not enough to support the family or where husbands are structurally denied access to positions at higher social levels is radically different from the work of mothers among of the more privileged. To see the difference, imagine the assumptions made about the "lack of drive" of a poor woman who chooses to care for her children full time, compared to the assumptions of "sacrifice" that tend to be made about middle- or upper-class women who do this. More important, the examination of context helps cement the argument that understanding mothering requires reframing the center of the analysis—moving away from simplistic work and family dichotomies—to viewing the work of mothers as being uniquely socially constructed, where all American women are located as members of culturally diverse groups, situated in social-class strata.

Children as Active
Agents in Social Processes

A growing body of literature on children in culturally diverse families acknowledges their roles in helping their immigrant families adapt (Orellana, 2001, 2003; Orellana, Dorner, & Pulido, 2003; Orellana, Thorne, Chee, & Lam, 2001; Park, 2001; Song, 1999; Valenzuela, 1999). This work has primarily investigated how children's lives are situated in the acculturation process. This scholarship challenges the predominant view of American childhood as "a set-apart and protected time of life" (Thorne, Orellana, Lam, & Chee, 2003, p. 244), emphasizing diverse experiences of American childhood.

Insight about children in culturally diverse families and their contributions to their families comes from various viewpoints. One view is that of the social construction of childhood of Prout and James (1997). Its emphasis is to understand children's social worlds from their own perspectives by examining their active roles in social processes within families and communities. Thus children are not conceptualized as passive subjects of adults' socialization or products of parenting. Rather, as Orellana (2001, 2003), who conducted studies on Hispanic children's household involvement, argued, "Children's work is supporting and sustaining households, bridging homes and schools, helping their families to negotiate the cultural and institutional terrain in the United States, and volunteering their services in classrooms and communities" (2001, p. 386).

In addition, scholarship on immigrant children emphasizes locating children at the center of the analysis. Zhou (1997) asserted that until recently, scholarship has focused on adult immigrants. The lack of efforts to understand children of immigrants has created a gap between the importance of these children and our knowledge about their lives (p. 64). This further implies that, even when children were included in studies of first-generation immigrant parents' assimilating processes, children's experiences tended to be marginalized. Thus, Park's research on Asian immigrant children (2001) who work for their parents' businesses is important in unraveling the intersections of childhood, diversity, and family. Park argued that these children experience "premature adulthood and prolonged adulthood" (p. 132); this experience is reflected in their more complex and ambiguous developmental stages.

Studies on children from immigrant Asian or Hispanic American families have primarily investigated the construction of childhood in families made of working-class immigrants who are not native speakers of English. This new child-centered research illustrates the heterogeneity and range of experiences, indicating that the American, play-driven model of childhood is neither historically nor currently the only one in practice.

Work and Culturally Diverse Family Dynamics in the United States

Women's Work and Gender Relations

A significant body of literature focuses on whether women's work outside of the home enhances their power or potentially renegotiates gender ideology and relations in conjugal relationships. For example, in spite of inequalities at work, some literature argues that immigrant women tend to experience an increase of power and independence at home. Immigrant men, on the other hand, are seen as losing their sense of male privilege in a culturally specific way (Foner, 1998; Kibria, 1993; Pessar, 2003). Some argue that women's economic contributions can be a leverage point to gain power in decision-making (Pessar, 2003) and to lead men to do more housework (Espiritu, 1997; Pessar, 1995).

Despite the theoretical increase in women's clout due to employment (Moon, 2003), reality, it appears, is much more complex. Various studies, including Espiritu's (1997, 2003) on labor and gender relations in Asian American and Latino immigrant families, illustrate how gender relations intersect with occupational status. Espiritu (2003) posited, based upon several studies (Chen, 1992; Foner, 1998; Min, 1998), that Asian professionals (e.g., engineers, architects, doctors) have more egalitarian gender relations than low-income families. Although these women still do most of the housework, their male partners participate in vacuuming, garbage disposal, dishwashing, bathroom cleaning, and laundry. This sharing of housework was primarily explained through both the small size of the income gap between spouses and wives' successfully pressuring their husbands to contribute (Espiritu, 2003; Hondagneu-Sotelo, 1994; Kibria, 1993; Pesquera, 1993).

However, Glenn (1983) and Kibria (1993) pointed out that men's higher involvement does not necessarily mean professional women do less housework management. Considering that these "well-off" women have very "little or no access to social networks that exist in highly connected ethnic communities" (as cited in Espiritu, 2003, p. 86), these women's family management burden is not likely to lessen. Also, husbands whose incomes are lower than those of their wives have even more complicated gender relations. For example, in Kim's study of working Korean women (1996), one female nurse attempted to reduce her income by avoiding extra money from working overtime to lessen the threat to her husband's male ego because she out-earned him.

In contrast, in family businesses, women are not likely to gain family power (Dhaliwal, 1995; Espiritu, 2003; Lim, 1997; Min, 1998), even though their work is as important as that of their husbands in maintaining the businesses (Lim, 1997; Min, 1998; Moon, 2003). Husbands control ownership, finances, and strategic planning (Dhaliwal, 1997; Min, 1998). In addition, Taiwanese (Chen, 1992) and Korean immigrant men (Lim, 1997; Min, 1998) in working-class employment expect their wives to do housework and childrearing and to serve them.

In such situations, women must deal with their husbands' rigid gender ideology and reluctance to do housework. In Min's study (1998), instead of mounting active resistance against their husbands, Korean immigrant women in New York avoided conflict, remaining silent. Lim's study (1997), of Korean immigrant women working in family businesses in Texas, explains that this strategy of resignation was due to their "deep-seated belief that women should endure any marital relations no matter how unfair they perceive them" (p. 43), to the effect of mothers or mothers-in-law who insisted that men may lose respect when they do "female" work, and to husbands' constant resistance.

Espiritu (2003) further argued that when power dynamics change among wage-laborer husbands and wives due to overall job instability, women may suffer. When men feel threatened by their female counterparts, they sometimes attempt to burden women by diminishing their own participation in housework, as discovered in Menjivar's research (2003) on Guatemalan and Salvadoran female domestic workers. This is further complicated by exposure to the gendered, middle-class behavior of the women's employers, leading these women to put their employers' potentially subversive perceptions of traditional gender relations into practice. Adding to the negotiation pileup is the fact that their husbands are often doing very "male," strength-oriented work—such as gardening or construction with their Latino peers, whose reinforcement of traditional gender ideology further widens the perception gaps.

Sometimes, these women find themselves worse off when they earn higher wages than men; for example, a Korean man in Min's study (1998) expressed deep frustration about not being served by his wife as in Korea, leading him to physically abuse her. This potential is exacerbated when families are isolated from relatives or kin networks, because it may lead men to seek more control over their wives (Foner, 1998; Hagan, 1994).

In sum, the literature indicates that women's economic gain does not dissipate husbands' gender ideologies, especially among working-class families. These women are not as likely to use their economic gains or resources to change or subvert traditional gender structures (Espiritu, 2003; Kibria, 1993; Moon, 2003). Rather, they see their gain as an opportunity to increase the standard of living of their families. The lack of change in their status seems better interpreted as coping than as passivity. For example, Kibria found that Vietnamese immigrant women viewed their shifting gender relations as temporary. They hoped through their contributions to return to middle-class status, as others such as Cuban or Dominican immigrants have done. Moon argues that for Asian immigrants, pooling resources in a marriage takes precedence over gaining economic power, thus diminishing the likelihood of drastic gender renegotiation.

A major challenge to the scholarship on work and gender relations lies in its limited coverage of ethnic groups and geographic locations in the United States. Southeast Asians and South Americans have been particularly understudied. Also, the majority of studies on culturally diverse families and work were conducted in California and New York. Thus, many varied geographic locations need further exploration.

Mothering and Women's Work Outside of the Home

Studies on mothering among culturally diverse women have raised questions about the application of decontextualized, one-size-fits-all theories and have further highlighted the significance of examining women's experiences in regional contexts (Collins, 1994, 2001; Dill, 1988; Glenn, 1983, 1985, 1994; Hondagneu-Sotelo & Avila, 1997; Orellana et al., 2001). The need to contribute economically to their families often has led to the development of alternative childrearing arrangements beyond nuclear family boundaries. For example, when African American women perform domestic labor outside of the home to ensure their children's survival, this paid caregiving work simultaneously and ironically deprives them of daily access to their own children. As a result, grandmothers or "other-mothers" in communities become primary caregivers through informal support networks (Collins, 1994; Stack, 1974). Similarly, some mothers of Korean immigrant families seek social supports through their churches. For example, youth group pastors closely monitor children's behavior while their mothers work (Kim et al., 2006).

Among certain Latina domestic workers and Filipina live-in caregivers, childrearing occurs in transnational locations. Mothers in the United States earn money to send to their children back home, who live with extended families that provide the children's daily care (Hondagneu-Sotelo & Avila, 1997; Schmalzbauer, 2004; Tung, 2003). Filipino women in Tung's study send remittances for children's school, food, clothes, and family finances; their own mothers or aunts monitor their children. Among the children, older female siblings do household work and care for their younger siblings. Similarly, Honduran transnational women often rely on their mothers or mothers-in-law. When these mother figures or husbands are deceased, aunts or older siblings help with family caregiving (Schmalzbauer, 2004).

In spite of culturally diverse women's economic contributions, studies also report that these transnational women are faced with grave emotional challenges because of living apart from their children. Any working absent mother fears her children's developing affection for their foster or provisional mother and anticipates that the children may not respond to her authority (Hondagneu-Sotelo & Avila, 1997). Absent mothers also worry about reestablishing relationships with their children when returning home (Tung, 2003). Furthermore, they must cope with the "stigma, guilt or criticism" (Hondagneu-Sotelo & Avila, 1997) associated with "voluntary" separation.

Overall, women's development of alternative childrearing arrangements provides a rationale for reconceptualizing mothering. First, these women do not nurture exclusively through the traditional work of mothers. Economic provision becomes a primary component of mothering, and work done to care for one's family implies both emotional and instrumental provision (Seery & Crowley, 2000). Moreover, in contrast to assumptions that childrearing occurs with the mother and children in close physical proximity, studies of socially and ethnically diverse mothers show that their childrearing sometimes has to occur where social or economic necessity blocks them from daily access to their children.

The greatest scholarly challenge in this area remains the understanding of work, gender, and motherhood in the multitudinous contexts of different families and practices. For example, few studies (Kim et al., 2006; Menjivar, 1995) have examined mothering strategies among working-class immigrant women. Especially underexplored are ways that refugee women or illegal immigrant women who lack family or kin networks define mothering and accomplish childrearing. Also, considering the increasing number of first- and second-generation professional immigrant women in the United States, investigating their mothering experiences will contribute greatly to a broader understanding of upper-class work, gender, and motherhood. Similarly, the lives of American women of color, whose choices are vastly limited by economic necessity and shrinking formal social supports, are underexplored. We especially need to examine these families in ways that go beyond detailing their dire straits.

Promising studies illustrate successful coping strategies for parenting in extreme poverty and suggest new paths for scholarship. For example, research by Edin and Kefalas (2005) and Edin and Lein (1997) focuses on economic strategies of single mothers transitioning from the welfare system. Their works' use of feminist frameworks is exemplary, as they examine women's families and the raw materials with which they seek resilience. Because women of color are overrepresented in low-income groups, this work advances the understanding of many ethnic minority women's lives. As Walker (2000) asserts in her discussion of the contribution of feminist frameworks to family science, Edin and Lein's exploration of "low skill" single mothers' financial strategies, combining formal and informal social supports, exemplifies research that will broaden our understanding of diversity in all our lives.

Contributions of Immigrant and Culturally Diverse Children to Their Families

Studies on relationships between mothers and children in culturally diverse families have tended to focus on working poor families. Despite this, these children's distinctively different experiences are compared to those from middle- or upper-class or White families—most often unfavorably. Children in these working-poor families do not have a responsibility-free, ideal American childhood, and they have distinctively different experiences compared to those of children from middle- or upper-class or White families. And like all children, they are not passive beings, nurtured without negotiating social transactions with their families. Their family labor is essential; for example, from the time of slavery to after World War II, young African American children did agricultural work outside the home (Collins, 1994). Contemporary Asian American children traded fields for storefronts, helping to run family businesses (Song, 1999).

Also, a growing body of recent research on children in families from Mexico and Central America addresses their family contributions in terms of interpreting language for their non-English-speaking relatives to help gain access to formal support systems (Orellana, 2001; Orellana et al., 2003; Valenzuela, 1999; Weisskirch & Alva, 2002). Valenzuela found three roles that Mexican children appear to perform in their families' settlement. First, they act as tutors, translating for parents and younger siblings during, for example, doctor's visits, school conferences, or processing immigration-related documents. Second, they advocate for their families in times of financial and legal difficulty. Their third role is acting as surrogate parents by doing household tasks. These roles are further differentiated by gender or age (Orellana, 2001; Valenzuela, 1999). For example, young girls perform more detailed translations and are assigned different household responsibilities than their male counterparts. Eldest boys and girls cook for and dress younger siblings and take them to school.

These studies suggest the importance of children's contributions. As Rogoff (2003) argued, worldwide, children participate in various family-related tasks; immigration keeps these practices normative as children adjust to new societies (Orellana et al., 2003). Children play a pivotal role in establishing their families and communities, and the scholarship on children in ethnic families illuminates their work, illustrating family processes in ethnically diverse immigrant families. However, given their importance, there is a comparative dearth of research about family contributions of American-born, culturally diverse children.

Implications of the Findings for the Field of Family Science

The research on work, gender, and family in culturally diverse families discussed here indicates that the lives of all families, regardless of their composition, cannot be fully understood without considering their social locations. Meanings of family structure, work-opportunity structures, work and motherhood, gender relations, and children's contributions are all socially and historically contextualized. This is equally true for mainstream families.

The research and theories discussed in this chapter have significant implications for the field of family science, raising critical questions about conceptualizing diversity and difference.

Studies of family diversity seem to include a prevalence of topics such as lifestyle differences and cultural values (Baca Zinn & Dill, 1998), forms of "exotica" (special or titillating cases; hooks, 1992, p. 21), "pluralit[ies] of views and experiences" (Anderson, 2005, p. 445), and special cultural cases (Baca Zinn, 1994). Although this approach to diversity provides some valuable information, it fails to clarify human experiences as being constructed in systems of power and privileges (Anderson, 2005) and how each group has differing degrees and qualities of power within the intersections of race, class, and gender. As Baca Zinn (1994) argued, diversity is not "an intrinsic property of groups that are different. Rather, it is the product of concrete social relationships that structure the experience of all families in different ways" (p. 305). For instance, if we could not understand why Vietnamese working women do not renegotiate gender roles with their husbands despite their economic contributions to the family, we might draw too simplistic a conclusion. We may not comprehend that the enactment of gender hierarchies within their homes reflects great complexity, interweaving personal and societal issues. Similarly, without seeing the meanings and costs of transnational motherhood and acknowledging mothers as the primary caretakers of their children, we might think these mothers are negligent. Without knowledge of informal social supports in African American families, we may misunderstand coping strategies of seemingly highly unavailable mothers as they care for their children's instrumental and emotional needs inside the opportunity structure available to them. Therefore, diversity, work, and families need to be understood and approached in relation to many differing contexts.

Also, considering the importance of examining the social contexts of work and family, this discourse should not be limited just to the way women divide themselves between their paid work and their families. This discourse is not always applicable and clearly results in a distortion of the experiences of many populations. Instead, it would be more productive to ask questions about the ongoing negotiation of meanings and arrangements surrounding work and family.

Conclusion and Discussion

Instead of approaching issues on the basis of national origin, race, or ethnicity, we propose that there are scholarly ways to discuss family issues across groups without losing the varied scholarly approaches' contributions to the understanding of work and family. Similarly, we argue for more examination of diversity within groups. These approaches do not undervalue the diverse experiences of American ethnic groups. Rather, they underscore how American-born and immigrant citizens share experiences of constantly renegotiating personal and family roles and how their work and family experiences are uniquely constructed within their social conditions.

Many fascinating questions remain to be answered. An important area needing exploration is that of immigrant men and their experiences within family contexts. The majority of early immigration research was male-centered, and its findings were generalized from men's experiences to those of all immigrants (Pessar, 2003). However, research on men within the context of immigrant families is rarely conducted, with the exception being a study by Strier and Roer-Strier on Israeli immigrants from Ethiopia and the former Soviet Union (2005). With respect to African American fathers, the situation is slowly improving. A body of research is emerging on how men negotiate their identities as fathers inside two-parent families, or in consort with households headed by a single female (Haynes, 2000). However, countless questions remain. How do men whose masculinity has been challenged due to severe job instability define and negotiate fatherhood? How do middle-class men of color do fathering? How do any men father in situations where their core identities as men are constantly jeopardized by the dynamics of their social locations? Understanding men as family members, whether they reside with their families or not, will enhance our understanding of families in the United States.

Also, many men and women of color are now socially mobile in America, working in professional and managerial fields; their experiences at work and influences on family life remain underexplored. For instance, Asian Americans have been portrayed as a "model minority," or "successful" compared to other immigrants, but reality is not so simple. One study (Dhaliwal, 1995) told of an engineer from India who was not promoted as quickly as his colleagues. His wife spoke of the effects of this extreme stressor on the family system. Greater exploration of workplace racism, social assumptions, and work and family will generate knowledge of people in various social hierarchies across many social locations based on ethnicity.

Given the increasing number of immigrant and American-born households headed by women experiencing marital disruption, more research is needed on factors contributing to marital instability and disruption (Pessar, 2003). For example, Asian American families are portrayed as harmonious and problem-free (Ishii-Kuntz, 2000), but they show a high incidence of violence and divorce, attributable to men's loss of status as U.S. immigrants. Also, considering the growth in the literature on violence against women in South Asian American communities, more attention should be given to how women's work intersects with acts of violence against women.

This review seeks to promote greater understanding of the evolving dialectic on diversity in the intersection of work and families. Deconstructing traditional models of work and family used in the study of culturally diverse women helps show that real lives do not often fit preexisting dichotomous models. As Collins (1994) argued, these traditional models have resulted in the distortion and misinterpretation of the reality of culturally diverse women and families and, further, in the exclusion of their lives from public discourse. By shifting the center of analysis, scholars, such as Collins, argue for the continual refinement and development of frameworks that better capture families' realities. Perhaps this can lead to a greater understanding of *all* families' lives.

References

Anderson, M. (2005). Thinking about women: A quarter century's view. *Gender and Society, 19*(4), 437–454.

Baca Zinn, M. (1994). Feminist rethinking from racial-ethic families. In M. Baca Zinn & B. Dill (Eds.), *Women of color in U.S. society* (pp. 303–314). Philadelphia: Temple University Press.

Baca Zinn, M., & Dill, B. (1998). Theorizing difference from multiracial feminism. *Feminist Studies, 22*(2), 321–332.

Chan, S. (1991). *Asian Americans: An interpretive history.* Boston: Twayne.

Chen, H. (1992). *Chinatown no more: Taiwan immigrants in contemporary New York.* Ithaca, NY: Cornell University Press.

Chodorow, N. (1989). *Feminism and psychoanalytic theory.* New Haven, CT: Yale University Press.

Collins, P. (1994). Shifting the center: Race, class, and feminist theorizing about motherhood. In E. Glenn, G. Chang, & L. Forcey (Eds.), *Mothering: Ideology, experience, and agency* (pp. 45–65). New York: Routledge.

Collins, P. (2001). *Black feminist thought: Knowledge, consciousness, and the politics of empowerment* (2nd ed.). New York: Routledge.

Dhaliwal, A. (1995). Gender at work: The renegotiation of middle-class womanhood in a South Asian–owned business. In W. Ng, S. Chin, J. Moy, & G. Okihiro (Eds.), *Reviewing Asian America: Locating diversity* (pp. 75–85). Pullman: Washington State University Press.

Dill, B. (1988). Our mothers' grief: Racial ethnic women and the maintenance of families. *Journal of Family History, 13*(4), 415–431.

Dill, B. (1994). Fictive kin, paper sons, and compadazgo: Women of color and the struggle for family survival. In M. Baca Zinn & B. Dill (Eds.), *Women of color in U.S. society* (pp. 149–169). Philadelphia: Temple University Press.

Edin, K., & Kefalas, M. (2005). *Promises I can keep: Why poor women put motherhood ahead of marriage.* Los Angeles: University of California Press.

Edin, K., & Lein, L. (1997). *Making ends meet: How single mothers survive welfare and low-wage work.* New York: Russell Sage Foundation.

Espiritu, Y. (1997). *Asian American women and men: Labor, laws, and love.* Thousand Oaks, CA: Sage.

Espiritu, Y. (2003). Gender and labor in Asian immigrant families. In P. Hondagneu-Sotelo (Ed.), *Gender and U.S. immigration: Contemporary trends* (pp. 81–100). Berkeley: University of California Press.

Firestone, S. (1970). *The dialect of sex.* New York: Bantam Books.

Foner, N. (1998). Benefits and burdens: Immigrant women and work in New York City. *Gender Issues, 16*(4), 5–24.

Glenn, E. (1983). Split household, small producer and dual wage earner: An analysis of Chinese-American family strategies. *Journal of Marriage and the Family, 45,* 35–46.

Glenn, E. (1985). Racial ethnic women's labor: The intersection of race, gender and class oppression. *Review of Racial Political Economics, 17*(3), 86–108.

Glenn, E. (1994). Social construction of mothering: A thematic overview. In E. Glenn, G. Chang, & L. Forcey (Eds.), *Mothering: Ideology, experience, and agency* (pp. 1–29). New York: Routledge.

Hagan, J. (1994). *Deciding to be legal: A Maya community in Houston.* Philadelphia: Temple University Press.

Haynes, F. E. (2000). Gender and family ideals: An exploratory study of Black middle-class Americans. *Journal of Family Issues, 21*(7), 811–837.

Hondagneu-Sotelo, P. (1994). *Gendered transitions: Mexican experiences of immigration.* Berkeley: University of California Press.

Hondagneu-Sotelo, P. (2003). Gender and immigration: A retrospective and introduction. In P. Hondagneu-Sotelo (Ed.), *Gender and U.S. immigration: Contemporary trends* (pp. 3–19). Berkeley: University of California Press.

Hondagneu-Sotelo, P., & Avila, E. (1997). "I'm here, but I'm there": The meanings of Latina transnational motherhood. *Gender and Society, 11*(5), 548–571.

Hood, J. (1986). The provider role: Its meaning and measurement. *Journal of Marriage and the Family 48,* 349–359.

hooks, b. (1992). *Black looks: Race and representation.* Boston: South End Press.

Ishii-Kuntz, M. (2000). Diversity within Asian American families. In D. Demo, K. Allen, & M. Fine (Eds.), *Handbook of family diversity* (pp. 274–292). New York: Oxford University Press.

Kibria, N. (1993). *Family tightrope: The changing lives of Vietnamese Americans.* Princeton, NJ: Princeton University Press.

Kim, A. (1996). *Women struggling for a new life: The role of religion in the cultural passage from Korea to America.* Albany: State University of New York Press.

Kim, S., Conway-Turner, K., Sherif-Trask, B., & Woolfolk, T. (2006). Reconstructing mothering among Korean immigrant working class women in the United States. *Journal of Comparative Family Studies, 37*(1), 43–56.

Kunz, W., & Parson, M. (1997). Complicating the contested terrain of work/family intersections. *Signs, 22*(2), 440–452.

Lim, I. (1997). Korean immigrant women's challenge to gender inequality at home: The interplay of economic resources, gender, and family. *Gender and Society, 11*(1), 31–51.

Lowe, L. (1997). *Immigrant acts: On Asian American cultural politics.* Durham, NC: Duke University Press.

Menjivar, C. (1995). Kinship networks among immigrants: Lessons from a qualitative comparative approach. *International Journal of Comparative Sociology, 36*(3/4), 219–232.

Menjivar, C. (2003). The intersection of work and gender: Central American immigrant women and employment in California. In P. Hondagneu-Sotelo (Ed.), *Gender and U.S. immigration: Contemporary trends* (pp. 101–126). Berkeley: University of California Press.

Min, P. (1998). *Changes and conflicts: Korean immigrant families in New York.* Boston: Allyn & Bacon.

Moon, S. (2003). Immigration and mothering: Case studies from two generations of Korean immigrant women. *Gender and Society, 17*(6), 840–860.

Orellana, M. (2001). The work kids do: Mexican and Central American immigrant children's contributions to households and schools in California. *Harvard Educational Review, 71*(3), 366–387.

Orellana, M. (2003). Responsibilities of children in Latin immigrant homes. In C. Suárez-Orozco & I. Todordva (Eds.), *Understanding the social world of immigrant youth* (pp. 25–39). Cambridge, MA: Jossey-Bass.

Orellana, M., Dorner, L., & Pulido, L. (2003). Accessing assets: Immigrant youths' work as family translators or "para-phrasers." *Social Problems, 50*(4), 505–524.

Orellana, M., Thorne, B., Chee, A., & Lam, W. (2001). Transnational childhoods; The participation of children in processes of family migration. *Social Problems, 48*(4), 572–591.

Park, L. (2001). Between adulthood and childhood. *Berkeley Journal of Sociology, 45,* 114–135.

Pesquera, B. (1993). "In the beginning he wouldn't lift a spoon": The division of household labor. In A. de la Torre & B. Pesquera (Eds.), *Building with our hands: New directions in Chicana studies* (pp. 181–195). Berkeley: University of California Press.

Pessar, P. (1995). On the home front and in the workplace: Integrating immigrant women into feminist discourse. *Anthropological Quarterly, 68*(1), 37–47.

Pessar, P. (2003). Engendering migration studies: The case of new immigrants in the United States. In P. Hondagneu-Sotelo (Ed.), *Gender and U.S. immigration: Contemporary trends* (pp. 20–42). Berkeley: University of California Press.

Prout, A., & James, A. (1997). A new paradigm for the Sociology of childhood? Provenance, promise and problems. In A. James & A. Prout (Eds.), *Constructing and reconstructing childhood* (pp. 7–33). Washington, DC: Falmer Press.

Rogoff, B. (2003). *The cultural nature of human development.* New York: Oxford University Press.

Romero, M. (1997). Epilogue. In E. Higginbotham & M. Romero (Eds.), *Women and work: Exploring race, ethnicity, and class* (pp. 235–248). Thousand Oaks, CA: Sage.

Schmalzbauer, L. (2004). Searching for wages and mothering from afar: The case of Honduran transnational families. *Journal of Marriage and Family, 66,* 1317–1331.

Seery, B., & Crowley, M. S. (2000). Women's emotion work in the family: Relationship management and the process of building father-child relationships. *Journal of Family Issues, 21*(1), 100–127.

Song, M. (1999). *Helping out: Children's labor in ethnic businesses.* Philadelphia: Temple University Press.

Stack, C. (1974). *All our kin: Strategies for survival in the black community.* New York: Harper Row.

Strier, R., & Roer-Strier, D. (2005). Fatherhood and immigration: Perceptions of Israeli immigrant fathers from Ethiopia and the former Soviet Union. *Families in Society, 86*(1), 121–133.

Thorne, B., Orellana, M., Lam, W., & Chee, A. (2003). Raising children, and growing up, across national borders: Comparative perspective on age, gender, and migration. In P. Hondagneu-Sotelo (Ed.), *Gender and U.S. immigration: Contemporary trends* (pp. 241–262). Berkeley: University of California Press.

Tung, C. (2003). Caring across borders: Motherhood, marriage, and Filipina domestic workers in California. In S. Hune & G. Nomura (Eds.), *Asian Pacific Islander American women: A historical anthology* (pp. 301–317). New York: NYU Press.

Valenzuela, A. (1999). Gender roles and settlement activities among children and their immigrant families. *American Behavioral Scientist, 42*(4), 720–742.

Walker, A. (2000). Refracted knowledge: Viewing families though the prism of social science. *Journal of Marriage and the Family, 62*(3), 595–608.

Weber, L. (1998). A conceptual framework for understanding race, class, gender, and sexuality. *Psychology of Women Quarterly, 22,* 13–32.

Weisskirch, R., & Alva, S. (2002). Language brokering and the acculturation of Latino children. *Hispanic Journal of Behavioral Sciences, 24*(3), 369–378.

Zhou, M. (1997). Growing up American: The challenge confronting immigrant children and children of immigrants. *Annual Review of Sociology, 23,* 63–95.

7

Parenting in Color

Culturally Diverse
Perspectives on Parenting

Kimberly A. Greder and William D. Allen

F amily research and clinical practice indicate that culture plays an integral role in shaping parenting values, beliefs, goals, and practices. This chapter addresses why it is important to consider the role of culture in parenting; how culture shapes parenting; and assumptions, key principles, and strategies to consider when working with culturally diverse families. Given space limitations of this chapter, we are able to address some cultural influences on parenting (socioeconomics, religion) only briefly; we deeply examine one other aspect, ethnicity. However, the key ideas presented in the chapter, including the assumptions, principles, and strategies discussed at the end of the chapter, are relevant for working with all culturally diverse families.

Why It Is Important to Consider the
Role of Culture and Ethnicity in Parenting

Parenting has been described as the process of nurturing, protecting, and guiding a child through the course of development (Brooks, 1991), and as preparing the next generation for life and success (Allen, 2003; Garcia-Coll & Patcher, 2002). Parenting involves a series of interactions between a parent and a child that influence the attitudes and behaviors of both the parent and child. The process of parenting has been extended to include behaviors of others who regularly interact with children such as relatives, friends, and teachers (Brooks, 1991).

There are several reasons why it is important to understand the role of culture in parenting today. The United States is becoming increasingly diverse with respect to ethnicity, religious beliefs, and socioeconomic status. Yet, much of the theory and research on parenting has been shaped primarily by middle-class, White researchers studying families from similar backgrounds (Garcia-Coll, 2003; Greder et al., 2002; *History of Parenting Practices*, 1999). This relatively narrow empirical focus inhibits our ability to confidently predict or understand cross-cultural parenting practices. All theories are socially constructed and emerge from specific cultural contexts. Therefore, one must carefully inspect the theory being applied in order to ensure an appropriate fit with any family.

Although the term *ethnicity* is often used interchangeably with *culture,* it should more accurately be seen as a subset of culture. In this chapter, we are defining *ethnicity* as the shared sense of group identity that results primarily from factors such as a common history, shared life experience, or common demographic characteristics such as skin color (Allen, 2003). In contrast, when we refer to *culture* we mean the sum of the experiences and learned behavior patterns of a given group (Hamner & Turner, 2001). Thus, *culture* is a collective term describing the outward manifestations of the inner beliefs, values, and shared identity that define ethnic, religious, or social groups.

The small but growing body of scholarship on culturally diverse families suggests that though all parents may share key characteristics, ethnic minority parents in particular experience unique conditions that influence parenting values, beliefs, and practices. As the United States becomes increasingly ethnically diverse (particularly in the younger segments of the population), scholarly work focused on ethnic minority parenting will become even more important. It is clear that a deeper, more broadly based understanding of parenting across ethnic boundaries will better inform legislative and program policies, services, and effective interventions for families.

Another significant factor in the growing cultural diversity within the United States is religion. According to the American Religious Identification Survey (ARIS), between 1990 and 2001, the percentage of the U.S. adult population that regards themselves members of a non-Christian religion (e.g., Jewish, Muslim, Buddhist) or not as a member of any religious group has increased (3 percent to 4 percent and 8 percent to 14 percent, respectively). The percentage of the U.S. adult population that regards themselves as a member of a Christian religion (e.g., Catholic, Baptist, Protestant) decreased (86 percent to 77 percent) between 1990 and 2001 (U.S. Census Bureau, 2004–2005).

Religious beliefs shape people's values and behaviors, including their parenting practices. For example, while the parenting practices of many Christian parents are influenced by their interpretation of the Bible (and passages in it like "spare the rod, spoil the child"), many Muslim and Jewish parents may base their parenting practices on different spiritual teachings (e.g., from the Qur'an and Torah, respectively). In addition to shaping a shared sense of identity, beliefs of a religious group may elicit strong reactions from people outside of the group who do not share the same values and beliefs. Also, there is considerable diversity within the population regarding the practice of religious beliefs. Formalized religion (as exemplified by the major denominations) could be described as a subset of spirituality. This broader category describes the wide range of beliefs and faith-seeking activities seen throughout the United States and indeed around the world. Using this approach, even atheism can be seen as a belief system that potentially shapes values and behaviors. It is also probable that proxies for religion (e.g., church attendance) may be insufficient to gauge the depth of religiosity in the U.S. population. For example, many people who consider themselves "believers" do not regularly attend churches, synagogues, or mosques.

In addition to the growing ethnic and religious diversity in the United States, the variance in socioeconomic status (SES) among families continues to increase. Ethnic minority families experience higher rates of poverty than White families. The percentage of those living in poverty is highest among American Indians and Alaskan Natives (25.7 percent) followed by African Americans (24.9 percent), Hispanics (22.6 percent), Native Hawaiians or other Pacific Islanders (17.7 percent), and Asian Americans (12.6 percent); it is lowest among non-Hispanic Whites (8.1 percent) (Bishaw & Iceland, 2003).

Although the United States is often cited as a classless society, socioeconomic status has clear and often predictable consequences for individuals and families. This is particularly true for individuals at the extremes of the socioeconomic spectrum. For example, children from poor families are as unlikely to have access to resources such as high-quality health care or educational opportunity as children from upper-income families are likely to have such access. Parental motivation and efficacy can be negatively affected by real or perceived disparities in health and educational opportunities for their children. These factors add to the stress of parenting in low-income or ethnically marginalized families. As in the cases of ethnicity and religion, socioeconomic class can potentially shape cultural values and behaviors that become associated with specific SES levels (e.g., the "jet set," or the "culture of poverty") and influence parenting practices.

The increasing ethnic, religious, and socioeconomic diversity of families in the United States presents challenges and opportunities for family professionals. While information regarding general characteristics of different ethnic, religious, and SES groups may be helpful, caution is needed. As there are differences between groups, there are also variances among members of each group.

How Culture Shapes Parenting

To fully understand parenting, one must understand how culture influences parenting values, beliefs, goals, and practices. Parents develop their parenting style based on their cultural group and socialization as well as their individual and family experiences, their personalities, and the characteristics of their children (Belsky, 1984; Brooks, 1991).

Culture is a key component of the psychological, social, and physical environments of individuals and families. These environments reflect cultural values and practices that guide human behavior and provide a socialization framework that shapes interactions (Lynch & Hanson, 1998). Thus views on parenting and parenting practices must always be seen in the various cultural contexts in which they occur. This is particularly important as practitioners attempt to assess parental functioning as part of the process of engaging parents (e.g., in school settings), or as a prelude for behavioral interventions (e.g., providing social or therapeutic services).

Although culture shapes parenting, the various cultural contexts parents live in are constantly evolving and being reworked (Anderson & Fenichel, 1989) as people and society change. Parenting behaviors are influenced by many factors other than culture such as socioeconomic status, gender, age, and education. Some people adhere strongly to a set of cultural parenting patterns, and others combine parenting practices from several cultural groups (Lynch & Hanson, 1998). Thus, people of the same cultural background may share tendencies and not have the same parenting values, beliefs, goals, and practices.

While it is important for family professionals to be aware of the cultural background and associated parenting practices of families they are working with, it is just as critical for professionals to be aware of individual characteristics of the parents and family members with whom they are working. Most parents are similar in the sense that they share certain basic feelings toward their children (e.g., affection, a desire to nurture) and basic aspirations (e.g., to provide economic support for their offspring). However, parents often have needs that are specific to the environments in which they raise families. Thus, they may have unique parenting goals and needs for specific resources that support their growth (Lynch & Hanson, 1998).

Parental aspirations that are applicable to all parents regardless of ethnic, cultural, or socioeconomic diversity include but are not limited to the following:

1. Ensuring the physical safety of their children

2. Meeting the material needs of their children (e.g., food, shelter)

3. Socializing their children to live successfully with others

4. Providing an environment that nurtures their children's progression through developmental stages

5. Transmitting cultural values and practices between generations (Garcia-Coll & Patcher, 2002; Harkness & Super, 1995)

Although these aspirations may be thought of as universal, parents may employ different styles and practices to achieve them based on the contextual demands of their environments.

Many parents from ethnic minority groups experience contexts that are qualitatively different from those of their peers (both in the so-called majority population and also in other ethnic minority groups). These contexts may arise from different ethnic, religious, or historical backgrounds and thus be reflected in different attitudes toward childrearing. Institutional racism and its consequences (prejudice, discrimination, segregation) make up part of the unique context many ethnic and minority parents experience (Garcia-Coll & Patcher, 2002). For recent immigrants, the reasons for their immigration and migration experience, assimilation, and acculturation are also significant components of the contexts from which parenting attitudes and practices emerge.

Factors such as SES or geographic location (e.g., urban versus rural) can also shape attitudes and adaptations in parenting behavior. Although useful for the parent in these specific contexts, these adaptations can potentially result in childrearing practices that appear inappropriate or even harsh to outside observers. White parents may also experience some of the contextual problems that ethnic minority parents do (e.g., economic hardship, gender bias); however, the effects on family functioning and parental decision-making are different. This is due to the accumulative effect of unique stressors that ethnic minority parents face (e.g., ethnic bias) that Whites do not experience. Thus ethnic minority parents must typically cope with additional contextual factors that are the direct result of their ethnic minority status.

For example, the experience of poverty may differ for ethnic minority parents as compared to that of White parents. Ethnic minority parents, in addition to economic deprivation, must cope with ethnic bias. Similarly, recent immigrants may need to cope with additional contextual factors such as language barriers and geographic isolation from extended family support. This is in addition to lack of economic resources and access to education or employment opportunities.

Cultural Heritage and Acculturation

Cultural traditions shape parenting by influencing childrearing practices, expectations of roles of children at different ages and stages of development, where families live, family structure, and roles and responsibilities of adults in families. However, the degree to which cultural heritage influences parenting is often based on a family's level of acculturation, where the family resides (e.g., their proximity to or isolation from other group members), how close or involved traditional relatives are, and the potential match between specific cultural practices and the social norms of surrounding communities (Garcia-Coll & Patcher, 2002).

Acculturation is a dynamic process that occurs over time in which families combine ethnic, minority, and dominant cultural values (Garcia-Coll & Patcher, 2002). Family members who regularly interact with members of the majority culture (e.g., children attending school, parents working outside the home) are exposed to acculturation opportunities. When family members acculturate at different rates (e.g., when children attend school and parents have little contact with the majority culture), disagreements about family values and parenting practices often occur (Szapocznik & Hernandez, 1988; Zuniga, 1992). For example, a teenager whose family has immigrated from another country may want to dress like his peers and ask parents to purchase clothing that the parents do not believe reflects their family values. The baggy pants that became popular among teen males in the United States during the late 1990s and early 2000s are an example of this. The parents may believe that pants that are loose and hang low on the hips do not reflect respect and honor. Therefore, the parents may refuse to purchase the pants for their teen. The teen may become upset and not understand why his parents cannot be like other parents of his peers who let their youth wear baggy pants.

Ethnic minority families become acculturated to the cultural norms of other groups in various degrees. The level of family acculturation can influence parenting style by influencing the developmental expectations of children. It can also shape parent-child behaviors, such as feeding and other caregiving practices, and regulate the degree to which extended family members influence parenting decisions. These issues can cause conflict in families in regard to the appropriateness of parenting practices among less and more acculturated family members (Garcia-Coll & Patcher, 2002). An example of a conflict around feeding practices and the role of extended family members is illustrated in the following scenario:

> A Vietnamese grandmother who recently immigrated to the United States lives with her son and his family. She goes to her six-year-old grandson's school every day to feed him. She values spending time with her grandson and believes it is her role to make sure he eats a nutritious meal and gets enough food. Her son realizes that his mother loves her grandson and wants the best for him. However, he doesn't believe that it is in the best interest of his son to have his grandmother feeding him at school. He believes that other children may not understand why the grandmother is doing this and may make fun of his son. He also believes that the act of the grandmother feeding his son every day may lessen the ability of his son to become independent.

Studies suggest that parents who are bicultural have the ability to embrace and profit from membership in two divergent cultures (Allen & Connor, 1997). Bicultural parents are able to retain social, psychological, and attitudinal linkages with their original culture while simultaneously adapting to and navigating the majority culture(s). Biculturalism does not mean abandoning one culture or absorption into another; the ideal is for both constituent cultures to be accessible and useful. Bicultural parents and their families may experience the healthiest adjustments to the multicultural contexts of their lives (Szapocznik, Kurtines, & Fernandez, 1980). An example of bicultural parenting would be a parent who has immigrated to the United States from Mexico and has been able to maintain basic traditional family values (e.g., values of cohesiveness and expressiveness) and roles (e.g., father as primary income provider) while learning to navigate and use the formal social support system in his new community to help him meet the basic needs of his family. Traditional ways of celebrating birthdays (e.g., coming-out parties for teens), honoring dead relatives (e.g., altars with candles and pictures of deceased family members in the home), and spending time together (e.g., visiting relatives together, going for walks in parks) are maintained.

Economic Hardship

Households headed by single mothers, individuals, and families from ethnic minority groups and families with preschool children are overrepresented among those in the population who live in poverty (DeNavas-Walt, Proctor, & Mills, 2004). Geography and generation also play important roles in determining who becomes poor, as do factors such as adolescent parenting, insufficient education, lack of job training, and chronic unemployment. Limited access to health care (and resulting poor health outcomes), inadequate housing and homelessness, and violent or unsupportive neighborhoods all contribute to the economic barriers confronting poor families. Moreover, the subjective experience of poverty can be heavily influenced by race, ethnicity, and gender (Garrett, Ng'andu, & Ferron, 1994; Huston, McLoyd, & Coll, 1994).

Poor families, especially families experiencing multigenerational poverty, may develop unique cultural behavior patterns (Payne, 2001; Wilson, 1987), some of which are erroneously attributed to ethnic or religious causes. However, these behaviors are more accurately seen as attempts to cope with the many problems that poverty either causes or exacerbates. In addition, a child's home environment is known to be a major contributor to preschoolers' language development and later to children's overall academic success. Studies reveal that the quality of the environment in families with limited incomes, regardless of race and ethnicity, is generally lower than the quality of the environment in families with middle and upper incomes. Mothers in lower-income homes were found to be less instructive; more controlling, critical, and restrictive; and less sensitive to their children's needs than mothers in middle-income homes. Studies also revealed that the availability of toys and books and encouragement and support for cognitive development (such as playing games to promote language development) occur less often in homes of families living in poverty than in homes of families who have middle and upper incomes (Walker, Greenwood, Hart, & Carta, 1994). Thus, SES is a key variable relating to parenting practices in any ethnic or cultural group (Hamner & Turner, 2001). Parents who struggled academically or who felt rejection by teachers or school administrations often find it difficult to provide their children with support and encouragement for intellectual accomplishments, unless their paternal aspirations for their children's academic success outweigh their own experiences.

Despite all that has been said about the potential harm poverty can cause, it is essential to bear in mind that social groups are seldom homogeneous. There is as much variation in parenting practices *within* groups (e.g., low-income parents) as *between* groups (e.g., low- and upper-income parents). One group of low-income parents may react to financial stress by overemphasizing parental techniques such as demanding obedience, using corporal punishment, or withholding affection (Garrett et al., 1994; McLeod & Shanahan, 1993), while another group might be overly permissive and fail to provide sufficient parental supervision. A third group from the same neighborhood may be able to give their children consistent, developmentally appropriate parenting, either alone or in cooperation with others. For this reason, one should think of the impact of social class on child development as representing probabilities, not inevitabilities (Hamner & Turner, 2001).

Minority Status

Regardless of ethnic or religious background or of socioeconomic status, cultural diversity has unique implications for parenting. Many ethnic minority parents experience various forms of prejudice and discrimination that can create psychological stress (Barbarin, 1999). Such stress can affect parenting behavior and thus indirectly influence child development. Parents' adaptations to racism, prejudice, and discrimination can also have direct implications for their children's development, including affecting children's sense of self-esteem, their response to stress, their academic performance, and their acquisition of good social skills (Garcia-Coll & Patcher, 2002).

Ethnic minority parents often strive to socialize their children about race and ethnicity (McAdoo, 1988; Peters, 1988). One strategy for doing this is to instill attitudes and values (such as a positive self-concept) that can buffer negative messages about their ethnic group in the wider society. Racial socialization can be deliberate as in the case of parents who provide positive information on ancestry. It can also be unintended as in the case of parents who actively seek positive engagements with members of other ethnic groups (and, as a result, raise children who value cultural diversity). Among other racial socialization techniques that parents employ are (a) teaching about cultural heritage, history, customs, and traditions; (b) creating an awareness of prejudice and discrimination; (c) alerting youth to be cautious of interacting with individuals outside their racial or ethnic group; and (d) promoting respect and appreciation for all people and cultural groups (Hughes & Chen, 1999).

Positive child outcomes are associated with parents emphasizing ethnic pride, self-development, awareness of racial barriers, and equality (Bowman & Howard, 1985). Most of the studies on racial socialization have been conducted with African American families, and a few studies have been made with Japanese American and Mexican American families (Phinney & Chavira, 1995; Quintana & Vera, 1999). Additional research with other ethnic groups is needed to see if similar findings are revealed.

As outlined previously, parenting practices of ethnic and minority parents are influenced by traditional childrearing practices associated with their cultural background, their degree of acculturation to the majority society, and the context of the environments in which they live, which frequently include racism and poverty. These factors have combined effects on parenting, but they must each be considered independently, as they each create unique contexts for individual parents and their families. For example, Mexican immigrant households often have more than one family that lives in the household, especially during the early years of settling in the United States. This could be due to the cohesiveness and informal social support that is common among Mexican families as well as to the scarcity of financial resources of immigrant families.

Parents learn about parenting from their environments, starting with what they learned as children by observing their own parents. The learning process continues with observations of parenting and childcare behavior of other family members (e.g., aunts, uncles, grandparents) as well as other adults in the community (e.g., neighbors). The media (e.g., magazines, television, the Internet) also influence perceptions about parenting and (potentially) parental practices. Finally, parents make continual adjustments over time in their parenting behavior as a result of interaction(s) with their children and other parents. Thus, parental attitudes and behaviors should be seen as somewhat dynamic, even though people have been shown to adopt preferred styles (Baumrind, 1996).

Assumptions, Principles, and Strategies for Working With Culturally Diverse Families

In addition to being aware of the cultural background of families and variances within cultures, professionals need to be aware of how their own cultural heritage (e.g., ethnicity, race, religion, socioeconomic status) and individual characteristics (e.g., values, beliefs, temperament) influence how they perceive parenting (e.g., assumptions, expectations, goals, roles) and their interactions with families. Understanding oneself and how one perceives parenting helps one to be more open to understanding others' parenting practices. These concepts relate to developing cultural competence, a lifelong process.

Cultural competence is the ability to learn from and relate respectfully to people of your own culture as well as people from other cultures. Having a better understanding of how other people think about things helps one find common ground. Gaining this knowledge helps professionals adjust their own behavior as well as adjust to the organizations they represent. Developing cultural competence is a first step one can take to better assist families of diverse cultures (Greder et al., 2002).

Cultural practices and individual characteristics of both professionals and families influence interactions between professionals and families (Greder et al., 2002). Thus, it is important for professionals to be aware of families' values, beliefs, concerns, and priorities regarding parenting and to tailor interventions and other services to meet the needs and resources of the families with whom they are working. Being aware and respectful of the cultural practices of families can strengthen the professional-family relationship and lead to the development of services and supports that are most effective for families (Greder et al., 2002; Lynch & Hanson, 1998).

Assumptions

Following are the authors' assumptions about parenting, based on clinical experiences and relationships the authors have developed with families of various cultural backgrounds.

1. Parents are the primary socializing agents in the lives of children.

2. Social and cultural contexts influence both parenting and the parent-child relationship.

3. All parents have strengths and weaknesses (as do their families).

4. All parents need support and encouragement. (Good parenting is a rewarding but difficult process.)

5. Most parents are motivated by the desire to improve the prospects for their children's lives.

6. Most parents have needs that if met could improve their parenting; however, parents do not have equal access to the resources to fill such needs.

7. On their own, demographic characteristics (such as ethnicity, socioeconomic status, or religion) are poor predictors of a person's parenting ability or capability.

8. Parenting skills can be learned and improved.

As mentioned previously, parents hold values that are influenced by many factors (e.g., cultural heritage, SES, educational attainment, environmental contexts, acculturation, past experiences). However, below are key values expressed by a sample of ethnic minority parents living in the Midwest (Greder, 2002, 2003a–c; Greder et al., 2002) as well as in the western United States (Chen, Brekken, & Chan, 1997).

Key Values Expressed by Ethnic Minority Parents

The Importance of Education

Many ethnic minority parents cite education as a key value in ensuring success in society (particularly in the workplace) for their children. "Getting an education is the key to my child's future" was a sentiment frequently stated by parents interviewed for a recent parenting education project in the Midwest (Greder, 2003a–c).

According to one Hispanic father, the term *educación* reflects something much more than simply academic education. He stressed the importance of teaching children to behave well and that good interpersonal skills are more important than anything else.

> The basic concept we use to raise our children is a concept called *educación*. Now literally translated, we think that means *education*, but we see a difference from formal education to that which we call *knowledge*. And knowledge is knowing how to be in life—how to greet somebody, how to treat an elder, how to treat a child, how to ask for something, how to know when not to ask for something, how to speak out, and how to be quiet when you need to be. It really has to do with character development rather than learning facts about things. So that's why many, many times when we have Latino children in school, parents seem to be much more concerned with behavior and whether they are getting along and not causing trouble as opposed to whether they are getting As and Bs or learning those other things. Because our feeling is that as long as you can get along with people and do well in life, then you will learn what you need to learn. (Chen et al., 1997)

The Importance of Family

Parents in the same project cited previously indicated that family relationships were most important in their lives. Phrases like "family comes first" and "keeping the family together" demonstrated the significance these parents placed on establishing and maintaining blood and fictive kin bonds. Parents reported that their families enjoyed leisure activities such as eating meals together, visiting relatives together, and spending recreation time together (e.g., going to the park together) as well as family support activities such as working to earn money for their families (including difficult, low-wage employment and multiple jobs) (Chen et al., 1997; Greder, 2002, 2003b).

Respect for Elders

Almost all of the parents interviewed in the aforementioned project stated that respect for elders was another key value. This entailed honoring older members of the immediate family (as well as community elders) and acknowledging the value of their experience and wisdom. Some interviewees stated that they would often specifically seek the parenting advice of older family members (Chen et al., 1997; Greder, 2003c). Respect for elders has been shown to be a significant aspect of family life within several ethnic minority groups (Greder, 2003a–c; McAdoo, 1988; Xiong, Detzner, & Cleveland, 2004). Instilling a respect for elders appears to be an important component of the socialization of children, preparing them for successful (honorable) interactions with members of the family and ethnic group(s) and society as well.

The Significance of Work, Particularly Hard Work

Work, and particularly the exchange of work for economic and social benefit, represents another key value for most ethnic minority parents. Like education, work is seen as both a means (as in "one must work to survive") and an end (as in "there's dignity in work"). Providing economic resources for support of their families is a hallmark of both fatherhood (McAdoo, 1993) and male identity (Hunter & Davis, 1994). Allen and Connor (1997, p. 66) cited messages they heard from African American fathers regarding work, including, "No work can hurt you" and "You can learn about life and yourself from whatever work you do.

The willingness to do hard work (often for relatively low wages) and to sacrifice is an underappreciated strength of many ethnic minority parents. Along with love of family and children, parents typically explain their motivation for hard work with phrases like "No one is gonna give you anything." This key value was particularly illustrated through interviews with Hispanic immigrant parents (Greder, 2003a, 2003c).

Principles and Strategies to Guide Work With Parents

The assumptions and key values mentioned previously can serve as a basis to inform the principles and strategies to guide work with parents of various cultural backgrounds.

I. Principles and strategies related to service

A. The work professionals do for parents and families should focus on understanding the family's concerns, assessing the family's strengths, and identifying the resources that can augment the family's ability to meet its needs.

B. Practitioners should attempt to support parents' abilities to identify and utilize resources rather than simply provide services.
   1. Taking into account the family's cultural construction(s) of family functioning is vital to successful development and implementation of any intervention.
   2. The family's informal systems of social support should be strengthened and used in favor of professional services when possible.

C. Professional support and resources need to be flexible, individualized, and responsive to the changing needs of families.
   1. Consider the ecological and psychosocial contexts in which families live (e.g., neighborhood characteristics, economic stresses, perceived racism, extended family involvement, etc.) as important factors that can potentially affect service delivery and effectiveness.
   2. Those doing the primary parenting should optimally be the ultimate decision-makers regarding the type and quantity of support they need and use.

D. Successful working relationships are built on mutual trust, respect, honesty, and open communication. The most important tool you have is your relationship with the parents. In all social service, the relationship is everything.

E. Practitioners are responsible for the quality of their work with parents and families. Regardless of organizational constraints or the client family's problems and actions, practitioners must treat clients with respect and dignity.

II. Principles and strategies related to cultural competence

A. Acquiring cultural competence is a lifelong process.
   1. Start by understanding how your own cultural contexts affect your work.
   2. Everything we do is cross-cultural. (That is, all family work is cross-cultural.)
   3. It is critical to recognize and learn from one's mistakes in cross-cultural encounters.

B. Understanding one's own culture is a prerequisite to understanding other cultural perspectives.
   1. Unacknowledged cultural biases can obscure our ability to recognize strengths and values of members from other groups.
   2. Explore and learn to appreciate different worldviews.

C. Constantly seek out reliable information about other cultures.
   1. Avoid relying on stereotypes or commonly held beliefs that have no factual basis, even if they are widely held.

    2. Remember, there is at least as much diversity within groups as between groups due to factors such as differences in level of acculturation, generation, SES status (current or past), migration experience, educational level, and national origin.

    3. Keep an open mind, letting families of other cultures teach you about their culture and parenting practices.

D. Balance is a key concept when working in multicultural environments.

    1. Always be aware of the probability of cultural similarities in addition to cultural differences. Ethnic minority families need to successfully achieve normative family developmental goals (e.g., preparing young children for school entry) while also accomplishing group specific objectives (e.g., socializing children about race and ethnicity).

    2. Be aware of families' attempts to balance mainstream values with their own cultural values and norms.

    3. Be aware of the extent to which families adhere to mainstream developmental goals, are able to navigate formal social support systems, and have assimilated or acculturated to mainstream culture.

    4. Try not to judge, but to understand.

E. Historical relationships between groups can present cross-cultural barriers unless acknowledged and managed.

    1. Be aware of how you perceive members of other groups and how they perceive you. Cultural mistrust can hinder the ability of either party to work effectively.

    2. Cultivate an attitude of openness by being respectful and collaborative and by managing intercultural anxiety.

Adapted from Allen, 2003; Garcia-Coll & Patcher, 2002; Greder et al., 2002; Pletcher & McBride, 2000.

Summary

Culture plays an integral role in shaping parenting values, beliefs, goals, and practices. As the United States becomes increasingly diverse, it is critical to understand and respect cultural influences on parenting and to identify ways to help families meet their goals that is respectful of their cultural contexts.

All parents, regardless of culture, want good things for their children. Universal parenting aspirations include ensuring the physical safety of children; meeting children's basic physical (e.g., food, shelter, clothing) and psychological needs (e.g., sense of belonging and self-worth); helping children adapt successfully to their environment; providing a stimulating environment that nurtures children's growth; and passing on cultural values, beliefs, and practices to the next generation. Although the basic aspirations of parents across cultures are similar, the behaviors parents employ to carry out these aspirations vary based on the contextual demands of their environments as well as the degree of acculturation the parent experiences. Ethnic minority parents face unique parenting challenges due to the various forms of prejudice and discrimination that can create psychological stress. Such stress can affect parenting behavior and thus indirectly influence child development.

Cultural practices and individual characteristics of both professionals and families influence interactions between professionals and families. Thus, it is important for professionals to be aware of families' values, beliefs, concerns, and priorities regarding parenting and to tailor interventions and other services to meet the needs and resources of families with whom they are working. In this chapter the authors have put forth specific principles and strategies related to professional service and cultural competence to consider when working with culturally diverse families.

References

Allen, W. D. (2003, October). *Cultural perspectives on parenting*. Paper presented at Cultural Perspectives on Parenting, a national satellite conference, Ames, IA. (Available from Educational Materials and Marketing Services, Iowa State University Extension, 3630 Extension 4-H Youth Building Ames, IA 50011-3630)

Allen, W. D., & Connor, M. (1997). An Afrocentric perspective on generative fathering. In A. Hawkins & D. Dollahite (Eds.), *Generative fathering: Beyond deficit perspectives* (pp. 52–70). Thousand Oaks, CA: Sage.

Anderson, P. P., & Fenichel, E. S. (1989). *Serving culturally diverse families of infants and toddlers with disabilities*. Washington, DC: National Center for Clinical Infant Programs.

Barbarin, O. A. (1999). Social risks and psychological adjustment: A comparison of African American and South African children. *Child Development, 70,* 1348–1359.

Baumrind, D. (1996). The discipline controversy revisited. *Family Relations, 45,* 405–414.

Belsky, J. (1984). The determinants of parenting: A process model. *Child Development, 55,* 83–96.

Bishaw, A., & Iceland, J. (2003). *Poverty: 1999 census 2000 brief*. Retrieved April 22, 2005, from http://www.census.gov/prod/2003pubs/c2kbr-19.pdf

Bowman, P. J., & Howard, C. (1985). Race-related socialization, motivation, and academic achievement: A study of Black youth in three-generation families. *Journal of the American Academy of Child Psychiatry, 24,* 134–141.

Brooks, J. (1991). *The process of parenting* (3rd ed.). Palo Alto, CA: Mayfield.

Chen, D., Brekken, L., & Chan, S. (Producers). (1997). *Project CRAFT: Culturally responsive and family focused training* [Videotape 31207P-Vb-X]. (Available from Child Development Media, Van Nuys, CA)

DeNavas-Walt, C., Proctor, B. D., & Mills, R. J. (2004, August). *Income, poverty, and health insurance coverage in the United States: 2003* (Current Population Reports: Consumer Income, P60-226). Retrieved July 30, 2006, from http://www.census.gov/prod/2004pubs/p60-226.pdf

Garcia-Coll, C. (2003, November 13). *Cultural perspectives on parenting.* Paper presented at Cultural Perspectives on Parenting, a national satellite conference, Ames, IA. (Available from Educational Materials and Marketing Services, Iowa State University Extension, 3630 Extension 4-H Youth Building Ames, IA 50011-3630)

Garcia-Coll, C., & Patcher, L. M. (2002). Ethnic and minority parenting. In M. H. Bornstein (Ed.), *Handbook of parenting, Vol. 4: Social conditions and applied parenting* (pp. 1–20). Mahwah, NJ: Erlbaum.

Garrett, P., Ng'andu, N., & Ferron, J. (1994). Poverty experiences of young children and the quality of their home environment. *Child Development, 65*(2), 331–345.

Greder, K. (Executive Producer). (2002). *Sharing a family's story* [Videotape]. (Available from Educational Materials and Marketing Services, Iowa State University Extension, 3630 Extension 4-H Youth Building Ames, IA 50011-3630)

Greder, K. (2003a). Unpublished transcript of interview with Mexican parents in Marshalltown, IA.

Greder, K. (2003b). Unpublished transcript of interview with parents from India, Sudan, and Saudi Arabia and with African American and Caucasian parents in Ames, IA.

Greder, K. (2003c). Unpublished transcript of interview with Guatemalan parent in Perry, IA.

Greder, K., Oesterreich, L., Anderson, P., Kaufman, M. B., Santiago, A., Hegland, S., & McDonnell, S. (2002). *Partnering with parents: Walking the journey together* (Extension Publication SP 175). Ames: Iowa State University.

Hamner, T. J., & Turner, P. H. (2001). *Parenting in contemporary society* (4th ed.). Boston: Allyn & Bacon.

Harkness, S., & Super, C. (1995). Culture and parenting. In M. H. Bornstein (Ed.), *Handbook of parenting, Vol. 2: Biology and ecology of parenting* (pp. 211–234). Hillsdale, NJ: Erlbaum.

History of parenting practices. (1999). [Videotape 3014]. (Available from Learning Zone Xpress, P.O. Box 1022, Owatonna, MN 55060)

Hughes, D., & Chen, L. (1999). The nature of parents' race-related communication to children: A developmental perspective. In L. Balter & C. S. Tamis-Lemonda (Eds.), *Child psychology: A handbook of contemporary issues* (pp. 467–490). Philadelphia: Psychology Press.

Hunter, A. G., & Davis, J. E. (1994). Hidden voices of Black men: The meaning, structure, and complexity of manhood. *Journal of Black Studies, 25,* 20–40.

Huston, A., McLoyd, V., & Coll, C. (1994). Children and poverty: Issues in contemporary research. *Child Development, 65*(2), 275–282.

Lynch, E. W., & Hanson, M. J. (1998). *Developing cross-cultural competence: A guide for working with children and their families* (2nd ed.). Baltimore, MD: Paul Brookes.

McAdoo, J. (1988). The role of Black fathers in the socialization of Black children. In H. McAdoo (Ed.), *Black families* (pp. 257–269). Newbury Park, CA: Sage.

McAdoo, J. (1993). The roles of African American fathers: An ecological perspective. *Families in Society, 74,* 28–35.

McLeod, J., & Shanahan, M. (1993). Poverty, parenting, and children's mental health. *American Sociological Review, 58,* 351–366.

Payne, R. K. (2001). *A framework for understanding poverty.* Highlands, TX: aha! Process.

Peters, M. (1988). Parenting in Black families with young children: A historical perspective. In H. McAdoo (Ed.), *Black families* (pp. 228–241). Newbury Park, CA: Sage.

Phinney, J. S., & Chavira, V. (1995). Parental ethnic socialization and adolescent coping with problems related to ethnicity. *Journal of Research on Adolescence, 5,* 31–53.

Pletcher, L. C., & McBride, S. (2000). *Family centered services: Guiding principles and practices for delivery of family centered services* (Early ACCESS, Iowa Department of Education). Retrieved May 13, 2005, from http://www.extension.iastate.edu/culture/files/FamlCntrdSrvc.pdf

Quintana, S. M., & Vera, E. M. (1999). Mexican-American children's ethnic identity, understanding of ethnic prejudice, and parental ethnic socialization. *Hispanic Journal of Behavioral Sciences, 21,* 387–404.

Szapocznik, J., & Hernandez, R. (1988). The Cuban-American family. In C. H. Mindel, R. W. Habenstein, & R. Wright (Eds.), *Ethnic families in America* (pp. 160–172). New York: Elsevier.

Szapocznik, J., Kurtines, W. M., & Fernandez, T. (1980). Bicultural involvement and adjustment in Hispanic-American youths. *International Journal of Intercultural Relations, 4,* 353–365.

U.S. Census Bureau. (2004–2005). *Statistical abstract of the United States: 2004–2005* (p. 55). Retrieved April 21, 2005, from http://www.census.gov/prod/2004pubs/04statab/pop.pdf

Walker, D., Greenwood, C., Hart, B., & Carta, J. (1994). Prediction of school outcomes based on early language production and socioeconomic factors. *Child Development, 65*(2), 606–621.

Wilson, W. (1987). *The truly disadvantaged: The inner city, the underclass, and public policy.* Chicago: University of Chicago Press.

Xiong, Z. B., Detzner, D., & Cleveland, M. (2004). Southeast Asian adolescents' perceptions of immigrant parenting practices. *Hmong Studies Journal, 5,* 1–20.

Zuniga, M. E. (1992). Families with Latino roots. In E. W. Lynch & M. J. Hanson (Eds.), *Developing cross-cultural competence: A guide for working with children and their families* (pp. 151–179). Baltimore, MD: Paul Brookes.

8

Cultural Diversity and Aging Families

Rona J. Karasik and Raeann R. Hamon

> It is not by the gray of the hair that one knows the age of the heart.
>
> —Edward G. Bulwer-Lytton

In thinking about aging and older families, it is important to consider that aging is not a single experience. Many equate aging with the physiological changes our bodies go through over time. Some focus on diseases that, while not age related, are often thought to be associated with old age. Aging, however, is much more than the accumulation of wrinkles, gray hair, and the possibility of one or more chronic health conditions. Aging is also about how we view people (including ourselves) based on how we look and act and even by the number of candles on our birthday cakes. Aging is also about relationships—how they are sustained, how they change, and how new relationships are formed.

We have many stereotypes about aging and older persons. While our expectations are often negative, in reality, there are both positive and negative aspects to aging. The way in which we age is affected by a wide range of personal and social factors. Older persons are a highly heterogeneous group, and the family relationships of older persons are highly diverse as well. This chapter will focus on how culture and ethnicity interplay with a variety of factors to affect aging and older families.

Why Focus on Cultural Diversity in Older Families?

We do not grow absolutely, chronologically. We grow sometimes in one dimension, and not in another; unevenly. We grow partially. We are relative. We are mature in one realm, childish in another. The past, present, and future mingle and pull us backward, forward, or fix us in the present.

—Anaïs Nin

There are many reasons to try to understand the diverse impact of aging on families. First and foremost is the size and ongoing growth of the older population in the United States. In 2002, 35.6 million persons (12.3 percent of the U.S. population) were aged 65 and older (Administration on Aging, 2003). By 2030, the older population is expected to grow to 20 percent of the U.S. population—roughly 71.5 million persons will be aged 65 and older. Not surprisingly, the U.S. older population is not just growing in size but in ethnic diversity as well. In 2000, 17.2 percent of adults 65 and older in the United States reported being ethnic minorities. African American elders made up the largest ethnic minority elder group (8.1 percent), followed by 2.7 percent identifying as Asian or Pacific Islanders, and less than 1 percent identifying themselves as American Indian or Alaskan Native. Older persons identifying themselves as Hispanic (who may be of any race) composed 5.5 percent of the population, and 0.5 percent of older adults indicated being of two or more races. By 2030, the proportion of ethnic minority elders is expected to grow to 26.4 percent of the older population (Administration on Aging, 2003).

While these demographics clearly reflect a rapidly growing and increasingly diverse older population, numbers do not tell the whole story. Diversity within each racial and ethnic group is considerable. Most data on race and ethnicity, however, are reported in the overly broad categories of White, Black, American Indian/Alaskan Native, Asian or Pacific Islander, and Hispanic (U.S. Bureau of the Census, 2002). Moreover, while the census requests write-in information on a "person's ancestry or ethnic origin," rarely are these data included in descriptions of the aging population. As such, we know very little about how culture and ethnicity affect the aging experiences of many groups in the United States.

Salari (2002), for example, notes the invisibility in aging research of the diverse groups in the United States who have Middle Eastern origins as well as of those who practice Islam. For many groups, religion is a vital concern in how we understand the impact of cultural diversity on aging. Thus, a second reason to explore the cultural diversity of the older population is to understand how factors of culture, ethnicity, and race interplay with the other factors that make aging unique—including religion (Salari, 2002), gender (Conway-Turner, 1999), sexual orientation (Cooney & Dunne, 2001; Orel, 2004), health (Diwan & Jonnalagadda, 2001; Johnson & Smith, 2002; Li & Fries, 2005; Zhan & Chen, 2004), socioeconomic status (Angel, 2003), family relationships (Shawler, 2004), social support (Johnson & Tripp-Reimer, 2001; Jordan-Marsh & Harden, 2005), geographic location (Applewhite & Torres, 2003; Barusch & TenBarge, 2003; Himes, Hogan, & Eggebeen, 1996), and life experiences (Moriarty & Butt, 2004). None of these factors alone makes a person or family. Rather, all are important for us to understand who our older population is and what their increasing numbers will mean.

Finally, considerations for how best to meet the needs of this rapidly growing and changing population are a third reason for exploring the impact of cultural diversity. Many call attention to the need for *cultural competence*—a system that provides appropriate, effective, high-quality services for all persons regardless of racial or ethnic background (Geron, 2002). Defining what constitutes cultural competence and how we can achieve it, however, can be challenging and perhaps a bit overwhelming. Capitman (2002), therefore, suggests starting with *cultural humility,* where we begin by "acknowledging what we do not know about each other as individuals and members of multiple cultural groups" (p. 12). Such an approach, however, still requires working not only toward understanding the needs of all older adults, but also toward the improved provision of culturally appropriate services. Saying we know little about a group is not enough. We must continuously seek to learn more about the diverse experiences, strengths, and needs of older adults and their families.

Theoretical Approaches to Understanding Cultural Diversity and Aging Families

It is theory that decides what can be observed.

—Albert Einstein

In selecting a framework to examine cultural diversity in older families, we must be sensitive to how our own expectations and biases affect not only the questions we ask but also the way in which we interpret the responses. Currently, much of the research on diversity in aging takes a preliminary, primarily descriptive approach (e.g., "what?" "who?" and "how many?"). Several studies, however, have taken the next step of grounding their research into a particular theoretical framework.

Many theories focus on the problems experienced by culturally diverse aging families. Sands and Goldberg-Glen (2000), for example, employ stress theory to explore factors that affect levels of stress experienced by grandparents who serve as parents to their grandchildren. Not surprisingly, research conducted under such an approach can result in lists of problems to be "fixed" by programs, services, and more research.

Other studies employ broader theoretical frameworks, such as the life course perspective, where the focus is on age norms and the timing of life transitions (Hagestad & Neugarten, 1985). From this perspective, family life transitions (e.g., marriage, widowhood, grandparenthood) are placed into social and historical context (e.g., as "on-time" or "off-time"). Individual life experiences and their outcomes are then interpreted with regard to the impact of such timing. Some recent studies using this framework have expanded the perspective to include how factors such as race and ethnicity affect the timing and interpretation of such experiences (Burton, 1996).

While also considering changes over the life span, selectivity theory focuses on the evolving function of social interaction and emotional closeness within relationships. Carstensen (2001) suggests that older persons become more selective in their choice of social partners, often directing their attention to, and thus placing more importance on, relationships with available close family and friends. Such an approach may be seen as an adaptive way to deal with shrinking social networks.

Also seeking to focus on positive adaptation, some frame their research in terms of the shared strengths and challenges certain social and historical circumstances bring about. Conway-Turner (1999) uses a feminist perspective to examine the lives of older women of color. Her approach is grounded in the notion that while women of color may come from very different backgrounds, they share experiences of discrimination based on race, ethnicity, gender, and age. Conway-Turner's approach also calls for exploring the cumulative effects of these variables as they both positively and negatively interact with the later-life and family experiences of women of color.

More recently, Pillemer and Lüscher (2004) suggest that "societies, and the individuals within them, are characteristically ambivalent about relationships between parents and children in adulthood" (p. 6). They propose an ambivalence framework "for studying dilemmas and contradictions in late-life families" in an empirical and systematic fashion, both at the socio-logical and psychological levels. Though it has not yet been explicitly applied to family relationships among ethnically or culturally diverse families, Boss and Kaplan (2004) assert that "the ambiguous loss of a parent with dementia provides fertile ground for increased ambivalence in intergenera-tional relations" (p. 207), making the model particularly relevant. So, too, ambivalence is a useful construct when considering adult children's filial role or sense of responsibility for the well-being of their aging parents (Lang, 2004).

Finally, Gibson's work (2005) is one of a handful of studies looking at aging families from an Afrocentric perspective. Such an approach "focuses on traditional African philosophical assumptions, which emphasize holistic, interdependent, and spiritual conceptions of people and their environment" and "focuses on family strengths within the culture of people of African descent" (p. 293). Thus, in contrast to a life course perspective that might view the event of grandparents parenting their grandchildren as "off-time," or stress theory, which might look at the negative impact parenting duties have on grandparents (Sands & Goldberg-Glen, 2000), Gibson looks at the positive aspects gained from this "grand-parenting" role and focuses, instead, on ways to strengthen the existing grandparent-as-parent relation-ships. Similarly, Minkler and Fuller-Thomson (2005) emphasize the value of "theories of intersectionality" or those that stress the connection of class, race, and gender (p. S82), particularly when examining later-life family top-ics like care provided by grandparents in African American communities.

Each of the above theoretical frameworks has a place in helping us to understand the experiences of culturally diverse older families. Certainly, aging families face many challenges as well as possess unique strengths. These theoretical approaches help to place the current research findings into context as well guide new research questions.

Research on Diversity in Later-Life Families

We have become not a melting pot but a beautiful mosaic. Different people, different beliefs, different yearnings, different hopes, different dreams.

—Jimmy Carter

Despite the rather large but separate bodies of research on aging families (Allen, Blieszner, & Roberto, 2000; Walker, Manoogian-O'Dell, McGraw, & White, 2001) and diversity in older populations (Capitman, 2002; Harris,

1998) there has been only limited research focusing on the intersections of race, ethnicity, and cultural background in aging families. Thus, much of the research presented here was not specifically designed to address culturally diverse aging families.

Additionally, in examining this research, it is important to recognize that culture and ethnicity do not operate in a vacuum. Time, history, immigration (Wilmoth, 2001), acculturation (Silverstein & Chen, 1999), and societal pressure continuously make and remake culture's role. For example, while Harris (1998) notes that the traditions of many groups (e.g., African American, Asian, Hispanic, Native American) focus on collectivity and interdependence—placing the needs of the family above the needs of the individual—changing societal influences have altered the meaning and outcome of these traditions. Whereas elders in such families might expect to hold central roles (e.g., teacher, guide, tradition bearer), many find themselves in conflict with current societal pressure to focus on youth and individualism. Many also face the paradox of wanting their children and grandchildren to become fully assimilated into the dominant culture and to have a better life than they did, while still adhering to their cultural traditions as well (Patterson, 2003). The goal of this section, therefore, is to highlight areas where culture, ethnicity, and aging families intersect, while also considering how such influences continue to change in today's society.

Partnerships in Later Life

Newlyweds become oldyweds, and oldyweds are the reasons that families work.

—Author unknown

Despite media images of lonely older adults, over half of adults age 65 and over are married. There are, however, significant discrepancies in marital status between men and women. Older women, who outnumber older men by a ratio of 141:100, are much less likely to be married than older men. In fact, in 2002, 73 percent of older men and only 41 percent of older women were currently married (Administration on Aging, 2003). These gender disparities also hold true when looking across broad racial and ethnic categories. While older White males were more likely to be married (74.3 percent) than older Hispanic males (67.5 percent) and older Black males (53.9 percent), males in general were still more likely to be married than females. As such, 42.9 percent of White older women, 38 percent of Hispanic older women, and 25 percent of older Black women were currently married (U.S. Bureau of the Census, 2002).

Conversely, older women (46 percent) were over four times as likely to be widowed as older men (14 percent) (Administration on Aging, 2003). With regard to race and ethnicity, older Black women (54.6 percent) were the most likely to be widowed, followed by White older women (44.4 percent) and Hispanic older women (39.4 percent). Similarly, older Black men (21 percent) were more likely to be widowed than older Hispanic men (15 percent) and older White men (13.9 percent) (U.S. Bureau of the Census, 2002).

Some of the gender difference in marital status has been attributed to the discrepancy in overall numbers and life expectancy between men and women, with women living an average of six years longer than men (Administration on Aging, 2003; Arias, 2004). Life expectancy differences, however, are not the only factor here. Social and cultural expectations about marriage and remarriage, which can vary among different groups, have also been cited in the higher rates of continued widowhood for women. The pool of socially acceptable potential mates for widowed women (their age and older) continues to diminish, while the pool for men (their age and younger) is potentially endless. Social norms about race and acceptable marriage partners may also contribute to this disparity (Pienta, Hayward, & Jenkins, 2000), as well as pervasive media images of older women as unattractive and men as ageless. Regardless of the cause, women of all ethnic groups are much more likely to live alone in later life than men (Administration on Aging, 2003; Himes et al., 1996). Furthermore, older women living alone, particularly older Hispanic women, have the highest rates of poverty among older adults (Administration on Aging, 2003). Factors of education and employment status, however, are also found to interact with marital status and ethnicity in regard to rates of income and poverty (Wilson & Hardy, 2002).

In addition to widowhood, divorce is another factor that places older women of all ethnic backgrounds at higher risk both of living alone and experiencing poverty. In 2002, approximately 10 percent of older persons were currently divorced, a rate that has almost doubled since 1980 (Administration on Aging, 2003). With regard to data on race and ethnicity, however, some gender differences appear, with the percentage of currently divorced older Hispanic women (11.1 percent) being somewhat higher than for older Hispanic men (8.4 percent) and older Black women (8.9 percent) and older Black men (8.4 percent). The number of currently divorced older White women (7.1 percent) was also slightly higher than for older White men (6.0 percent) (U.S. Bureau of the Census, 2002).

Finally, an often overlooked area is the highly diverse group of older adults who have remained ever-single (Cooney & Dunne, 2001), accounting for about 4 percent of older men and 4 percent of older women (Administration on Aging, 2003). Older Black men (9.1 percent) were the most likely group not to marry, followed by older Black women (5.9 percent) and older Hispanic women (5.6 percent). An equal percentage of older White men (3.8 percent) and older Hispanic men (3.8 percent) remained ever-single, while older White women (3.5 percent) were the least likely to never marry. Currently, few studies focus on older ever-singles—and even fewer, if any, focus on culture and ethnicity in older ever-singles. The reasons why a person might remain single, however, and also in who we as a society label as single, are important factors in later-life experiences. Careers, lack of opportunity, and relatively high percentage of Latinos who live in informal unions; these individuals may not appear in demographic studies as married. Similarly, some stay single because marriage is not a legal option, not because they are not involved in a partnership. While growing attention is being given to gay and lesbian partnerships in later life (Grossman, D'Augelli, & Hershberger, 2000; Orel, 2004), few studies focus specifically on issues of culture and ethnicity (McFarland & Sanders, 2003).

Beyond the above demographic descriptions, research directed specifically at the intersections of race, culture, ethnicity, and later-life family partnerships is limited. Pienta et al. (2000) looked at the effects of marriage on health for White, African American, and Latino adults and found that married older adults had better health than widowed and divorced persons, although these findings were less distinct for Whites than for persons of color. Kitson (2000) found similarly complex outcomes looking at how widows adjust to the death of their spouses, with age, race, and cause of death interacting. Of note is that Black widows of spouses who died of suicide expressed more distress than similar White widows, suggesting a greater stigma against suicide among Blacks.

Siblings in Later Life

To the outside world we all grow old. But not to brothers and sisters. We know each other as we always were.

—Clara Ortega

The sibling relationship is typically one of the longest lasting of all family relationships, with most current older adults having at least one living sibling—something that may change as smaller families become the norm. Later-life sibling relationships tend to decrease in intensity and contact during the childbearing and rearing years, followed by increased contact in the later years (Goetting, 1986). Studies suggest gender, geographic proximity, and individual differences mediate the amount and type of contact siblings have in later life (Connidis & Campbell, 2001). Campbell, Connidis, and Davies (1999) discovered the centrality of the confidant role as well as emotional and instrumental support among siblings; companionship is a less critical function for siblings. So, too, they found that single, childless, and widowed women tend to have greater involvement with their siblings. Gold (1990) found that race also had an impact on later sibling relationships, finding that Black sibling dyads tended to be more positive than White sibling dyads. Other findings that include culture and race, however, are somewhat mixed. For example, many studies find that sister-sister ties hold the strongest bonds (Connidis & Campbell, 2001). John (1991), however, found ties between brothers to be stronger in his study of siblings in the Prairie Band Potawatomi, a Native American tribe.

While few studies focus directly on the impact of culture and ethnicity on later-life sibling relationships, several studies on the social support networks of culturally diverse older adults also find that siblings play an important role. Becker, Beyene, Newsom, and Mayen (2003) found that siblings were an important part of mutual support networks for older African Americans, Latinos, and Filipino Americans. Similarly, Johnson (1999) found strong bonds between older Black men and their siblings. Williams (2001), on the other hand, found that the impoverished older Mexican American men in her sample had little interaction with their extended families, including their siblings.

Grandparenthood

> *Grandchildren are the dots that connect the lines from generation to generation.*
>
> —Lois Wyse

While there have always been some who have lived long enough to become grandparents, the evolution of grandparenthood is fairly new. Today's ever-increasing life expectancies have created unprecedented numbers of three-, four-, and even five-generation families. Szinovacz (1998) calls grandparenthood a "near universal experience" (pp. 48–49), with most older adults having an average of five to six grandchildren. Szinovacz also notes, however, that "about 15 percent of Black and Hispanic men report that they are not grandparents" (p. 49). In suggesting that some of these men may be unaware of their grandparent status due to loss of contact with their families (via immigration, divorce, and other means), Szinovacz raises two important concerns.

First, much of the data on grandparenthood is self-reported. Even the census, which recently added questions on the number of grandparents living with grandchildren, relies on measures of self-report (Simmons & Dye, 2003). A second concern is the question of who is a grandparent. Is grandparenthood solely a biological event, or must one acknowledge the bond for it to exist? Also, is a biological bond required? In some groups, the titles "mother" and "grandmother" are used as a sign of respect for all elder women or to designate fictive kin (Gibson, 2005; Jordan-Marsh & Harden, 2005) and is not necessarily reserved for blood kin.

Additionally, the roles grandparents play and their impacts on families are quite varied. Several factors can influence the shape grandparent roles may take, including gender, age, culture, and ethnicity (Bengtson, 1985; Fingerman, 2004). Cherlin and Furstenberg (1992) describe three grandparenting styles—remote, companionate, and involved. Remote relationships were characterized as largely symbolic, with little if any direct contact. Often geographic distance and/or divorce were factors in limiting the amount of grandparent-grandchild contact. Companionate grand-relationships tend to focus more on leisure activities and friendship, while involved grandparents took a more active role in their grandchildren's lives, often taking on a more parental role. Weibel-Orlando (2001) found similar grandparenting styles among Native American elders, adding two additional styles—*ceremonial grandparents,* who lived distant from their grandchildren but had frequent, culturally endowed contact, and *cultural conservator grandparents,* who actively sought contact and temporary coresidence with their grandchildren "for the expressed purpose of exposing them to the American Indian way of life" (p. 143).

In another study, Silverstein and Chen (1999) examined how acculturation, defined as "the erosion of traditional cultural language, values, and practices" (p. 196) affected the quality of the grandparent-grandchild relationship in Mexican American families. Using data from the study of three-generational Mexican American families, Silverstein and Chen found that gaps in cultural values between generations reduced the social interaction and intimacy of these Mexican American grandparents and grandchildren over time. While language barriers appeared to add to this gap, language was not the sole cause of the relationship distance. Of additional note is that while the grandchildren in this study reported a reduction in their grandparent-grandchild relationship, their grandparents did not.

Other research focuses on the small but growing trend involving coresidence among grandparents and grandchildren. The 2000 census found that 3.6 percent of adults (or 5.8 million people) were living with grandchildren under the age of 18 (Simmons & Dye, 2003). Some of these relationships may be characterized as coparenting (where the parent also lives with the grandparent and grandchild) and others (2.4 million, or 42 percent) were described as custodial grandparent caregivers. Census rates of coresidence, either as coparent or as caregiver, varied considerably by racial and ethnic category. Only 2 percent of non-Hispanic Whites reported coresiding with a grandchild, compared with 6 percent of Asian Americans, 8 percent of American Indian and Native Alaskans, 8 percent of people who are Black, 8 percent who are Hispanic, and 10 percent of Pacific Islanders (Simmons & Dye, 2003).

Several researchers have looked at the phenomenon of grandparents raising grandchildren (Erera, 2002). Fuller-Thomson, Minkler, and Driver (1997) note that while custodial grandparenting was not limited to any single group, a disproportionate number of single women, African Americans, recently bereaved parents, and persons with low income were found in this role. African American grandparent caregivers, especially grandmothers, were particularly vulnerable in that they experienced elevated rates of poverty and "were more likely than their noncaregiving peers to report functional limitations" (Minkler & Fuller-Thomson, 2005, p. S90). Examinations of the impact on grandparents providing care for grandchildren suggest that the role involves some level of stress (Musil, 1998), but that a variety of factors, including caregiving context and family support (Sands & Goldberg-Glen, 2000) as well as ethnicity (Goodman & Silverstein, 2002), moderate just how much stress caregiving grandparents experience.

Taking a somewhat different approach, Gibson (2005), focused on the positive impact parenting African American grandparents can have on their grandchildren and identified seven themes or potential strengths of such relationships, including maintaining effective communication, taking a strong role in their grandchildren's education, providing socioemotional support, involving the extended family, involving grandchildren in the community, working with the vulnerabilities of the grandchildren, and acknowledging the absence of the grandchildren's biological parent(s). Strom, Carter, and Schmidt (2004) and Strom, Heeder, and Strom (2005) similarly found that African American grandparents often take a strong role in their grandchildren's lives, particularly with regard to being a teacher and role model. These studies suggest that teaching is a strength of Black grandmothers, and that grandparents should be encouraged to help support the education of their grandchildren.

Taken together, these findings suggest that grandparenthood is an important yet highly variable aspect of later-life families. The range of variables, including cultural and ethnic diversity, that affect grandparenthood suggest further research with broader samples from a variety of backgrounds is warranted (Fingerman, 2004; Hayslip & Kaminski, 2005).

Family Caregiving and Future Research

> *You don't choose your family. They are God's gift to you, as you are to them.*
>
> —Desmond Tutu

Family caregiving is a vastly broad area that includes but is not limited to areas of social support and resources (Williams & Dilworth-Anderson, 2002), filial responsibility or obligation (Hamon & Whitney, 2003; Jolicoeur & Madden, 2002), health and ability of care recipients (Johnson & Smith, 2002; Li & Fries, 2005) and informal care providers (Dilworth-Anderson, Goodwin, & Williams, 2004), health-seeking practices and use of formal services (Pang, Jordan-Marsh, Radina, & Barber, 2004; Silverstein, & Cody, 2003; Sohn & Harada, 2004), and medication practices (Zhan & Chen, 2004) as well as cultural interpretations of disease (Diwan, Jonnalagadda, & Gupta, 2004); caregiver stress, burden, and coping (John, Hennessy, Dyeson, & Garrett, 2001; Ramos, 2004); and end-of-life decisions and transition to death (Settles, 2005). Dilworth-Anderson, Williams, and Gibson (2002), in their extensive review of two decades of research on race, ethnicity, and culture in caregiving research, found that the experience of caregiving varied across different racial and ethnic groups. Fairly consistent, however, was the finding that caregivers to ethnic minority elders were more likely to use informal than formal support mechanisms and that family members (both close and extended) provided much of the informal support.

Perhaps even more important than their synthesis of the caregiving findings, however, is that Dilworth-Anderson et al. (2002) call attention to the significant problems in interpreting findings across studies that lack consistency in their definitions, methods, and approaches to studying caregiving for older adults in ethnically diverse families. They call for better studies on family caregiving that are grounded in culturally sensitive theoretical approaches (e.g., life course, symbolic interaction, and social constructivism) and that can take into account "the cultural-historical background (values, beliefs, identities, and meanings assigned to experiences) and sociopolitical conditions (economic status and access to goods and services) of diverse groups" (p. 267). Such studies need also to consider the issues of immigration, migration, acculturation, socioeconomic status, education, and other factors that lead to differences within as well as between various groups. The concerns Dilworth-Anderson and colleagues raise about caregiving research can and should be applied to future efforts to understand the influence of culture and ethnicity on later-life partnerships, sibling relationships, grandparenthood, and other aspects of later-life families as well.

Applying What We Know About Cultural Diversity and Later-Life Families

Everyone thinks of changing the world, but no one thinks of changing himself.

—Lev Nikolayevich Tolstoy

Given that the population of older adults in the United States is rapidly growing and becoming increasingly diverse, it is vital that we seek to understand the strengths, concerns, and needs of aging families so that we may better provide adequate and appropriate services and support. As discussed throughout this chapter, numerous factors affect the experiences of aging families. While we do not have all the answers, we can start by enhancing our own cultural sensitivity and by thinking about the questions that are raised. Rather than assuming all older adults are the same, or that all persons of a particular background have similar experiences and needs, it is important to inquire about relevant individual circumstances. For example, when providing food service, it is appropriate to ask about food preferences—a question that is likely to garner health concerns as well as cultural or religious restrictions. Be mindful, however, not to phrase questions in such a way as to single a person out or to make generalized assumptions (e.g., "Since you are Jewish, are there foods you do not eat?"). Rather, open, sincere inquiries such as "Do you have any food preferences or special dietary needs?" allow older adults and their families to be the guide for providing culturally sensitive services. Similarly, in examining potential family support, one should inquire broadly about who is included in a person's household and social network rather than making assumptions about likely familial assistance.

When assessing older adults' situations or intervening on their behalf, it is also helpful to be informed by the most recent scholarship relative to certain potential strengths (e.g., close and extended family members may be an important source of informal support to ethnic minority elders) and vulnerabilities (e.g., older Hispanic women who live alone have the highest rates of poverty among older adults) that might be present among elders of certain ethnic or racial groups. It is vital, however, to be careful not to generalize such findings to the point of developing stereotypes. All elder clients deserve careful and thorough assessment of their own life circumstance when determining the best health care, social support, and care plan. By adopting an attitude of *cultural humility*, we can work toward creating a *culturally competent* system that provides effective, appropriate, high-quality services for all regardless of racial or ethnic background (Capitman, 2002; Geron, 2002).

References

Administration on Aging. (2003). *A profile of older Americans: 2003*. Washington, DC: U.S. Department of Health and Human Services.

Allen, K. R., Blieszner, R., & Roberto, K. A. (2000). Families in the middle and later years: A review and critique of research in the 1990s. *Journal of Marriage and the Family, 62*(4), 911–926.

Angel, J. L. (2003). Devolution and the social welfare of elderly immigrants: Who will bear the burden? *Public Administration Review, 63*(1), 79–89.

Applewhite, S. L., & Torres, C. (2003). Rural Latino elders. *Journal of Gerontological Social Work, 41*(1/2), 151–174.

Arias, E. (2004). United States life tables, 2002. *National Vital Statistics Reports, 53*(6), 1–39.

Barusch, A., & TenBarge, C. (2003). Indigenous elders in rural America. *Journal of Gerontological Social Work, 41*(1/2), 121–136.

Becker, G., Beyene, Y., Newsom, E., & Mayen, N. (2003). Creating continuity through mutual assistance: Intergenerational reciprocity in four ethnic groups. *Journal of Gerontology: Social Sciences, 58B*(3), S151–S159.

Bengtson, V. L. (1985). Diversity and symbolism in grandparental roles. In V. Bengtson & J. Robertson (Eds.), *Grandparenthood* (pp. 11–25). Beverly Hills, CA: Sage.

Boss, P., & Kaplan, L. (2004). Ambiguous loss and ambivalence when a parent has dementia. In K. Pillemer & K. Lüscher (Eds.), *Intergenerational ambivalences: New perspectives on parent-child relations in later life* (pp. 207–224). Amsterdam: Elsevier.

Burton, L. M. (1996). Age norms, the timing of family role transitions, and intergenerational caregiving among African American women. *The Gerontologist, 36*(2), 199–208.

Campbell, L. D., Connidis, I. A., & Davies, L. (1999). Sibling ties in later life: A social network analysis. *Journal of Family Issues, 20*(1), 114–148.

Capitman, J. (2002). Defining diversity: A primer and a review. *Generations, XXVI*(3), 8–14.

Carstensen, L. L. (2001). Selectivity theory: Social activity in life-span context. In A. Walker, M. Manoogian-O'Dell, L. McGraw, & D. White (Eds.), *Families in later life: Connections and transitions* (pp. 265–275). Thousand Oaks, CA: Pine Forge Press.

Cherlin, A., & Furstenberg, F. (1992). *The new American grandparent*. Cambridge, MA: Harvard University Press.

Connidis, I., & Campbell, L. (2001). Closeness, confiding, and contact among siblings in middle and late adulthood. In A. Walker, M. Manoogian-O'Dell, L. McGraw, & D. White (Eds.), *Families in later life: Connections and transitions* (pp. 149–155). Thousand Oaks, CA: Pine Forge Press.

Conway-Turner, K. (1999). Older women of color: A feminist exploration of the intersections of personal, familial and community life. *Journal of Women and Aging, 11*(2–3), 115–130.

Cooney, T. M., & Dunne, K. (2001). Intimate relationships in later life. *Journal of Family Issues, 22*(7), 838–858.

Dilworth-Anderson, P., Goodwin, P. Y., & Williams, S. W. (2004). Can culture help explain the physical health effects of caregiving over time among African American caregivers? *Journal of Gerontology: Social Sciences, 59B*(3), S138–S145.

Dilworth-Anderson, P., Williams, I. C., & Gibson, B. E. (2002). Issues of race, ethnicity, and culture in caregiving research: A 20-year review (1980–2000). *The Gerontologist, 42*(2), 237–272.

Diwan, S., & Jonnalagadda, S. S. (2001). Social integration and health among Asian Indian immigrants in the United States. *Journal of Gerontological Social Work, 36*(1/2), 45–62.

Diwan, S., Jonnalagadda, S. S., & Gupta, R. (2004). Differences in the structure of depression among older Asian Indian immigrants in the United States. *Journal of Applied Gerontology, 23*(4), 370–384.

Erera, P. I. (2002). *Family diversity: Continuity and change in the contemporary family.* Thousand Oaks, CA: Sage.

Fingerman, K. L. (2004). The role of offspring and in-laws in grandparents' ties to their grandchildren. *Journal of Family Issues, 25*(8), 1026–1049.

Fuller-Thomson, E., Minkler, M., & Driver, D. (1997). A profile of grandparents raising grandchildren in the United States. *The Gerontologist, 37*(3), 406–411.

Geron, S. M. (2002). Cultural competency: How is it measured? Does it make a difference? *Generations, XXVI*(3), 39–45.

Gibson, P. A. (2005). Intergenerational parenting from the perspective of African American grandmothers. *Family Relations, 54*(2), 280–297.

Goetting, A. (1986). The developmental tasks of siblingship over the life cycle. *Journal of Marriage and the Family, 48*, 703–714.

Gold, D. T. (1990). Late-life sibling relationships: Does race affect typological distribution? *The Gerontologist, 30*(6), 741–748.

Goodman, C., & Silverstein, M. (2002). Grandmothers raising grandchildren: Family structure and well-being in culturally diverse families. *The Gerontologist, 42*(5), 676–689.

Grossman, A. H., D'Augelli, A. R., & Hershberger, S. L. (2000). Social support networks of lesbian, gay, and bisexual adults 60 years of age and older. *Journal of Gerontology: Psychological Sciences, 55B*, P171–P179.

Hagestad, G., & Neugarten, B. (1985). Age and the life course. In R. Binstock & E. Shanas (Eds.), *Handbook of aging and the social sciences* (2nd ed., pp. 35–61). New York: Van Nostrand Reinhold.

Hamon, R. R., & Whitney, K. R. (2003). Filial responsibility. In *International encyclopedia of marriage and family* (Vol. 2, pp. 673–679). New York: Macmillan Reference.

Harris, H. L. (1998). Ethnic minority elders: Issues and interventions. *Educational Gerontology, 24*(4), 309–323.

Hayslip, B., & Kaminski, P. L. (2005). Grandparents raising their grandchildren: A review of the literature and suggestions for practice. *The Gerontologist, 45*(2), 262–269.

Himes, C. L., Hogan, D. P., & Eggebeen, D. J. (1996). Living arrangements of minority elders. *Journal of Gerontology: Psychological Sciences and Social Sciences, 51B*(1), S42–S48.

John, R. (1991). Family support networks among elders in a Native American community: Contact with children and siblings among the Prairie Band Potawatomi. *Journal of Aging Studies, 5*(1), 45–59.

John, R., Hennessy, C. H., Dyeson, T. B., & Garrett, M. D. (2001). Toward the conceptualization and measurement of caregiver burden among Pueblo Indian family caregivers. *The Gerontologist, 41*(2), 210–219.

Johnson, C. (1999). Family life of older Black men. *Journal of Aging Studies, 13*(2), 145–160.

Johnson, J. C., & Smith, N. H. (2002). Health and social issues associated with racial, ethnic, and cultural disparities. *Generations, XXVI*(3), 25–32.

Johnson, R. A., & Tripp-Reimer, T. (2001). Aging, ethnicity, and social support. *Journal of Gerontological Nursing, 27*(6), 15–21.

Jolicoeur, P. M., & Madden, T. (2002). The good daughters: Acculturation and caregiving among Mexican-American women. *Journal of Aging Studies, 16*(2), 107–120.

Jordan-Marsh, M., & Harden, J. T. (2005). Fictive kin: Friends and family supporting older adults as they age. *Journal of Gerontological Nursing, 31*(2), 25–31.

Kitson, G. C. (2000). Adjustment to violent and natural deaths in later and earlier life for Black and White widows. *Journal of Gerontology: Social Sciences, 55B*(6), S341–S351.

Lang, F. R. (2004). The filial task in midlife: Ambivalence and the quality of adult children's relationships with their older parents. In K. Pillemer & K. Lüscher (Eds.), *Intergenerational ambivalences: New perspectives on parent-child relations in later life* (pp. 183–206). Amsterdam: Elsevier.

Li, L. W., & Fries, B. E. (2005). Elder disability as an explanation for racial differences in informal home care. *The Gerontologist, 45*(2), 206–215.

McFarland, P. L., & Sanders, S. (2003). A pilot study about the needs of older gays and lesbians: What social workers need to know. *Journal of Gerontological Social Work, 40*(3), 67–80.

Minkler, M., & Fuller-Thomson, E. (2005). African American grandparents raising grandchildren: A national study using the census 2000 American Community Survey. *Journal of Gerontology: Social Sciences, 60B*(2), S82–S92.

Moriarty, J., & Butt, J. (2004). Inequalities in quality of life among older people from different ethnic groups. *Ageing and Society, 24*(5), 729–753.

Musil, C. M. (1998). Health, stress, coping, and social support in grandmother caregivers. *Health Care for Women International, 19*, 441–455.

Orel, N. A. (2004). Gay, lesbian, and bisexual elders: Expressed needs and concerns across focus groups. *Journal of Gerontological Social Work, 43*(2–3), 57–77.

Pang, E. C., Jordan-Marsh, M., Silverstein, M., & Cody, M. (2003). Health-seeking behaviors of elderly Chinese Americans: Shifts in expectations. *The Gerontologist, 43*(6), 864–874.

Patterson, F. M. (2003). Heeding new voices: Gender-related herstories of Asian and Caribbean-born elderly women. *Affilia, 18*(1), 68–79.

Pienta, A. M., Hayward, M. D., & Jenkins, K. R. (2000). Health consequences of marriage for the retirement years. *Journal of Family Issues, 21*(5), 559–586.

Pillemer, K., & Lüscher, K. (2004). Introduction: Ambivalence in parent-child relations in later life. In K. Pillemer & K. Lüscher (Eds.), *Intergenerational ambivalences: New perspectives on parent-child relations in later life* (pp. 1–19). Amsterdam: Elsevier.

Radina, M. E., & Barber, C. E. (2004). Utilization of formal support services among Hispanic Americans caring for aging parents. *Journal of Gerontological Social Work, 43*(2/3), 5–23.

Ramos, B. M. (2004). Culture, ethnicity, and caregiver stress among Puerto Ricans. *Journal of Applied Gerontology, 23*(4), 469–486.

Salari, S. (2002). Invisible in aging research: Arab Americans, Middle Eastern immigrants, and Muslims in the United States. *The Gerontologist, 42*(5), 580–588.

Sands, R. G., & Goldberg-Glen, R. S. (2000). Factors associated with stress among grandparents raising their grandchildren. *Family Relations, 49*(1), 97–105.

Settles, B. H. (2005). U.S. families. In B. N. Adams & J. Trost (Eds.), *Handbook of world families* (pp. 560–601). Thousand Oaks, CA: Sage.

Shawler, C. (2004). Aging mothers and daughters: Relationship changes over time. *Ageing International, 29*(2), 149–177.

Silverstein, M., & Chen, X. (1999). The impact of acculturation in Mexican American families on the quality of adult grandchild-grandparent relationships. *Journal of Marriage and the Family, 61*(1), 188–198.

Simmons, T., & Dye, J. L. (2003). *Grandparents living with grandchildren: 2000* (Census 2000 Brief). Washington, DC: U.S. Census Bureau.

Sohn, L., & Harada, N. D. (2004). Time since immigration and health services utilization of Korean-American older adults living in Los Angeles County. *Journal of the American Geriatric Society, 52*(11), 1946–1950.

Strom, R., Carter, T., & Schmidt, K. (2004). African-Americans in senior settings: On the need for educating grandparents. *Educational Gerontology, 30*(4), 287–303.

Strom, R. D., Heeder, S. D., & Strom, P. S. (2005). Performance of Black grandmothers: Perceptions of three generations of females. *Educational Gerontology, 31*(3), 187–205.

Szinovacz, M. (1998). Grandparents today: A demographic profile. *The Gerontologist, 38*(1), 37–52.

U.S. Bureau of the Census. (2002). *Current population survey.* Washington, DC: U.S. Government Printing Office.

Walker, A., Manoogian-O'Dell, M., McGraw, L., & White, D. (Eds.). (2001). *Families in later life: Connections and transitions.* Thousand Oaks, CA: Pine Forge Press.

Weibel-Orlando, J. (2001). Grandparenting styles: Native American perspectives. In A. Walker, M. Manoogian-O'Dell, L. McGraw, & D. White (Eds.), *Families in later life: Connections and transitions* (pp. 139–145). Thousand Oaks, CA: Pine Forge Press.

Williams, N. (2001). Elderly Mexican American men: Work and family patterns. In A. Walker, M. Manoogian-O'Dell, L. McGraw, & D. White (Eds.), *Families in later life: Connections and transitions* (pp. 202–207). Thousand Oaks, CA: Pine Forge Press.

Williams, S. W., & Dilworth-Anderson, P. (2002). Systems of social support in families who care for dependent African American elders. *The Gerontologist, 42*(2), 224–236.

Wilmoth, J. M. (2001). Living arrangements among older immigrants in the United States. *The Gerontologist, 41*(2), 228–238.

Wilson, A. E., & Hardy, M. A. (2002). Racial disparities in income security for a cohort of aging American women. *Social Forces, 80*(4), 1283–1306.

Zhan, L., & Chen, J. (2004). Medication practices among Chinese American older adults. *Journal of Gerontological Nursing, 30*(4), 24–33.

9

Parent-Child Ties of Culturally Diverse Aging Families

Paula M. Usita

Intergenerational relationships, or the relationships between aging parents and adult children, are among the most interesting and noteworthy family ties to investigate because they are among the longest-enduring social relationships in people's lives. Adult intergenerational relationships are dynamic ties that are affected by earlier parent-child interactions (Bedford, 1992; Hoyert, 1991; Whitbeck, Hoyt, & Huck, 1994) as well as events of the adult life course including changes in marital status, declines in mental and physical health, and a return to coresidential living arrangements (Goldscheider & Lawton, 1998; Ward & Spitze, 1996). The intergenerational ties of the various ethnic and racial groups in the United States are particularly interesting, because the cultural values, traditions, norms, and customs of group members uniquely shape familial expectations and behaviors (Becker, Beyene, Newsom, & Mayen, 2003; Ishii-Kuntz, 1997; Usita, 2005). Capturing the ways in which culture influences the intergenerational expectations and interactions of diverse families is important because by 2030, minority older adults will represent 26.4 percent of the elderly population in the United States, an increase of 17.2 percent from 2002 (Administration on Aging, 2003).

The aims of this chapter are multifold: to examine theory and contemporary research in the family sciences and gerontology related to ethnic and racial minority intergenerational ties in the United States, to explore the pressing issue of culturally competent care with older minority families, and to offer recommendations to enhance future research with minority elders and their offspring. It will be shown that although adult intergenerational research in the family sciences and gerontology has made some positive advancement toward understanding intergenerational issues for families of color, much more additional research is required for developing a deeper understanding of the diverse views, expectations, and interactions of these families in the United States.

Theoretical Approaches and Aging Families

A variety of theoretical approaches have been used to study intergenerational relationships in adulthood, among them solidarity, ambivalence, socioemotional selectivity, and life course models. Each of these theoretical approaches has helped unravel the intricacies of adult parent-child relationships. The solidarity model has emphasized various types of cohesion and the dialectics such as intimacy and distance, agreement and dissent, and dependence and autonomy that exist between aging parents and adult children (Bengtson, Giarrusso, Mabry, & Silverstein, 2002; Bengtson & Roberts, 1991). The ambivalence model has drawn attention to the tensions between individual desires and social structural influences, and they are manifested in a variety of situations such as financial transfers between the generations and caregiving to frail elders (Lüscher, 2002; Lüscher & Pillemer, 1998). The socioemotional selectivity model has suggested that over the adult years, individuals limit their social support systems to consist of partners who provide the most emotionally supportive interactions (Carstensen, 1992).

The life course perspective has offered one of most engaging lenses from which one can understand family life for people of color. Life course models attend to historical factors, social processes, cultural factors, individual transitions, and family trajectories (Dilworth-Anderson, Burton, & Johnson, 1993; Elder, 1998). In studies of culturally diverse families, the linkages between personal choices related to age, race or ethnicity, gender, family outcomes, geographic residences, and historical time frames have been highlighted (Becker, 2002; Burton, 1996; Usita & Blieszner, 2002). A life course lens was used as the leading framework in selecting studies for inclusion in this chapter.

Contemporary Research on
Culturally Diverse Aging Families

Contemporary research findings in the fields of family science and gerontology have shed light on the intergenerational ties of people of color. Given space limitations, this chapter highlights research in six areas: communication challenges in immigrant families; living arrangements in old-age families; helping networks in late-life families; health of family caregivers; cultural expectations of elder helping in families; and death, dying, and aging families.

Communication Challenges
in Immigrant Families

Effective communication is important for healthy family relationships. Among immigrant families, research has shown that when language proficiency weakens across family generations, communication breakdown occurs and families struggle. Studies have repeatedly illustrated this conclusion with various populations including immigrants from Asian and Latin countries (Kendis, 1989; Kibria, 1993; Lubben & Becerra, 1983; Osako, 1979; Schmidt & Padilla, 1983; Simon, 1983; Strom, Buki, & Strom, 1997). These studies document various dilemmas such as loss of parental authority (Buriel & DeMent, 1997; Detzner, 1996; Gozdkiak, 1989; Kibria, 1993), children's resistance to sharing confidential information (Osako, 1979), parental frustration with being unable to express ideas (Glenn, 1986), and emotional distance between grandparents and grandchildren (Kendis, 1989).

Few studies have looked at the effects of language acculturation on communication intimacy among parents and adult children, however. Moreover, little research has been conducted on immigrant family strengths and cultural strengths of aged minorities (Becker & Newsom, 2005; Seller, 1994; Williams & Wilson, 2001), such as how families deal with language acculturation and communication problems. In a study of the relationship quality of immigrant Japanese mothers and their adult daughters, mothers and daughters were found to have strained communication because they were not able to fluently speak each other's native language. Mothers were native Japanese speakers and daughters were native English speakers; neither had full command of the other's native language. Conversations were often marked by misunderstanding and feelings of frustration. However, importantly, mothers and adult daughters engaged in a variety of problem-solving strategies to increase their communication skills and relationship quality.

Among the strategies were humor and reciprocal assistance (e.g., mothers help daughters with childcare and daughters help mothers to improve oral and written English skills) (Usita & Blieszner, 2002). Thus, although language acculturation poses communication challenges for parents and adult children, they find ways to build intimacy in their relationships.

Living Arrangements in Old-Age Families

Due to choice or a variety of circumstances (e.g., divorce, widowhood, physical health problems, mental health problems, financial strain), aging parents and adult children may share a residence. Studies that have focused on the topic of living arrangements across ethnic and racial groups indicate that these groups possess varying expectations about intergenerational coresidence, and that, consistent with other research (Becker et al., 2003), coresident family patterns are affected by socioeconomic and native/ immigrant characteristics. For example, older Blacks and older Hispanics are more likely than older Whites to believe that members of the younger generation should make coresidence available if it is needed (Burr & Mutchler, 1999). The economic standing as well as the recent immigration history of parents is associated with coresidence patterns in old age. In the United States, Asian and Central and South American immigrant parents are more likely to live in households where their adult children earn most of the household income (Glick & Van Hook, 2002). However, the longer immigrant parents have lived in the United States, the less likely they are to live with their adult children (Glick & Van Hook, 2002).

Helping Networks in Late-Life Families

The potential lifelong quality of intergenerational relationships, the cultural prescriptions for family care that exist in many minority communities, and the tendency for minority families to have backgrounds that include voluntary and forced international relocation all raise important questions about whether adequate types and levels of assistance are available from adult children to their aging parents. Filial responsibility encompasses adult children's sense of duty to provide aid to their aged parents in ways that maintain parental well-being (Hamon & Whitney, 2003). Among Asian families, filial piety is a salient familial concern. Filial piety refers to adult children's emotional, financial, and residential support to aged parents (Ishii-Kuntz, 1997; Osako & Liu, 1986).

In a study investigating filial piety among Japanese American, Chinese American, and Korean American families, researchers found that structural

variables and social factors offered the best explanation of filial duty enactment. Structural factors such as geographic proximity, financial standing,
and parental need for assistance, along with social factors such as parental
need for emotional support, were key to understanding when care was most
likely to be provided from adult children to aging parents (Ishii-Kuntz,
1997). Importantly, researchers noted group differences: Korean American
adult children were more likely to provide various types of support
to elderly parents compared with their Chinese American and Japanese
American counterparts. Korean American elderly were the most recent immigrants among the three groups, and they may have required the greatest
level of support from adult children in order to adapt to living in the United
States (Ishii-Kuntz, 1997).

The evolving nature of culture is relevant to studies of filial responsibility
and intergenerational bonds. And where immigrant families are concerned,
the internal variation in family organization and adherence to prescribed cultural behaviors must be recognized (Ishii-Kuntz, 2000). Generational positioning influences the strength of association that each generation has to filial
responsibility expectations in ways that might not be expected.

Research with Japanese families shows that immigrant parents claimed
that they did not expect to live with their adult children or to receive care
from them, whereas their adult children reported that their parents expected
them to display filial duty (Yanagisako, 1985). Other research offers additional evidence of transformations to filial duty among Japanese families
(Osako & Liu, 1986), and more recent research points to the role of hired
non-kin homecare workers in filial duty roles in ethnic Chinese families. In
a study of elder care in ethnic Chinese immigrant families in California, Lan
(2002) reported that immigrant adult children hired ethnic Chinese homecare workers to provide intensive and quality care to their aged parents.
By hiring the homecare workers, immigrant adult children were able to
continue working outside the home. Working enabled the adult children to
afford to purchase the help needed by their parents and to support the family
in other ways through their economic earnings. Thereby, the adult children
were able to fulfill the cultural ideal of filial duty.

Whereas the cultural norm of filial piety has been used to understand
caregiving within Asian families, cultural, economic, and household or family
structure arguments have been proposed to explain the observed differences
in the helping networks of Blacks and Whites. According to the cultural
argument, Blacks' emphasis on filial duties and responsibilities accounts for
the number of informal helpers available to Black elders (Hatch, 1991;
Mutran, 1985; Taylor & Chatters, 1991). The economic argument suggests
that Blacks' economic disadvantage leads them to rely more heavily upon

informal support networks, compared with Whites (Chatters, Taylor, & Jackson, 1985; Hatch, 1991; Mutran, 1985). A slightly different though related argument is that the household and family structure of Blacks may also explain the presence of more informal helpers to elder Blacks during times of assistance. Variations in household and family structure exist between Blacks and Whites: Blacks are more likely to live without a spouse, have more children, have larger extended families, and live in multigenerational households, compared with Whites (Beck & Beck, 1989; Coward, Lee, Netzer, Cutler & Danigelis, 1986; Hofferth, 1984; Taylor & Chatters; Taylor, Chatters, Tucker, & Lewis, 1990).

Tests of the household and family structure argument have revealed that among a sample of older Blacks and older Whites all living within the same community, family and household structure do matter in the delivery of care to dependent elders. In families where the elder did not live with a spouse, elder Blacks were more likely to receive assistance from adult children compared with elder Whites (Peek, Coward, & Peek, 2000). Elder Blacks had larger families, and a greater number of elder Blacks also lived with family members compared with elder Whites (Peek et al., 2000).

Household and family structure variables may influence the delivery of care from Black and White families to dependent elder family members, but the gender and coupling status of the adult child caregiver matters as well. For example, in a study with Latin Americans, it was found that Puerto Rican son caregivers were more likely to provide transportation and financial management services, whereas Puerto Rican daughter caregivers were more likely to provide personal care for their elder parents (Delgado & Tennstedt, 1997). Further, in a study of race, gender, and hours of caregiving, it was found that nonpartnered Black sons provided substantially more hours of help to their dependent elderly parents than their White counterparts and that partnered Black daughters provided more help than their White counterparts (Laditka & Laditka, 2001).

Health of Family Caregivers

Protecting the health of adult child caregivers is important to the functioning of the elder family unit. Ways in which adult child caregivers can be assisted include providing informational support and relief from care. Research with Cuban American adult child caregivers shows that they desire to have more caregiving training, family caregiver support groups, case management assistance, and respite care than White caregivers (Mintzer et al., 1992). When respite care is not available, caregivers may experience feelings of strain. Indeed, the unavailability of respite care has been shown to predict role strain among African American female caregivers of dependent elderly parents (Mui, 1992).

Cultural Expectations of Elder Helping in Families

A large majority of caregiving studies in gerontology and family science focus on the care that dependent elders receive from their adult children (Allen, Blieszner, & Roberto, 2000). Yet, there is a growing need to recognize the help that elders provide to families or the ways that help is exchanged across family generations (Usita & Blieszner, 2002). When researchers have studied elder perceptions of helping across family generations of Latino Americans, African Americans, Filipino Americans, and Cambodian Americans, they have found different group norms (Becker et al., 2003). African American elders were very involved in the lives of their children, grandchildren, and other family members, yet they valued their personal autonomy; Latino Americans valued emotionally interdependent relationships with their extended family; Filipino Americans discussed the importance of economic support to the extended family; and Cambodian Americans valued multigenerational households and expected financial support from their adult children. Each group's position regarding elder roles in the family was connected to the group's unique culture and history.

These histories were varied and included survivorship as oppressed people, immigrants with family scattered throughout the United States and in other countries, immigration for better economic and health offerings, and escaping oppressive regimes to arrive in the United States with remnants of their families (Becker et al., 2003). Evident throughout the narratives of family and aid that were provided by elders was the influence of culturally prescribed gender roles on patterns of mutual aid. Across the groups, family continuity was ensured for women through their caregiving role, whereas for men, their social standing within the family and sense of family continuity was more ensured when they exhibited role flexibility. Life disruptions such as migration had affected elders' role satisfaction, and forced or voluntary separation from their native country and families had disrupted elders' lives. However, elders were intent on sustaining ties to their families in whatever ways were possible. In other studies, researchers have found that aid patterns become more reciprocal when parents and adult children live in communities with families that are ethnically or racially similar to their own (Usita, 2001).

Death, Dying, and Aging Families

Death is a natural part of the human life cycle. Yet surprisingly, in the fields of gerontology and family science, minimal attention has been given to perceptions and expectations of death and dying among culturally diverse families. Studies that have been completed reveal that countries and cultures outside the United States attach clear psychological and cultural significance to the ways of thinking about dying and death among minority elders. In gerontology, this was demonstrated in research that showed the fluidity of place to immigrants and refugees in the United States who were asked about their views of death and rituals associated with it. Researchers found that underlying refugees' and immigrants' views of death were struggles that had occurred in their homelands, religious belief systems, cultural practices of families, and the personal losses they had encountered (Becker, 2002). Cambodian Americans' discussion of dying was understandably linked to the genocide committed by the Communist Khmer Rouge regime. They reported about the deep personal losses they encountered, and they told stories about the regime's destruction of their sense of an orderly and morally operative world. Their discussions of death also included the personal desire to visit or live in Cambodia where they believed there would be more family and friends surrounding and supporting them.

In contrast with Cambodian Americans, most of whom were Buddhists, the majority of Filipino Americans were Catholics. Filipino Americans discussed death in relation to their religious belief and its customs and rituals associated with proper deaths. As immigrants, the location of the extended family also mattered to Filipinos, with the presence of the extended family determining where they would eventually die and have their remains kept. Intergenerational implications of the findings of this type of research are numerous including the role that family members such as adult children might play in ensuring that the dying wishes of the elder parents are successfully carried out.

Summary of Research Findings

In summary, contemporary research findings on intergenerational relationships and aging in culturally diverse communities suggest that adult parent-child relationships among ethnic and racial minorities is affected by a multitude of factors such as location in time and history, race, gender, and immigrant or refugee status. Compared with each other, ethnic minority families have differing perspectives about expected levels of elder involvement within families and differing viewpoints regarding when adult children should help dependent elders. Compared with families in the ethnic majority in the United States, minority families do not report more burden, but they do desire to have more assistance with caregiving responsibilities. Studies that have placed their samples within sociopolitical, cultural, and historical contexts have been particularly important, because they have revealed how those contexts matter in the ways that intergenerational ties are thought about and lived.

Cultural Competence With Aged Minority Families

The goal of cultural competence is to create a healthcare system and workforce that are capable of delivering the highest-quality care to every patient regardless of race, ethnicity, culture, or language proficiency.

—Betancourt, Green, Carrillo, & Park, 2005, p. 499

Though applied to the health care system, the above can and must also be applied to other systems of care, such as the mental health, family, and social work fields. The need to create and deliver culturally competent care has gained strong momentum in recent years owing to the increased ethnic and racial diversity of the United States, knowledge that health outcomes are improved if services are more culture-friendly, and that racial and ethnic health disparities exist and must be eliminated (Betancourt et al., 2005).

Several practices are involved in creating and delivering culturally competent care. These include carefully examining and reexamining value systems at the personal, interpersonal, organizational, and cultural or societal levels; seeking opportunities to enhance knowledge and skill sets; and working with individuals while maintaining an "informed not-knowing" stance (Laird, 1998; Yee, 2002). The last refers to preparing specific questions for clients that are consistent with what is generally known about the client's ethnic or racial group's history but also recognizing that those questions may not be relevant for any individual client (Laird, 1998).

The dynamic nature of culture, coupled with the limited research that has been conducted with aged minority families, requires that family practitioners be innovators who seek out readily available information from a variety of sources in order to enhance their knowledge and delivery of services to diverse groups. The literature in a variety of academic fields has often been suggested to be a rich and untapped source of information on the intricacies of life among minority persons. In addition to the literature in the family sciences and gerontology, the literature in the fields of humanities, ethnic studies, and women's studies has the potential to offer much-needed insight into the lives of ethnic and racial minorities (Dilworth-Anderson, Burton, & Turner, 1993; Ray, 1996). Reviewing the literature from a variety of fields may help practitioners to better understand the goals and challenges of minority families. Another rich and untapped resource is minority families themselves. Collins (1991) maintained that by searching through and discussing their personal experiences, marginalized persons select the stories that reveal important information about their lives. Listeners such as researchers and practitioners are privileged by the opportunity to hear those stories, and they may be able to identify important themes about minority person's lives that could be shared with other researchers and practitioners in ways that advance social science and improve service delivery to minority families.

Recommendations for Future Research

For the fields of family science and gerontology, three research avenues involving families of color are suggested: using frameworks and methods that provide a lens through which to consider the interlocking systems of gender, race, and class and that also capture the meaning of concepts in their cultural context; extending research studies to include ethnic or racial immigrant and refugee groups that have been previously excluded in scientific investigations; and conducting studies with families whose members include members of more than one racial or ethnic group.

Frameworks and methods that call attention to individuals and families within historical and cultural contexts should be used in future studies with minority groups. Aside from life course models, symbolic interaction, feminist, and social constructivism perspectives are invaluable investigative tools for research on older people of color and women (Allen et al., 2000; Calasanti, 1996; Dilworth-Anderson, Williams, & Gibson, 2002; Ray, 1996). These perspectives provide a lens through which to examine the ways that gender, race, and class inequalities in economic and political institutions at a given time in history have led to restricted roles, beliefs, or stereotypes about certain groups in society. They also enable researchers to question the research that supports existing knowledge systems and power structures, including the questions that are asked in studies, the people who are included in studies, and the information about various people that is or is not included in written texts. Importantly, these tools also enable attention to be drawn to the shared meanings assigned to concepts and the ways in which concepts are interpreted from a cultural frame of reference.

Research on adult intergenerational ties among minority groups must include studies with the numerous ethnic and racial groups living in the United States, indigenous populations such as American Indians and Native Hawaiians, and immigrant and refugee groups that have made international moves at various stages in life. A better understanding of the intergenerational issues of ethnic and racial minorities and immigrant and refugee populations in the United States is very important, because in some geographic regions of the United States, the minority population has or will soon compose the majority of the elderly population (Hayes-Bautista, Hsu, Perez, & Gamboa, 2002). Practitioners in those locales have already begun or will soon begin to work extensively with ethnic and racial elderly and their offspring.

By midcentury, 20 percent of the U.S. population will be of mixed ancestry. This percentage is likely to be higher among some groups with histories of intermarriage such as Asian Americans (Cutler & Hendricks, 2001). Subsequently, research with multiracial families will be increasingly important. Studies have begun to shed light on the aims, strengths, and challenges of multiracial family life (Dalmage, 2000; Root, 2001; Rosenblatt, Karis, & Powell, 1995). Yet, most of the multiracial family research revolves around couple and family formation, and coverage of mid- and late-life family issues is notably absent. Studies with multiracial families in mid- and late-life have the potential to illuminate the degree of intimacy or distance within multiracial families, ways that race has or has not mattered to parents' and children's expectations and interactions, and patterns of assistance across the generations given the variety of potential health scenarios and geographic locations in which multiracial families have lived (Usita & Poulsen, 2003). It is important to draw attention to and investigate the positive dimensions of multiracial relationships in the United States (Dalmage, 2000; Root, 2001). Narratives methods are suggested for use in studies with multiracial families, because they allow respondents to set the frames for their responses and offer their personal interpretations of important personal experiences.

Conclusion

Minority elderly and their offspring have a host of personal and familial matters to explore in their later years. According to existing research, ongoing changes in the quality of relationships, negotiation of caretaking responsibilities, and preparation for culturally informed dying and death processes are among the matters that will present themselves. Service professionals have and will continue to play a vital role in helping minority families to access help, improve short- and long-term stressful situations, and plan for the future needs of family members. Given the changing demographics of the United States and the knowledge of health disparities across ethnic and racial groups, researchers and service professionals must continue to engage themselves in the practice of developing, sustaining, and advancing cultural competence in their work.

References

Administration on Aging. (2003). *A profile of older Americans: 2003*. Washington, DC: U.S. Department of Health and Human Services.

Allen, K. R., Blieszner, R., & Roberto, K. A. (2000). Families in the middle and later years: A review and critique of research in the 1990s. *Journal of Marriage and the Family, 62*, 911–926.

Beck, R. W., & Beck, S. H. (1989). The incidence of extended households among middle-age African American and White women: Estimates from a 5-year panel study. *Journal of Family Issues, 10*, 147–168.

Becker, G. (2002). Dying away from home: Quandaries of migration for elders in two ethnic groups. *Journal of Gerontology: Social Sciences, 57B*, S579–S595.

Becker, G., Beyene, Y., Newsom, E., & Mayen, N. (2003). Creating continuity through mutual assistance: Intergenerational reciprocity in four ethnic groups. *Journal of Gerontology: Social Sciences, 55B*(3), S151–S159.

Becker, G., & Newsom, E. (2005). Resilience in the face of serious illness among chronically ill African Americans in later life. *Journal of Gerontology: Social Sciences, 60B*(4), S214–S223.

Bedford, V. H. (1992). Memories of parental favoritism and the quality of parent-child ties in adulthood. *Journal of Gerontology: Social Sciences, 47*, S149–S155.

Bengtson, V. L., Giarrusso, R., Mabry, J. B., & Silverstein, M. (2002). Solidarity, conflict, and ambivalence: Complementary or competing perspectives on intergenerational relationships? *Journal of Marriage and the Family, 64*, 568–576.

Bengtson, V. L., & Roberts, R. E. L. (1991). Intergenerational solidarity in aging families: An example of formal theory construction. *Journal of Marriage and the Family, 53*, 856–870.

Betancourt, J. R., Green, A. R., Carrillo, J. E., & Park, E. R. (2005). Cultural competence and health care disparities: Key perspectives and trends. *Health Affairs, 24*(2), 499–506.

Buriel, R., & DeMent, T. (1997). Immigration, sociocultural change in Mexican, Chinese, and Vietnamese American families. In A. Booth, A. C. Crouter, & N. Landale (Eds.), *Immigration and the family: Research and policy on U.S. immigrants* (pp. 165–200). Mahwah, NJ: Erlbaum.

Burr, J. A., & Mutchler, J. E. (1999). Race and ethnic variation in norms of filial responsibility among older persons. *Journal of Marriage and the Family, 61*, 674–687.

Burton, L. M. (1996). Age norms, the timing of family role transitions, and intergenerational caregiving among aging African American women. *The Gerontologist, 36,* 199–208.

Calasanti, T. M. (1996). Incorporating diversity: Meaning, levels of research, and implications for theory. *The Gerontologist, 36,* 147–156.

Carstensen, L. L. (1992). Social and emotional patterns in adulthood: Support for socioemotional selectivity theory. *Psychology and Aging, 7,* 331–338.

Chatters, L. M., Taylor, R. J., & Jackson, J. S. (1985). Size and composition of the informal helper networks of elderly African-Americans. *Journal of Gerontology, 40,* 605–614.

Collins, P. H. (1991). *Black feminist thought.* New York: Routledge.

Coward, R. T., Lee, G. R., Netzer, J. K., Cutler, S. T., & Danigelis, N. L. (1996). Racial differences in the household composition of elders by age, gender, and area of residence. *International Journal of Aging and Human Development, 42,* 205–227.

Cutler, S. J., & Hendricks, J. (2001). Emerging social trends. In R. H. Binstock & L. K. George (Eds.), *Handbook of aging and the social sciences* (5th ed., pp. 462–480). San Diego, CA: Academic Press.

Dalmage, H. M. (2000). *Tripping on the color line.* New Brunswick, NJ: Rutgers University Press.

Delgado, M., & Tennstedt, S. (1997). Puerto Rican sons as primary caregivers of elderly parents. *Social Work, 42,* 125–134.

Detzner, D. F. (1996). No place without a home: Southeast Asian grandparents in refugee families. *Generations, XX,* 45–48.

Dilworth-Anderson, P., Burton, L. M., & Johnson, L. B. (1993). Reframing theories for understanding race, ethnicity, and families. In P. G. Boss, W. J. Doherty, R. LaRossa, W. R. Schumm, & S. K. Steinmetz (Eds.), *Handbook of family theories and methods: A contextual approach* (pp. 627–646). New York: Plenum Press.

Dilworth-Anderson, P., Burton, L. M., & Turner, W. L. (1993). The importance of values in the study of culturally diverse families. *Family Relations, 42,* 238–242.

Dilworth-Anderson, P., Williams, I. C., & Gibson, B. E. (2002). Issues of race, ethnicity, and culture in caregiving research: A 20-year review (1980–2000). *The Gerontologist, 42*(2), 237–272.

Elder, G. H., Jr. (1998). The life course and human development. In R. M. Lerner (Ed.), *Handbook of child psychology: Vol. 1. Theoretical models of human development* (5th ed., pp. 939–991). New York: Wiley.

Glenn, E. N. (1986). *Issei, nisei, war bride.* Philadelphia: Temple.

Glick, J. E., & Van Hook, J. (2002). Parents' coresidence with adult children: Can immigration explain racial and ethnic variation? *Journal of Marriage and the Family, 64,* 240–253.

Goldscheider, F. K., & Lawton, L. (1998). Family experiences and the erosion of support for intergenerational coresidence. *Journal of Marriage and the Family, 60,* 623–632.

Gozdkiak, E. (1989). New branches, distant roots: Older refugees in the United States. *Aging, 359,* 2–7.

Hamon, R. R., & Whitney, K. R. (2003). Filial responsibility. In J. J. Ponzetti (Ed.), *International encyclopedia of marriage and family* (pp. 673–679). New York: Macmillan.

Hatch, L. R. (1991). Informal support patterns of older African-American and White women. *Research on Aging, 13,* 144–170.

Hayes-Bautista, D. E., Hsu, P., Perez, A., & Gamboa, C. (2002). The "browning" of the graying of America: Diversity in the elderly population and policy implications. *Generations, XXVI*(3), 15–24.

Hofferth, S. L. (1984). Kin networks, race, and family structure. *Journal of Marriage and the Family, 46,* 791–806.

Hoyert, D. L. (1991). Financial and household exchanges between generations. *Research on Aging, 113,* 205–225.

Ishii-Kuntz, M. (1997). Intergenerational relationships among Chinese, Japanese, and Korean Americans. *Family Relations, 46,* 23–32.

Ishii-Kuntz, M. (2000). Diversity within Asian immigrant families. In D. Demo, K. R. Allen, & J. Fine (Eds.), *Handbook of family diversity* (pp. 272–292). New York: Oxford University Press.

Kendis, R. J. (1989). *An attitude of gratitude: The adaptation to aging of the elderly Japanese in America.* New York: AMS Press.

Kibria, N. (1993). *Family tightrope: The changing lives of Vietnamese Americans.* Princeton, NJ: Princeton University Press.

Laditka, J. N., & Laditka, S. B. (2001). Adult children helping older parents: Variations in likelihood of hours by gender, race, and family role. *Research on Aging, 23*(4), 429–456.

Laird, J. (1998). Theorizing culture: Narrative ideas and practice principles. In M. McGoldrick (Ed.), *Re-visioning family therapy: Race, culture, and gender in clinical practice* (pp. 20–36). New York: Guilford.

Lan, P. C. (2002). Subcontracting filial piety: Elder care in ethnic Chinese immigrant families in California. *Journal of Family Issues, 23*(7), 812–835.

Lubben, J. E., & Becerra, R. M. (1983). Social support among Black, Mexican, and Chinese elderly. In D. E. Gelfand & C. M. Baressi (Eds.), *Ethnic dimensions of aging* (pp. 130–144). New York: Springer.

Lüscher, K. (2002). Intergenerational ambivalence: Further steps in theory and research. *Journal of Marriage and the Family, 64,* 585–593.

Lüscher, K., & Pillemer, K. (1998). Intergenerational ambivalence: A new approach to the study of parent-child relations in later life. *Journal of Marriage and the Family, 60,* 413–425.

Mintzer, J. E., Rupert, M. P., Loewenstein, D., Garnez, E., Millor, A., Quinteros, R., et al. (1992). Daughters caregiving for Hispanic and non-Hispanic Alzheimer patients: Does ethnicity make a difference? *Community Mental Health Journal, 28,* 293–303.

Mui, A. C. (1992). Caregiver strain among Black and White daughter caregivers: A role theory perspective. *The Gerontologist, 32,* 203–212.

Mutran, E. (1985). Intergenerational family support among African-Americans and Whites: Response to culture or socioeconomic differences. *Journal of Gerontology, 40,* 382–389.

Osako, M. M (1979). Aging and family among Japanese Americans: The role of ethnic tradition in the adjustment to old age. *The Gerontologist, 19,* 448–455.

Osako, M. M., & Liu, W. T. (1986). Intergenerational relations and the aged among Japanese Americans. *Research on Aging, 81,* 128–155.

Peek, M. K., Coward, R. T., & Peek, C. W. (2000). Race, aging, and care: Can differences in family and household structure account for race variations in informal care? *Research on Aging, 22*(2), 117–142.

Ray, R. E. (1996). A postmodern perspective on feminist gerontology. *The Gerontologist, 36,* 674–680.

Root, M. P. P. (2001). *Love's revolution: Interracial marriage.* Philadelphia: Temple University.

Rosenblatt, P. C., Karis, T. A., & Powell, R. D. (1995). *Multiracial couples: Black and white voices.* Thousand Oaks, CA: Sage.

Schmidt, A., & Padilla, A. M. (1983). Grandparent–grandchild interaction in a Mexican American group. *Hispanic Journal of Behavioral Sciences, 5,* 181–198.

Seller, M. S. (1994). *Immigrant women* (2nd ed.). Albany: State University of New York Press.

Simon, R. J. (1983). Refugee families' adjustment and aspirations: A comparison of Soviet Jews and Vietnamese immigrants. *Ethnic and Racial Studies, 6,* 492–504.

Strom, R. D., Buki, L. P., & Strom, S. K. (1997). Intergenerational perceptions of English speaking and Spanish speaking Mexican-American grandparents. *International Journal of Aging and Human Development, 45,* 1–21.

Taylor, R. L., & Chatters L. M. (1991). Extended family networks of older African American adults. *Journal of Gerontology: Social Sciences, 46,* S21–S217.

Taylor, R. L., Chatters, L. M., Tucker, M. B., & Lewis, E. (1990). Developments in research on African American families: A decade review. *Journal of Marriage and the Family, 52,* 993–1014.

Usita, P. M. (2001). Interdependency in immigrant mother-daughter relationships. *Journal of Aging Studies, 15,* 183–199.

Usita, P. M. (2005). Social geography and continuity effects in immigrant women's narratives of negative social exchanges. *Journal of Aging Studies, 19*(2), 221–239.

Usita, P. M., & Blieszner, R. (2002). Communication challenges and intimacy strategies of immigrant mothers and adult daughters. *Journal of Family Issues, 23*(2), 266–286.

Usita, P. M., & Poulsen, S. (2003). Interracial relationships in Hawaii: Issues, benefits, and therapeutic interventions. *Journal of Couples Therapy, 2*(2), 35–42.

Ward, R. A., & Spitze, G. (1996). Gender differences in parent-child coresidence experiences. *Journal of Marriage and the Family, 58,* 718–725.

Whitbeck, L. B., Hoyt, D. R., & Huck, S. M. (1994). Early family relationships, intergenerational solidarity, and support provided to parents by their adult children. *Journal of Gerontology: Social Sciences, 49,* S85–S94.

Williams, D. R., & Wilson, C. M. (2001). Race, ethnicity, and aging. In R. Binstock & L. George (Eds.), *Handbook of aging and the social sciences* (5th ed., pp. 160–178). San Diego, CA: Academic Press.

Yanagisako, S. J. (1985). *Transforming the past: Tradition and kinship among Japanese Americans.* Palo Alto, CA: Stanford University Press.

Yee, D. (2002). Introduction: Recognizing diversity, moving toward cultural competence. *Generations, XXVI(3),* 5–7.

PART III

Contextual Issues and Culturally Diverse Families

10

Human Services and Cultural Diversity

Tenuous Relationships, Challenges, and Opportunities Ahead

Donald G. Unger, Teresita Cuevas,
and Tara Woolfolk

There are many reasons why family service providers should be interested in cultural diversity. First, human service providers are likely to work with persons of different cultures, as clients, coworkers, or employers, by the nature of changes in population trends in the United States (Smeiser, Wilson, & Mitchell, 2000). Individuals and families in the United States have, as a group, become increasingly diverse. This diversity has emerged from many sources such as changes in immigration patterns, ethnic and racial distribution in the general population, greater inclusion of individuals with disabilities, increased longevity, and broadening views of gender appropriate behaviors (see Chapter 2 in this volume).

Second, many of the problems that human service delivery systems are expected to address are experienced more often by ethnic minorities. There are significant disparities between the socioemotional and physical health of the majority population and that of ethnic minorities and non-Hispanic Whites in the United States. Both race and ethnicity are key factors associated with these disparities in health (Keppel, Pearcy, & Wagener, 2002).

Third, ethnic minorities, such as Mexicans, Puerto Ricans, and African Americans, are more likely than non-Hispanic Whites to experience poverty in the United States. Poverty is a pervasive problem that contributes to numerous developmental, socioemotional, and physical health problems (Scott & Simile, 2005). The pervasive impact of poverty also partially explains the overrepresentation of ethnic minorities in the child welfare and criminal justice systems. This disproportionate involvement, however, goes beyond the needs of children and families to biases within these systems (Derezotes, Testa, & Poertner, 2004; Roberts, 2002).

Fourth, in contrast to their overrepresentation in mandatory services, ethnic minorities are underrepresented among those who receive voluntary, supportive, and preventive services (Scott & Simile, 2005). Families of ethnic minorities are believed to be reluctant to seek out professional services for family problems. Issues such as trust, insurance coverage, access to care, and expectations of disrespect, misdiagnoses, and mistreatment contribute to the extent to which families seek out help (Collins, 2000; Mayberry et al., 1999). When they do seek help, the scope and quality of this help may not adequately meet their needs. The quality of care received by ethnic minorities is often inferior to that received by non-Hispanic Whites, even when factors such as insurance coverage and socioeconomic status are equal (HRSA, 2000).

Last, professional organizations such as the American Psychological Association, the National Association for Social Workers, the National Council on Family Relations, and the National Organization for Human Services have standards that require that research with and services to individuals and families of diverse cultures be implemented competently (e.g., Fischer et al., 2002).

This chapter focuses on cultural diversity and human services with children and families within the context of a nonprofit service delivery system. Nonprofit agencies make up a significant segment of the human service delivery system. These agencies typically focus on serving a diverse group of children and families believed to be at risk for social, economic, and educational problems or who are experiencing problems. We believe that the relationship between cultural diversity and human services is tenuous, at best. This chapter highlights why, with so much cultural diversity in the United States, and so many professionals interested in understanding this topic, the needs of many of America's families are still not being met

(Sue, 2003). We offer some potential solutions and hope the reader will be challenged to identify others.

We propose that cultural competence in human services involves ensuring a good fit between the cultural diversity of those families involved in services and a quality human service delivery system. Cultural diversity involves not only the cultures of families receiving the services, but also the cultures represented by the staff and the organizations providing the services and the wider culture that educates those who work in human services. A good fit between families and family services results from addressing culture in purposive and meaningful ways in all phases of programming, including the development, delivery, and evaluation of family services as well as the training of providers.

Cultural competence includes the development and full inclusion of mechanisms for both families and staff of diverse backgrounds to play integral roles in what and how services are developed, implemented, and evaluated so that culture is meaningfully interwoven throughout family services. Correspondingly, cultural competence includes proactively addressing existing barriers to the meaningful inclusion of cultural diversity that contribute to a misfit between a family's cultural values and needs and those of the service intervention or agency. Last, cultural competence involves a reflective, inquiring process that seeks an understanding of culture as a complex, multidimensional construct with no universal, preconceived, singular determinants or qualities. For a discussion of the controversies around the use of the term *cultural competence,* see Dean (2001) and Sue (2003).

For the purposes of this chapter, culture (a) is viewed as an abstract concept that is human-made rather than a manifestation of any natural social order; (b) provides a context for the development and functioning of individuals, families, and communities as well as human service delivery systems; and (c) is characterized by social and instrumental transactions between individuals, families, organizations, communities, and societies over multiple generations as well as within generations. These transactions (a) are influenced by race, class, gender, nation, language, and ability or disability; (b) are influenced by, and contribute to, assumptions and beliefs about individuals and families and the meanings of their behaviors as well as values and beliefs about power, social class, equity, and marginalization; and (c) are characterized by adaptations to demands, stressors, and supports that arise through these transactions. This view of culture builds upon the theoretical frameworks of life course (Hareven, 2000) and developmental contextualism (Lerner & Castellino, 2002) as well as the work of Guzman (2003) and Lonner (1994).

Cultural Diversity and Family Services: A Tenuous Relationship

We propose nine assumptions that are commonly held in the United States about families and human services that lead to difficulties with integrating cultural diversity and family services. These are not exhaustive but illustrative of the major challenges ahead.

Assumption #1: By understanding different groups of people, we can adapt our services to different people, or we can target our services for specific groups.

Approaches to service delivery and cultural competence are often based upon looking at cultural diversity through the lens of group differences. Distinctive characteristics have become associated with specific groups whose members are, for example, monolithically identified by their race, sex, nation of origin, or the nature of their abilities or disabilities. These characteristics suggest (a) ways of behaving and thinking that are rather routinely enacted by members of specific ethnic and minority cultures, e.g., parent expectations and beliefs about parenting; (b) patterns of help-seeking, i.e., how problems are perceived, and views toward appropriate sources and types of help; (c) needs that individuals and families may have and the resources and supports that are typically used to meet those needs; (d) expectations felt by members of ethnic and minority groups of service providers and agencies; and (e) the functions of language and the distinctive uses of language to convey meaning and emotion. Researchers have documented the presence of group differences, and practitioners have written convincingly about the importance of being aware of these differences when working with families (McGoldrick, Giordano, & Garcia-Preto, 2005).

Troubles arise when this way of understanding cultural diversity becomes a stopping point. Attention also needs to be given to the diversity within these groups. Contextual differences related to class and socioeconomic issues, religion, and geographic region of residence (rural versus urban), for example, may be equally important in understanding family functioning. When group differences are taken out of context, there is the danger of stereotyping and misunderstanding. In the good intention to be culturally sensitive to a particular group, certain types of programming may be put into place that may not meet the needs of group members who do not share these group views and practices.

Problematic responses to group differences can also be seen in certain personnel practices. For example, individual(s) of similar race, ethnicity, or disability ("cultural contacts") may be hired to address the needs of particular groups of persons. While this helps diversify an agency's staff, often the unspoken implication is that the other staff of differing cultural membership are not responsible for addressing the needs of clients who are culturally different. Moreover, the cultural contact gets stereotyped as the one to use for cultural matters specific to a particular group and is called upon much less for her other areas of expertise, leading to burnout and resentment.

Group differences may also be applied incorrectly to individuals from one group whose members appear similar to those of another group, such as Mexicans and Puerto Ricans or West Africans and East Africans. In addition, individuals within the same group may experience membership differently in terms of their ethnic identities (Phinney, 1990). Ethnic identity is a multidimensional construct composed of a sense of belonging, involvement in activities associated with one's identified group, and/or knowledge and interest in one's heritage. Ethnic identity evolves over time, and the label one uses to describe oneself varies depending upon the setting or circumstance (Phinney, 1996). For example, immigrants from some countries in the Caribbean may self-identify as Latina or African American.

In summary, group differences are one way to understand cultural diversity. While group characteristics may help to distinguish differences and unique characteristics between groups, they may be quite limited in contributing to an understanding of specific individuals and their families within a cultural context.

Assumption #2: There is equal opportunity for all Americans to live the American dream, regardless of culture, i.e., sex, class, race, ethnicity, ability, or disability.

A consequence of the assumption that people are all on an equal playing field in America is that problems are then often incorrectly attributed to failures of the individual, or of a specific cultural group, to take initiative, work hard enough, or be morally strong enough. Culturally competent practice alternatively views behavior as occurring within the context of barriers to equal opportunity, some of which are discussed as follows.

Marginalization

Some people find themselves experiencing marginalization, i.e., being outside the mainstream culture, whether it be defined by race, gender, ethnicity, social class, or ability. Marginalized individuals and their families are at risk for reduced opportunities for accessing and enjoying the social and economic resources of the mainstream culture and experiences of prejudice, racism, and oppression. This risk is further compounded by the psychological toll that marginalized individuals and their families experience on their physical health and sense of self (Kagan & Burton, 2005).

Because of *involuntary* conditions, such as ethnicity or minority status or having a cognitive disability, some individuals are predisposed to being marginalized in a society that places higher value and acceptance on other conditions that they do not have (Kagan & Burton, 2005). Marginalization is not a condition of the individual, nor an indication of weakness or fault of the individual, but a phenomenon of interaction between community culture and the individual and family's status in that culture. For example, highly respected citizens within other nations often experience marginalization upon immigration or acquiring a student visa in the United States. Moreover, the marginalized status of an individual or family within a culture may change over time depending upon a complex interplay of factors such as a change in social class or the acquisition of a disability due to an accident or illness.

Born Into Privilege

Culturally competent practice involves understanding the experience of membership in a racial and ethnic minority group in the United States and an awareness of the benefits and privileges that are often taken for granted by White heterosexuals. Whites, for example, rarely experience racial profiling and increased suspicion by police and store security due to their skin color, whereas such experiences are normative across social classes for many people of color. Helms (1992) proposes that Whites have difficulty acknowledging that "it is better to be perceived as White than not" (p. 24) in the United States. "Whites are taught to think of their lives as morally neutral, normative and average, and also ideal" (McIntosh, 1998). White standards have become so much part of the American culture that Whiteness is normative. Subsequently, membership in a majority culture impacts one's perceptions and expectations of the acceptability of minority culture behaviors and ideas.

Born Into Power

Along with privilege comes power. Those who have power, like those who have privilege, would rather not acknowledge and discuss it. Those in power typically assume that this is the normal state of affairs and have little motivation to challenge the status quo.

Power is often associated with one's gender. Normative practices and social policies pair women with caregiving responsibilities for children, ill family members, and elderly parents. It is more natural to assume that men have work outside the home as their primary responsibility (Goodrich, 1991). Such assumptions help support beliefs that women "choose" more virtuous, noble life goals, such as motherhood, not that they are denied the power to build meaningful lives that might expand on these realms. However, when a woman becomes a mother, she does not also "choose" to run into a maternal wall beyond which opportunities for career advancement may need to be traded for responsibilities of family care (Williams & Cooper, 2004). Crosby, Williams, and Biernat (2004) conclude that "mothers' *choices* are framed within a discriminatory system" [italics added] (p. 678). The consequences of these perceptions of motherhood and women as caregivers are perpetuated by a society that enables men to view employment and fatherhood as a right and caregiving as optional.

Born Into Prejudice

Prejudice can have both historical and contemporary significance for individual and family functioning. The oppression of African American ancestors through slavery and racist practices still affects families in very practical ways. For example, the prior economic, political, and social status of African Americans precluded opportunities for African American families to acquire wealth by passing on resources from one generation to another. Today, prejudice negatively impacts the health of African Americans through issues such as stress and the quality of health care services received (Clark, Anderson, Clark, & Williams, 1999). Phinney (1990) concludes that racism and oppression inherently contribute to the identity of African Americans.

Poverty and Classism

Families in poverty live in neighborhoods with higher rates of violence and crime, fewer quality childcare facilities and after school programs, increased chances for exposure to environmental toxins, and limited access to health care. Family caregivers in poverty struggle to raise a family with few financial resources, and many experience stress, depression, low self-esteem, marital conflict over money, and substance abuse (Brooks-Gunn & Duncan, 1997).

In a country increasingly characterized by wide differences in family wealth, social class has become an even greater influence on attitudes and values (Lareau, 2003). Social-class differences are similarly reflected in beliefs about services for families of lower socioeconomic status. Those with power and resources, for example, assume that families of lower socioeconomic status need greater initiative (i.e., they are lazy), help with family life (i.e., they don't know how to be good parents), and greater self-reliance (i.e., they want to be dependent on welfare programs) (Friedman, 2000).

A "Typical" World

Children with disabilities and their families experience a world with many challenges including physical barriers, social exclusion, bullying, and attitudinal barriers such as a lack of awareness or knowledge on the part of "typical" individuals (Pivik, McComas, & LaFlamme, 2002). "Typicals" take for granted everyday privileges that those with disabilities struggle with on a daily basis.

Services for Diverse Families

Family services are needed that acknowledge and build upon the strengths of individuals and families experiencing marginalization, support families in challenging and influencing social structures, and join in efforts to change a status quo that supports marginalizing individuals and their families. New human service paradigms are needed to redesign human services so that they address the current inequities that have become associated with cultural diversity. Human services should provide opportunities to validate the client's struggles with inequities, help families strengthen their diverse coping strategies, and assist them in acquiring the resources that are needed to negotiate the differences in opportunities and constraints in their environments (Pinderhughes, 1995–1996). Empowerment-focused intervention strategies are needed to bring about changes in the systems that contribute to oppression and prejudice. While culturally competent interventions with individuals and families are important, changes in social policy, along with changes in who makes decisions and allocates resources, are essential to bring about lasting change.

Assumption #3: Child and family services should be designed to remedy problems and focus on the individual with the problem.

There is a predominant human service culture that views the purpose of human services as remedying individual problems and reducing risky behaviors in order to repair broken families. Social services to families have traditionally followed what has been referred to as a *deficit* model: Services have focused on identifying problems of the child and parent and then providing services to remediate these problems.

Problems of families are commonly attributed to individual deficits, when many of the causes of problems are actually beyond the family system. People without power, whether women, ethnic minorities, or the poor, are often viewed as defective by those with power or deserving of blame for their inability to be successful. Such a strategy has been referred to as *blaming the victim*. A failure to understand the cultural context of a behavior, for example, can result in an individual's and family's coping behaviors being labeled as dysfunctional instead of being understood as adaptive to a dysfunctional environment. Within this perspective, human services are designed to emphasize remediating or fixing the individual rather than bringing about changes in the systems and other individuals and cultures that contribute to the disadvantaging of persons. Similarly, the strengths of these individuals, families, and cultural practices—and their successful adaptations to difficult and prejudiced environments and cultures—go overlooked.

This culture of service provision that is organized around specific individual problems usually relies upon a diagnosis of a problem or some eligibility criterion specific to a circumscribed problem. Services are carried out by agencies and organizations that have missions that are focused on helping the individual diagnosed with a particular problem. This individually focused service delivery culture is problematic for at least three reasons.

First, problems typically have multiple determinants, associated risk factors, and co-occurring problems. For example, a low-income family caring for a child with a disability may need educational and medical assistance. At the same time, they may also benefit from after-school programs and childcare, housing assistance, and family counseling. However, access to this array of services becomes difficult because services typically focus only on the primary individual experiencing the problem. Services have yet to fully embrace family-centered practices to address the multiple impacts of a problem on the whole family system and its diverse membership.

Second, services are provided within a service delivery culture made up of distinct problem-focused agencies, all with differing eligibility requirements, fee schedules, waiting lists, and culturally different practices. This has encouraged a social service system characterized by specialized turfs, with agencies competing for a limited pool of funding (Minuchin, Colapinto, & Minuchin, 1993). While some progress has been made with efforts to develop systems of care for child mental health problems, these efforts have proven very complex given the pervasive culture and related funding of service delivery systems and the differing abilities of these agencies to address the needs of culturally diverse families.

Third, compounding the problems of accessing segregated services that are designed to address singular, individual problems, the human service culture in the United States is also organized around the separation of at least two different types of children: "typical" children and those diagnosed with disabilities. It is common for agencies to be segregated through the lens of disability or "typical" (sometimes referred to as "normal"). Some agencies, for example, work exclusively with persons with disabilities. In other agencies, services are oriented toward the needs of "typical" individuals. While these latter agencies do not refuse to serve individuals with disabilities, they benignly defer *primary* responsibility for services to individuals with disabilities to disability organizations. For example, they comply with federal physical accessibility requirements. However, adapting after-school programming to the needs of children with learning and physical disabilities may be perceived as beyond their capabilities and resources. A director of a community center explains: "We serve people with disabilities when it is not at the expense of other families" (Cuevas, 2002, p. 31).

As a result, resources may exist in the community, but a family may face many struggles to access these services. Families with a member with a disability experience significant stress navigating within two highly segregated service delivery systems as well as trying to coordinate services of the two systems in order to meet their needs.

In summary, services would better meet the needs of individuals and their families if needs were not defined by one individual's diagnosis but were addressed from a family-centered perspective. That is, an individual's needs should be understood within the context of the family and community and their strengths and resources. Community-based, parent-directed, family support programs have developed, in part, in response to dissatisfaction with the existing individual, problem-focused, segregated service delivery systems. Similarly, there has been increasing interest in programs that promote health and strengths of families, where families are seen as having diverse assets and resources to be strengthened and developed rather than as having "problems to be managed" (Lerner, 2001, p. 255).

Assumption #4: There is sufficient knowledge today about child development, parenting, and family functioning to know what is dysfunctional.

While this may appear true for White middle-class families, it is not the case for families with different cultural backgrounds in the United States. Dilworth-Anderson and Burton (1996) propose that existing theories of family development have limited utility for understanding ethnic minority families. Prior research has been guided by the assumption of a logical, linear, individual and family developmental progression. Researchers rarely take into account the social structural forces that shape different developmental pathways for families, particularly ethnic minority families. Omission of the context of the lives of families results in the failure to ask different types of questions, to include or exclude persons in research samples, and to accurately interpret the content and scope of what is observed.

Cautiousness is therefore required when applying existing theories and research in human service practice. Nondelinquent aggressive behaviors and "mutual verbal attacks," for instance, may indicate effective interpersonal skills with peers among African American youth growing up in urban poverty but not with middle-class suburban youth (Luthar & Burack, 2000). Learning how to negotiate the demands associated with being an adult, while still chronologically a teenager, may be a normative task in order for youth in poverty to succeed (Burton, Allison, & Obeidallah, 1995). Indicators of success may be dealing with situations of economic independence, survival, or even parenthood rather than (or in addition to) academic performance.

Immigrant families struggle to pave successful paths that vary, in part, from negotiating a balance between the values, beliefs, and behaviors of their country of origin or their ancestors, and the majority culture in the United States. Even within one immigrant family, there can be multiple adaptive processes co-occurring. Children may become more Americanized than their parents or grandparents and not want to comply with old obligations. Parents may become a squeezed generation, trying to take care of the family's cultural obligations and be Americanized for their kids. Parents with close ties to their homeland may send financial resources back home and try to immigrate other family members, adding to crowding and economic hardship.

Research has yet to clearly determine the exceptions to majority risk factors for child and family problems. A risk factor for the majority may actually be an adaptive and protective factor for an ethnic minority family. Sleeping arrangements where children sleep in the same bed or same room as their parents may seem inappropriate in regard to some emotional health and safety issues, but typical in terms of custom and nurturance (Fontes, 2005). Fluid and flexible family and household boundaries may be seen as a risk factor for family dysfunction. However, such fluid boundaries may be an expression of closeness of kith and kin (Boyd-Franklin, 2003), and, in the case of immigrant families, a way to respond to the transitions and needs experienced by families with members in two or more countries.

Assumption #5: The nuclear family is still the ideal family structure in America.

Simply put, family diversity is a reality in the United States. Different family structures and processes have evolved over time within various cultures to care for family members. Rather than continually comparing families to the nuclear form assumed to be the gold standard, human service providers need to learn who *families* perceive to be family members and how roles are carried out. Thinking beyond those living in a household or who are biologically related to identify significant family members and caregiving systems is necessary (Jones & Unger, 2000). The importance of kinship, fictive kin, and extended family members is influenced by cultural practices and norms. Roles may vary by gender and age of family members, and these roles may change over time with differing demands related to a family member's needs as well as the family's survival. Not only are those who are present important for understanding a family, those family members who are significant but absent are important also. Boss (1999), for example, describes the ambiguous loss experienced by family members when a significant person is not involved in family activities.

Assumption #6: Good helpers are well-trained professionals who are objective and who leave their issues and values at the door.

Higher Education and Training

In the past decade, there has been an overall endorsement for the importance of cultural diversity in higher education. However, higher educational institutions have not yet mastered cultural competency training. One of the great challenges for accomplishing this is that Eurocentric knowledge is emphasized and taught in most universities in the United States (excluding historically Black colleges and universities, also known as HBCUs). "The fundamental dogma of the American academy seems to rest upon the belief that the European culture is the world's only source of rational thought" (Asante, 1996, p. 22). The teachings and practices of Africans, American Indians, and other people are rarely as centrally included in curriculum as Eurocentric ideas.

Higher education institutions have yet to meet the frequent desire of families to have education providers of cultural backgrounds similar to theirs. Much progress has been made since *Brown v. Board of Education* (1954), and it is typical for predominately White colleges and universities to actively recruit minority students. However, it is much less common for predominately White higher education institutions to recognize and provide distinctive and unique supports that minority students need once they matriculate. This is particularly a problem for first-generation college students of color. Being African American in a predominately White college can exacerbate and add to the unique stresses and demands involved in coping with college (Brower & Ketterhagen, 2004).

Opportunities need to be provided for students of all cultural backgrounds to engage together in reflective and respectful discussions and exercises about prejudice and discrimination (Gaines, 2004). Such opportunities require an atmosphere of openness to addressing emotional reactions to the issues along with discussions of readings (Mio & Barker-Hackett, 2003). Similarly, students and faculty must feel safe that there will not be sanctions for their opinions by instructors or the academic institution or their peers (Gaines, 2004; Helms, Malone, Henze, Satiani, Perry, & Warren, 2003).

Service learning courses are needed that involve action, and just as important, reflection components. In these courses, students can be exposed to families and service organizations with values and operating principles that differ from the students' prior experiences or textbook readings. In this way, students may learn through "disconfirmatory experiences, which can initiate a reflective process whereby students try to integrate and understand a new and unexpected experience. Such experiences can suggest revisions, expansions, and modifications of preexisting, rules, principles, theories, or schemas" (Stukas, Clary, & Snyder, 1999, p. 5). Institutions of higher education must also achieve greater diversity among faculty, throughout departments, not just within, for example, a Black studies program (Gaines, 2004).

Objectivity and Professionalism

Objectivity has traditionally been a hallmark of professionalism. However, values are an integral part of a person's identity and the way a person views the world. Values are so much a part of a person's worldview that attempting to become objective is not only impossible, it may appear to others of differing cultural backgrounds as inauthentic and disingenuous.

A more realistic goal is for professionals to understand their own values, beliefs, and assumptions about individuals, families, and the nature of problems. Through cultural and life experiences, people develop specific ways of knowing and understanding their environments. This is typically referred to as their worldview or the lens by which they understand themselves and others. Such self-awareness is central for working with people of all cultures.

Professionals need to also rethink their views about relationships between professionals and culturally diverse families. Woolfolk and Unger (2004) describe how some African American families look at professionals who provide parent education and support in the home as taking on roles such as a child's aunt or mother's sister. Minuchin et al. (1993) suggest that social service providers in the child welfare system become part of the family system by the nature of the powerful influence they have over families. Human service providers need to be aware of the family's view of their relationship and the impact of the relationship on the family, regardless of the intentions of the provider.

Supervision and mentoring can help staff to deal with these complex issues and to acquire culturally competent practices (Alvarado, 2004). Time and senior staff should be available to create opportunities to engage in reflective practices and to build climates of mutual respect and support between providers and supervisors. Supervisors also need to know that time devoted to supervision is respected and supported by an organizational climate that values cultural competence as a process requiring ongoing dialogue and commitment to resources (Brunelli & Schneider, 2004).

Assumption #7: A neighborhood is where people live.

The role of the neighborhood is actually quite diverse in the United States. For some, a desirable neighborhood is primarily a safe and affordable place to live; for others it can be an indication of social status or a place for informal support, socialization, and a sense of belonging (Unger & Wandersman, 1981). Cultural competence involves recognizing the complexity of community and its importance to families, particularly ethnic minority families with low socioeconomic resources.

Neighborhoods in low-income ethnic minority urban communities are often seen as places at risk for crime, violence, insufficient affordable housing, and inadequate quality childcare, educational, and after-school services. It is less evident from an outsider's perspective, however, that these same neighborhoods may be communities with infrastructures that strive to maintain and improve the well-being of their residents. Elders serve on church committees, long-standing residents take on city council positions, pastors of storefront churches have children's clothing drives in the winter, parents try to monitor neighbor children's activities, and community leaders commit their energies to keep afloat ethnic agencies (Holley, 2003) that predominately serve the local community. Neighborhood boundaries, often not shown on city maps, are well known by families. A sense of community and attachment to what once was, or what could be, is shared among some residents within these neighborhoods.

Staff in programs designed to provide culturally competent services in low-income communities need to identify and involve community leaders, respect neighborhood history and traditions, and learn about the informal organization and structure of neighborhoods. The ability to develop trusting relationships and legitimacy are critical for the long-term success of a community-based intervention. The success of these relationships may ultimately depend upon *mutual* satisfaction regarding who makes decisions about how the intervention is delivered and who controls the allocation of resources and services (Unger, Antal, Tressell, & Cuevas-Mejia, 2001).

Assumption #8: "If we build it, they will come."

Human service providers in nonprofit agencies frequently experience low attendance and a lack of participation by the underserved population they are trying to reach, even though they have tried to provide a high-quality service. Culturally competent practice recognizes that finding help with a problem is, in part, a social and cultural event (Green, 1982). In fact, even the identification of a situation as a problem or as normal is often culturally determined (Linen-Thompson & Jean, 1997). In the help-seeking process, people turn to family and friends who may use language and labels differently from professionals in the majority culture to identify and categorize a problem. The meaning attributed to certain labels, such as mental illness or disability, may be stigmatizing for some, based upon cultural beliefs and knowledge. The extent to which human service agencies understand and respect the beliefs and practices of the "client culture" will influence whether clients use an agency's services (Green, 1982, p. 30).

Finding help is also a problem of access. Given the disproportionate number of ethnic minorities who live in poverty, they often experience very pragmatic barriers to accessing services. Being uninsured or underinsured limits the types, if any, and quality of services available. Transportation and access to childcare are also major obstacles to obtaining services, particularly when services require repeated visits. Language is a similar significant barrier for those who are not fluent in English, given that many agencies do not routinely have bilingual staff available or materials available in languages other than English. For individuals with physical disabilities, access is more than having a ramp to enter a building. Students with disabilities in after-school programs, for instance, may have limited access because activities are located above the ground floor or because staff do not know how to accommodate their disabilities so they can be included in activities.

Underutilization may also be due in part to mistrust and suspicion (Collins, 2000; Diala et al., 2000). Latino and certain Asian populations may refrain from obtaining services due to fear of deportation. Others may not pursue services because of previous experiences with disrespectful agency personnel. Human services can begin to address some of these problems through hiring bilingual staff, involving community leaders in outreach efforts, and building an organizational climate perceived as welcoming by families (Unger, Jones, Park, & Tressell, 2001). Public relations materials need to emphasize the problem through the eyes of the population to be served. For example, Perez-Stable, Marin, and Posner (1998) recommend that smoking-cessation programs targeting Latino smokers emphasize quitting for the benefit of the family's health, rather than focusing on improving personal health. Churches and local community-based ethnic agencies can be important collaborators in reaching out to families as well as in providing services (Holley, 2003).

A culturally competent organizational environment is also achieved through representative leadership (Alvarado, 2004). Representation is key to promoting equity in hiring and decision-making. But representation cannot promote cultural competence

> if such representation exists within an inequitable system or environment that values *one* [italics added] set of experiences, knowledge, teaching, and learning methodology over all others. . . . Equity will be achieved when all populations gain the right to share in organizational benefits and are appreciated for the value that they add. (Alvarado, 2004, p. 37)

Assumption #9: Agencies receiving funds to provide family services have the infrastructure to effectively deliver culturally competent services.

Providing culturally competent services requires considerable organizational resources that many nonprofit organizations do not have or are unable to consistently and adequately provide. In the past several years, even fewer funds have been allocated to nonprofits by federal governmental and foundation sources (Boyle & Fratt, 2004). As a result, agencies struggle to provide adequate pay and benefits to maintain a quality staff and subsequently experience frequent staff turnover and disruptions in family-staff relationships (Nittoli, 2003). Agencies serving primarily White clients debate the utility of allocating resources for bilingual staff and translation services. Agency staff who do not view services to individuals with disabilities as the primary mission of their agencies may view devoting resources to increase accessibility as low priority. In an effort to be more cost effective, agencies may adopt a one-size-fits-all programming strategy, compromising the flexibility needed to meet the needs of a diverse population. Another strategy used to save costs is to contract out services to agencies that may provide specialized skills but that may not have the expertise to meet the needs of a community's diverse population, despite good inten-sions on the part of the providers. Agencies may also find themselves in competition to be "the" agency that provides services to a particular ethnic or minority group, potentially decreasing the choice of and diversity in ser-vices. Funds often are allocated for specific pilot projects to underserved groups, but when the pilot funding is gone, the agency may not be able to sustain these services.

Nonprofit agencies are continually devoting resources to fund-raising and grant-seeking activities. However, smaller ethnic agencies frequently do not have persons with the expertise or time to respond to the increasingly complex requirements of funding organizations (Holley, 2003). The ability to provide culturally competent services is further challenged by the limited time and staff resources available for supervision and mentoring. Agencies often compromise with one-time diversity training workshops.

Social service agencies are held accountable for documenting and pro-ducing predefined, desirable outcomes. However, agencies serving ethnic minorities often find their goals and objectives are quite different from those of their funding organizations, such as corporations, that tend to see problems through the worldview of the majority population. They may also have difficultly identifying culturally valid methods and measures to evalu-ate their programs (Guzman, 2003).

The strains of limited funding and the self-preservation interests of agencies compromise efforts toward representation and equity, a corner-stone of culturally competent organizations. As Meenaghan, Gibbons, and McNutt (2005) observe, "Unfortunately, the culture of many agencies, in today's political climate and the reality of scarce resources, stresses organi-zational needs and productivity in the context of significant power differ-entials among staff and managers" (p. 36). These power differences in an organization's culture also can influence the nature of staff and family relationships.

There are no short-term remedies to the economy and corresponding financial struggles experienced by nonprofit organizations. However, increased collaboration and cooperation across agencies may help agencies better meet the diverse needs of families. Through participation in coalitions, agencies may increase their capacity, as a unified group, to leverage resources and how they are allocated. Of critical importance is including community representation and community leaders who provide a strong and loud voice for a diverse group of families. Universities could also develop partnerships with agencies and provide service learning opportunities for graduate students to assist with grant-writing.

Conclusion

Much progress has been made in heightening the awareness and skills of human service providers in the nonprofit sector regarding families and cultural diversity. However, intervention approaches are still needed that are more culturally appropriate and meet the diverse needs of individuals and their families. The future provides opportunities to challenge assumptions underlying current human services that do not fit with the daily life experiences of many ethnic minority children and families. Improving services so they meet the needs of all families not only requires changes in the ways that professionals interact with children and families but also changes in the ways that programs are designed, administered, and evaluated. Alternative views, with sufficient resources, can enable families, together with service providers, supervisors, and administrators in the nonprofit human services sector, to develop and sustain culturally competent programs. Higher-education institutions, in partnership with communities and local leaders, can further impact the future by providing opportunities and environments that embrace learning about diversity.

References

Alvarado, C. (2004). Authentic leadership: Lessons learned on the journey to equity. *Zero to Three, 25*, 32–39.

Asante, M. K. (1996). Multiculturalism and the academy. *ACADEME, 82*, 20–23.

Boss, P. (1999). *Ambiguous loss: Learning to live with unresolved grief.* Cambridge, MA: Harvard University Press.

Boyd-Franklin, N. (2003). *Black families in therapy: Understanding the African American experience* (2nd ed.). New York: Guilford Press.

Boyle, P., & Fratt, L. (2004). Times are tough—get used to it. *Youth Today, 13*(1), 37–38.

Brooks-Gunn, J., & Duncan, G. J. (1997). The effects of poverty on children. *The Future of Children, 7*, 55–72.

Brower, A. M., & Ketterhagen, A. (2004). Is there an inherent mismatch between how Black and White students expect to succeed in college and what their colleges expect from them? *Journal of Social Issues, 60*, 95–116.

Brown v. Board of Education, 347 U.S. 483 (U.S. Supreme Court, 1954).

Brunelli, J., & Schneider, E. F. (2004). The seven Rs of team building. *Zero to Three, 25*, 47–49.

Burton, L. M., Allison K. W., & Obeidallah, D. (1995). Social context and adolescence: Perspectives on development among inner-city African-American teens. In L. J. Crockett & A. C. Crouter (Eds.), *Pathways through adolescence:*

Individual development in relation to social contexts (pp. 119–138). Mahwah, NJ: Erlbaum.

Clark, R., Anderson, N.B., Clark, V. R., & Williams, D. R. (1999). Racism as a stressor for African Americans: A biopsychosocial model. *American Psychologist, 54,* 805–816.

Collins, P. H. (2000). *Black feminist thought: Knowledge, consciousness, and the politics of empowerment.* New York: Routledge.

Crosby, F. J., Williams, J. C., & Biernat, M. (2004). The maternal wall. *Journal of Social Issues, 60,* 675–682.

Cuevas, T. (2002). *The role of non-profit community centers in supporting people with disabilities.* Unpublished master's thesis/analytic paper, School of Urban Affairs and Public Policy, University of Delaware.

Dean, R. G. (2001). The myth of cross-cultural competence. *Families in Society, 82,* 623–630.

Derezotes, D. M., Testa, M. F., & Poertner, J. (2004). *Race matters: Examining the overrepresentation of African Americans in the child welfare system.* New York: Child Welfare League of America.

Diala, C., Muntaner, C., Walrath, C., Nickerson, K. J., LaVeist, T. A., & Leaf, P. J. (2000). Racial differences in attitudes toward professional mental health care and in the use of services. *American Journal of Orthopsychiatry, 70,* 455–464.

Dilworth-Anderson, P., & Burton, L. M. (1996). Rethinking family development: Critical conceptual issues in the study of diverse groups. *Journal of Social and Personal Relationships, 13,* 325–334.

Fisher, C. B., Hoagwood, K., Boyce, C., Duster, T., Frank, D. B., Grisso, T., et al. (2002). Research ethics for mental health science involving ethnic minority children and youths. *American Psychologist, 57,* 1024–1040.

Fontes, L. A. (2005). *Child abuse and culture: Working with diverse families.* New York: Guilford Press.

Friedman, D. H. (2000). *Parenting in public: Family shelter and public assistance.* New York: Columbia University Press.

Gaines, S. O., Jr. (2004). Color-line as fault-line: Teaching interethnic relations in California in the 21st century. *Journal of Social Issues, 60,* 175–193.

Goodrich, T. J. (1991). Women, power, and family therapy: What's wrong with this picture? In T. J. Goodrich (Ed.), *Women and power: perspectives for family therapy* (pp. 36–47). New York: Norton.

Green, J. W. (1982). *Cultural awareness in the human services.* New York: Prentice Hall.

Guzman, B. L. (2003). Examining the role of cultural competency in program evaluation: Visions for new millennium evaluators. In S. I. Donaldson & M. Scriven (Eds.), *Evaluating social programs and problems: Visions for the new millennium* (pp. 167–182). Mahwah, NJ: Erlbaum.

Hareven, T. K. (2000). *Families, history, and social change. Life-course and cross-cultural perspectives.* Boulder, CO: Westview Press.

Health Resources and Services Administration (HRSA). (2000). *Eliminating health disparities in the United States.* Washington, DC: U.S. Department of Health and Human Services.

Helms, J. (1992). *Race is a nice thing to have: A guide to being a White person or understanding the White persons in your life.* Topeka, KS: Content Communications.

Helms, J. E., Malone, L. T. S., Henze, K., Satiani, A., Perry, J., & Warren, A. (2003). First annual diversity challenge: "How to survive teaching courses on race and culture." *Journal of Multicultural Counseling and Development, 31,* 3–11.

Holley, L. C. (2003). Emerging ethnic agencies: Building capacity to build community. *Journal of Community Practice, 11,* 39–57.

Jones, C. W., & Unger, D. G. (2000). Diverse adaptations of single parent, low-income families with young children: Implications for community-based prevention and intervention. *Journal of Prevention and Intervention in the Community, 20,* 5–24.

Kagan, C., & Burton, M. (2005). Marginalization. In G. Nelson & I. Prilleltensky (Eds.), *Community psychology: In pursuit of liberation and well-being* (pp. 293–308). New York: Palgrave Macmillan.

Keppel, K., Pearcy, J., & Wagener, D. (2002). *Trends in racial and ethnic specific rates for the health status indicators: United States, 1990–98* (Healthy People Statistical Notes, no. 23). Hyattsville, MD: National Center for Health Statistics.

Lareau, A. (2003). *Unequal childhoods: Class, race, and family life.* Berkeley: University of California Press.

Lerner, R. M. (2001). Promoting promotion in the development of prevention science. *Applied Developmental Science, 5,* 254–257.

Lerner, R. M., & Castellino, D. R. (2002). Contemporary developmental theory and adolescence: Developmental systems and applied developmental science. *Journal of Adolescent Health, 31,* 122–135.

Linen-Thompson, S., & Jean, R. E. (1997). Completing the parent participation puzzle: Accepting diversity. *Teaching Exceptional Children, 30,* 46–50.

Lonner, W. (1994). Culture and human diversity. In E. Trickett, R. Watts, & D. Birman (Eds.), *Human diversity: Perspectives on people in context* (pp. 230–243). San Francisco: Jossey-Bass.

Luthar, S. S., & Burack, J. A. (2000). Adolescent wellness: In the eye of the beholder. In E. Cicchetti, J. Rappaport, I. Sandler, & R. P. Weissberg (Eds.), *The promotion of wellness in children and adolescents* (pp. 29–57). Washington, DC: Child Welfare League of America Press.

Mayberry, R. M., Mili, F., Vaid, I. G. M., Samadi, A., Ofili, E., McNeal, M. S., et al. (1999). *Racial and ethnic differences in access to medical care: A synthesis of the literature.* Washington, DC: Henry J. Kaiser Family Foundation.

McGoldrick, M., Giordano, J., & Garcia-Preto, N. (2005). *Ethnicity and family therapy* (3rd ed.). New York: Guilford Press.

McIntosh, P. (1998). White privilege: Unpacking the invisible knapsack. In M. McGoldrick (Ed.), *Revisioning family therapy: Race, culture, and gender in clinical practice* (pp. 147–152). New York: Guilford Press.

Meenaghan, T. M., Gibbons, W. E., & McNutt, J. G. (2005). *Generalist practice in larger settings: Knowledge and skill concepts* (2nd ed.). Chicago: Lyceum Books.

Minuchin, P., Colapinto, J., & Minuchin, S. (1993). *Working with families of the poor.* New York: Guilford Press.

Mio, J. S., & Barker-Hackett, L. (2003). Reaction papers and journal writing as techniques for assessing resistance in multicultural courses. *Journal of Multicultural Counseling and Development, 31,* 12–19.

Nittoli, J. (2003). *The unsolved challenge of system reform: Condition of the frontline human services workforce.* Baltimore, MD: Annie E. Casey Foundation.

Perez-Stable, E., Marin, G., & Posner, S. (1998). Ethnic comparison of attitudes and beliefs about cigarette smoking. *Journal of General Internal Medicine, 13,* 167–174.

Phinney, J. (1990). Ethnic identity in adolescents and adults: A review of research. *Psychological Bulletin, 108,* 499–514.

Phinney, J. S. (1996). When we talk about American ethnic groups, what do we mean? *American Psychologist, 51,* 918–927.

Pinderhughes, E. (1995–1996). Difference and power in therapeutic practice. *Family Resource Coalition Report, 14,* 20–23.

Pivik, J., McComas, J., & LaFlamme, M. (2002). Barriers and facilitators to inclusive education. *Exceptional Children, 69,* 97–107.

Roberts, D. (2002). *Shattered bonds: The color of child welfare.* New York: Basic Civitas Books.

Scott, G., & Simile, C. (2005, May 12). Access to dental care among Hispanic or Latino subgroups: United States, 2000–03. *Advance Data from Vital and Health Statistics* (No. 354). Hyattsville, MD: National Center for Health Statistics.

Smeiser, N. J., Wilson, W. J., & Mitchell, F. (Eds.). (2000). *American becoming: Racial trends and their consequences, Vol. 1.* Washington, DC: National Academy Press.

Stukas, A. A., Jr., Clary, E. G., & Snyder, M. (1999). Service learning: Who benefits and why. *Social Policy Report, 13.* Ann Arbor: Society for Research in Child Development, University of Michigan.

Sue, S. (2003). In defense of cultural competency in psychotherapy and treatment. *American Psychologist, 58,* 967–970.

Unger, D. G., Antal, P. W., Tressell, P. A., & Cuevas-Mejia, T. (2001). *Wilmington Healthy Start Final Evaluation Report.* Newark: Center for Disabilities Studies, University of Delaware.

Unger, D. G., Jones, W., Park, E., & Tressell, P. A. (2001). Promoting involvement between low income single caregivers and urban early intervention programs. *Topics in Early Childhood Education, 21,* 197–212.

Unger, D. G., & Wandersman, A. (1981). Neighboring in an urban environment. *American Journal of Community Psychology, 10,* 493–509.

Williams, J. C., & Cooper, H. C. (2004). The public policy of motherhood. *Journal of Social Issues, 60,* 849–865.

Woolfolk, T., & Unger, D. G. (2004, November). *Perceptions of African American mothers involved in Parents as Teachers.* Paper presented at the Annual Conference of the National Council on Family Relations, Orlando, Florida.

11

Family, School, and Community

Finding Green Lights at the Intersection

Judith A. Myers-Walls and Larissa V. Frias

Writing this chapter provided a formidable challenge: simultaneously addressing the issues of family, school, community, and diversity. The complexity of the overlap of these factors can be overwhelming, yet it is critical to remember that any separation of these domains is artificial. While each has been examined by separate academic disciplines, people's lives are lived within that complex overlap. Children from diverse backgrounds and situations wake up in the morning in their family homes or residences; participate in educational opportunities at home or in schools according to local, state, and federal policies; and spend afternoons and evenings in recreation, communication, or education with friends, family, neighbors, and media. While each realm of family, school, and community has its own characteristics, policies, history, and goals, each is impacted by the others. And all operate differently and are viewed differently by differing cultural groups.

This chapter views the intersection of family, school, and community through the lens of family diversity. It begins with a discussion of theoretical frameworks and then looks at cultural diversity from a historical perspective.

Models and frameworks and a brief research summary are provided next followed by recommendations for improving collaborative relationships among family, school, and community in a context of diversity.

Theoretical Perspectives

There are three theoretical perspectives that are especially useful in viewing this intersection: ecological theory, symbolic interactionism, and general systems theory. Urie Bronfenbrenner's *ecological theory* provides reminders of the importance of this intersection and the most general overview of how these realms work together. In his ecological view of development and behavior, Bronfenbrenner (1979, 1986) presented a picture of the development of an individual as occurring within the context of nested spheres of influence, including the family, school, and community (Bronfenbrenner, 1986; Bronfenbrenner & Morris, 1998). The *microsystem* is the context of roles and activities with which the developing child (or the parent) interacts face to face. The context that links microsystems with each other is called the *mesosystem*. The relationships and the communication that take place between a child's family and his or her teachers or the family's relationship with the child's peer group are examples of mesosystem influences. The *exosystem* includes the family's community environment and all other external systems and public agencies such as schools, faith organizations, and health services.

The larger social context in which all these settings are embedded is called the *macrosystem*. This includes overarching cultural patterns of beliefs and values that guide both families' and schools' goals and ways of raising and educating the children in each cultural group. An example of macrosystem influence is how belief systems impact the structures under which schools and families operate, although institutions and individuals may not always be conscious of that influence. The macrosystem influence of culture plays an important part in the roles that teachers, human service providers, children, and families take; in how people respond to each other; and in the values and attitudes that individuals bring to their families, work environments, schools, and communities. All these levels of contextual systems and subsystems—microsystem, mesosystem, exosystem, and macrosystem—interact and influence each other and provide a framework for looking at the family, school, and community intersection with a diversity lens.

Other theoretical perspectives that are helpful in framing the topic are symbolic interactionism and general systems theory. *Symbolic interactionism* explores how social interactions influence what meanings are assigned to events and situations. Based on this theory, individuals act upon things according to the meaning ascribed to them, and they express that meaning through symbols such as language and gestures. This framework of family science assumes that individuals and the context in which they exist are inseparable; thus, the diverse backgrounds of different families and individuals may prove to be a challenge. However, the interpretative process is dynamic and ever-changing (White & Klein, 2002).

General systems theory looks at family, school, and community as separate systems that are interlinked. Boundaries exist that separate them from each other, but their interconnectedness and interdependence mean that a change in one system creates changes in the others (Whitchurch & Constantine, 1993). Communication links the family, school, and community systems together. There is a feedback loop among the systems that communicates the expectations and demands of the situations that affect the goal setting and the actions of each individual. In systems theory, consistent with symbolic interactionism, these expectations are formed and molded according to the experiences of the person, his or her environment, and the social position attached to him or her. For example, an immigrant parent and the child's teacher may have very different understandings and expectation related to school field trips, leading both of them to make decisions that the other sees as either unusual or unreasonable.

These theoretical frameworks all view the three contexts of home, school, and community as nested and linked structures, all existing in a cultural context. Ideally, those contexts support and sustain each other. Each context may have different goals and different strategies in supporting the development of individuals, but one thing common among them is that the system contributes to the well-being of the individuals who are part of it.

Culture and Historical Reflections on the Intersecting Systems

As stated above, the intersection of family, school, and community occurs within a cultural context. Culture has been thought of as composed of meanings and symbols that groups of people share, or "recurring, common objects and events of a group of people and the shared meanings they create about such objects and events" (Strauss & Quinn, 1997, in Myers-Walls, Myers-Bowman, & Posada, 2006, p. 148). It refers to ethnic and racial groups but also groups of individuals in different family forms or socioeconomic and other varying social dimensions (Falicov, 1995).

Whether or not it was ever true, it is a common belief that families in the United States used to be more homogeneous than they are today. "Family" meant a married couple with a father who was employed, a mother who stayed home and managed the household, and any number of children. Stephanie Coontz, in her book *The Way We Never Were* (1992), has challenged these and other assumptions and pointed out that what is called the "typical" family was actually a small blip on the U.S. radar screen that came and went over a brief period in the 1950s and 1960s. Even during those years, there were single parents, families that did not speak English, families with special-needs children, and other atypical families, but they were often invisible.

Diversity of families and children actually has been a major feature of U.S. society since it was founded, even though it is often thought of as a recent trend. In fact, in the early 1900s, the mass immigration of people from other places in the world "represented what has been described as the greatest mass movement of people the world has ever known" (Goodman, 1977, p. 175). This migration led to two trends in schools and communities that have continued and that are at the same time complementary and in tension with each other. On one hand, one force directed the schools to help families maintain the culture and heritage of immigrants' home countries. In some ways this grew out of the fear that leaving behind the vestiges of home, both secular and religious, could render immigrants as wild and uncivilized as they thought this new land was (Handlin, 1977, p. 126). On the other hand, a contrasting trend focused on Americanizing the many disparate individuals with their varying languages, beliefs, and practices (Goodman, 1977). At an extreme, that meant melting all of these immigrants down and recasting them in a single mold. Considering these two trends together, schools and community agencies were faced with the challenge of helping new citizens hold on to their heritage at the same time that they created something new from the combination of the many colors, textures, and flavors of the world's cultures.

In spite of the diversity in U.S. families that surrounds us now and has since the country was founded, most people carry a clear and consistent image of a prototypical family in their heads—a nuclear family that is White and middle or upper class with two children. The percentage of the population that fits that prototype is diminishing steadily due to several trends, including acceptance of several types of lifestyles that were socially rejected in the past, continuing immigration and increased mobility of families, and increased insistence among individuals in a number of minority groups that they be recognized and included. But the stereotypical image remains—in the minds of families, school personnel, and community members and professionals. And that image (along with stereotypical images of schools and communities) can impair collaboration among multiple cultures and backgrounds.

Family, School, and Community Working Together

The intersection of families, schools, and communities can be either a collection of independent entities or a collaboration of groups working toward a common goal. In their presentation of a framework of collaboration, the National Network for Collaboration states that "when beginning the journey, it is critical that all existing and potential members share the vision and purpose" (National Network for Collaboration, 1995, p. 3). Families, schools, and communities tend to share a focus on the positive development of individuals, but finding a more specific common vision can be a significant challenge when dealing with forces as varied as families, schools, and communities. It is likely that schools see their primary or perhaps sole purpose as the academic preparation of children. Communities typically define success as social stability and economic growth. Simultaneously, families in the United States may have a vision that concentrates on the physical, psychological, and financial well-being of their own members. How does one find a common ground among these perspectives?

Not only may there be different goals and targets across the different groups, but the three domains may even use a different language and talk about different issues. Each discipline uses its own rhetoric and jargon. In addition, there is variation within the domains. Definitions of family, school, and community vary significantly across cultures, and those definitions are likely to change both across and within cultures over time (Andrews, 2002). For example, education in China traditionally meant that Chinese parents were responsible for their children's socialization and education about family regulations, daily family rituals and courtesies, and family education, including filial piety, brotherly love, and support for the elderly (Dai, 2001). Globalization and migration have required a shift away from those expectations. Traditional education in Africa has seen children as partners with adults, and they work alongside each other rather than adults providing verbal or formal instruction (Thioune, 2001). Although that tradition is being challenged in African countries as Western intervention imposes different education styles, the traditional expectations influence families and professionals as they operate in the home country and migrate abroad. Defining who the family is can often be a problem as well. Jones and Moomaw (2003) have highlighted the family terminology used in Native American culture, in which sisters-in-law may be called wives and uncles may be called grandfathers. These family definitions can cause misunderstandings and confusion unless cross-cultural communication takes place.

As outlined by the National Network for Collaboration (1995), the first step in building partnerships is dialogue and understanding. This is true whether building relationships between families and schools or communities or among different cultural groups. This process is grounded in valuing and respecting diversity and recognizing that the varying perspectives and resources that each group brings to the partnership are valuable and enrich the joint efforts. Rather than trying to make each realm operate like another, appreciation of unique contributions strengthens the partnership. That understanding can then lead to shared goals. Although common ground may vary, it is likely that a goal shared by families, schools, and communities across cultural groups will be the facilitation of the growth of healthy and capable children.

Research Findings Related to the Intersection

Perhaps due to the complexity of triadic research models, a lack of awareness of the contributions of all three domains, or the location of most researchers in single disciplines, very little research has been conducted looking at family, school, and community factors together. Even fewer have viewed the intersection in the light of diversity, although Boethel (2003) has identified many of the studies that have been conducted. Much of the work done in the area of the intersection has focused on the desired outcomes of a single domain, most often the educational system, and examined how the other domains facilitate or hinder the meeting of those goals. For example, Rogers, Light, and Curtis (2004) recognized the separate but overlapping domains and identities of children regarding literacy beliefs. They explored how narrow definitions of literacy in some populations and communities, specifically an African American sample, run counter to the goal of integrating local resources into the public school curriculum. Anderson-Butcher and Ashton (2004) focused on how collaborations among organizations, agencies, and families can benefit schools. They identified family and community needs that must be addressed in order to achieve teacher success and student learning. Riggs and Greenberg (2004) used hierarchical linear regression to determine what family and community factors were important in determining participation in after-school programs among Latino children. They concluded that after-school programs may serve a protective function for children in migrant populations, at least when looking at academic functioning.

Some studies have looked at negative child or family outcomes and used regression models to discover the relative contributions of each domain to those outcomes. Some of the dependent variables bridge goals of different domains. For example, Delizonna, Alan, and Steiner (2006) examined factors associated with a school shooting and concluded that it was best explained by a transactional model in which the individual influences and is influenced by his or her environment. They also recommended that intervention at all three levels, including family, school, and community, was necessary in order to reduce school violence. Focusing on a different level of violence, Jaffe, Baker, and Cunningham (2004) looked at family, community, and school factors that could reduce the likelihood of domestic violence.

Other researchers have looked at positive outcomes and identified ways to use all domains to reach those goals. Bennett (2006) described an early childhood program that places teachers in intimate contact with a family and community setting in order to provide better continuity of care. Martin and Halperin (n.d.) addressed the issue of out-of-school youth and how educators and community leaders can help them build useful lives in work, family, and citizenship. In a broad focus on community well-being, Zelniker and Hertz-Lazarowitz (2005) created a program involving parents in their children's literacy development and in building peaceful coexistence in a community in Israel that included both Jews and Arabs. Friedland and Morimoto (2005) looked at the role of young people in the community and examined how school and family factors influenced the likelihood of young people getting involved in civic engagement activities. They found that family socialization, school programs that facilitated involvement, and the future expectations of young people determined their levels of civic involvement.

In a summary of recommendations that arise out of research on family-school-community partnerships in diverse populations, Boethel (2003) recommends in part that schools and agencies honor families' hopes and concerns for their children, that they acknowledge both commonalities and differences among students and families, that staff be better prepared to work with all groups of families, that immigrant families receive extra support in understanding school policies and procedures, and that all parties recognize that it takes time to build trust.

Views of Partnership Styles

Research studies over a period of 25 years have found an important connection between parent and community involvement and academic performance of students (Ceperley, 2005), the primary outcome variable that has been measured. Due to such findings, the No Child Left Behind Act of 2001 and other regulations from the U.S. Department of Education (2004) require parent and community involvement. This shared responsibility is expected not only in organization and implementation of services but from the beginning steps of decision-making and planning through the evaluation and assessment of the programs. Although research involving family, school, and community factors together is limited, other authors have addressed the dyads involved: family and school, family and community, and school and community.

Levels and Types of Partnerships Between Parents and Schools

Several different authors have created models of levels or forms that home and school partnerships may take. One model describes a continuum from minimal to associative to decision-making levels of involvement (Barbour, Barbour, & Scully, 2005). For example, in addressing homework, teachers might need a minimal level of involvement from parents, asking them to check whether their children had done their assigned homework. At the associate level, teachers may invite families or resource people from the community to speak to a class, or parents may participate in the Parent-Teacher Association (PTA). The third level of involvement is the decision-making level. In this form, the parents, teachers, school personnel, community business persons, and social agencies help to make the decisions for programs that educate the children. Parents may serve on school committees, taking part in planning, organizing, implementing, and evaluating activities according to the goals set by the programs (Barbour et al., 2005).

Weiss, Kreider, Lopez, and Chatman (2005) have described another model of four frameworks. Rather than representing levels of involvement, they describe four different approaches to partnerships. One framework is a *family-school partnership,* in which familylike schools bring families and educators together to support and encourage children both at home and in the school. A second framework is *comprehensive school improvement.* In this approach, teams are formed that each include teachers, parents, and students to develop and monitor school programs, support learning at home, and deal with individual needs. The *funds of knowledge* framework assumes that parents bring skills and experiences that are valuable in the educational setting. The *empowerment approach* has as its goal the imparting of advocacy skills and knowledge to parents. It is likely that each of those approaches would be perceived differently by different cultural groups, and cultures would show different levels of skill with performing within those frameworks.

From a parent perspective, these models of involvement in schools are consistent with some of the critical parenting practices included in the National Extension Parent Education Model (Smith, Cudaback, Goddard, & Myers-Walls, 1994). The involvement models address primarily children's motivation: teach children about themselves, others, and the world around them; stimulate curiosity, imagination, and the search for knowledge; create beneficial learning conditions; and help children process and manage information. These parenting skills have been shown in numerous empirical studies to be crucial to the growth of healthy, confident, and competent children. The ways parents perform those skills will vary significantly across cultures, however.

Partnerships Between Families and Community Agencies

Another dyadic relationship within the family-school-community intersection is the parent or family with community agencies. Again, that relationship has been cited as important in outcomes for children, families, and communities. Lisbeth Schorr (1989), in her exploration of what works for overcoming risk in children and families, found that one of the characteristics of successful community programs was seeing "the child in the context of family and the family in the context of its surroundings" (p. 257). She highlighted the importance of mobilizing parents as partners in community programs and identifying family needs beyond the immediate identified problem, and she described the need for professionals to venture out of traditional hours and settings to meet the needs of parents and families. This mobilization is likely to be a foreign concept among many communalist cultures, however.

Again, the skills needed by parents to develop partnerships with communities have been identified as critical by the National Extension Parent Education Model (Smith et al., 1994). The skills related to this partnership concern advocacy: find, use, and create community resources when needed to benefit one's children and the community of children; stimulate social change to create supportive environments for children and families; and build relationships with family, neighborhood, and community groups. Connie Flanagan (2001) also has highlighted the importance of parents and families placing their childrearing approaches firmly in the context of culture and societal change, leading to connections between families and communities. As her research has shown, families raise their children in the context of social and cultural groups and with the perspective of what parents expect their children to encounter in the future. Changing parenting practices in response to those expected future realities is one of the mechanisms that stimulate social change.

Types of School-Community Partnerships

A third dyad involved in the family-school-community intersection is the relationship between schools and the community. A current perspective on connecting schools with the community is service learning (Campus Compact, 2006). Student involvement in the community is seen as ranging from volunteerism at one extreme where the needs of the community recipient are seen as primary, to internships where the training needs of the student are primary. A balance point in between these extremes is called *service learning*, and this level of involvement both advances the educational needs of the student and meets important needs of the community. Such programs are seen as beneficial to the student's grasp of academic content, beneficial in helping communities to meet needs, and beneficial to both students and communities by teaching civic responsibility and sensitivity to community needs. Ideally, this kind of connection with the community minimizes cultural conflict by incorporating the cultural characteristics into the partnerships.

Family, School, Community Involvement

The most complex and most complete partnership includes families, schools, and communities. Joyce L. Epstein, the director of the Center on School, Family, and Community Partnerships, outlined six types of involvement strategies that include families, schools, and communities as partners (Epstein, Coates, Salinas, Sanders, & Simon, 1997; Wright, Stegelin, & Hartle, 2007). Although it is from a school perspective, the typology can be adapted to other perspectives.

1. *Parenting skills* includes schools facilitating the development of diverse parents' childrearing skills, child development knowledge, and home conditions that support the academic learning of the children.

2. *Communicating with the school administrators and teachers* addresses parents' exchanges regarding school programs and the children's progress, strengths, and challenges.

3. *Volunteering* in school activities includes recruiting families to volunteer, training for volunteer jobs, providing for support to students and other families, and collaborating with business establishments for volunteer opportunities.

4. *Learning at home* helps families continue the learning process by providing supplemental educational activities at home, giving assistance and guidance for the children's homework, and using materials from the library for academic exercises.

5. *Decision-making* involvement is when families take part in the school's decisions, governance, and advocacy by being involved in the PTA or in the school's committees.

6. *Collaborating with the community* occurs when school resources and programs for families are coordinated with community businesses and agencies. Schools locate and contact business establishments to support their programs, while the business partners gain publicity through recognition in the school events and benefit from a well-trained future workforce.

Epstein's six types of involvement have been adopted in many settings. Each family, school, or community may have different ways of practicing their involvement, but it is important to establish a match among the domains regarding their goals and vision. Furthermore, the partnership will also be successful if the level and type of involvement are within the range of skills, resources, and interests of the parents, teachers, school administrators, and businesspeople (National Network for Collaboration, 1995).

Program Models

The next section presents two school models that exhibit key factors in collaborations among family, school, and community, Project Head Start and Comer's School Development Program.

Project Head Start, the early childhood program for low-income children, has emphasized parent and community involvement in its curriculum since it started (Washington & Bailey, 1995; Zigler & Muenchow, 1992). The parent-involvement feature of the program encourages the families and the centers to work together by providing opportunities for parents to work as either paid or volunteer staff in the center. This lets them observe different strategies in working with children, making them aware of what their children are learning (Barbour et al., 2005). At a more formal level, some parents serve on the policy committee where they can be active in the planning of the program, recruitment and hiring of staff, and budget planning. It has been reported that more than 950,000 Head Start parents have volunteered in their children's classrooms within a single year's time (U.S. Department of Health and Human Services, 1993). In addition to parent involvement, Project Head Start also pays attention to collaborating with community health and social service agencies. Head Start families have been able to maintain their immunizations and medical exam schedules, and children have enjoyed the nutritious diet program that is a part of this model (Barbour et al., 2005).

Comer's School Development Program (SDP) was started in 1968 by Dr. James Comer and colleagues from the Yale Child Study Center. The three guiding principles of this program are (1) consensus, which requires that all people concerned come to an agreement on the plans; (2) collaboration; and (3) no fault, which means that everybody shares responsibility for success or a need for improvement (Comer, Haynes, & Joyner, 1996). The school community includes three teams: the school planning and management team that coordinates school activities, the student and staff support team that attends to the concerns of the staff and students, and the parent team made up of the parents of students. Comer's approach emphasizes the importance of improving the social climate in school. This is achieved when there is a minimal culture gap between the teachers and their students (Cook, Hunt, & Murphy, 1999). To attain this, teachers avoid stereotyping their students based on their color and economic background. Similarly, students and their families understand the pressures that the school personnel face and take some responsibility for the students' behaviors. A primary aim of the program is to link school goals closely with home values, so that both parties will be able to support the education and development of the children.

In an evaluation study conducted in Comer's inner-city schools in Chicago, the elementary school SDP students performed better than a control group in math and reading and on certain behavioral measures such as anger control and acting out (Cook et al., 1999). Based on the perceptions of the students and teachers, the social climate in schools that adopted the SDP model was reported to have improved once the program started.

Recommendations

Successful partnerships across the domains are not automatic. "Forming relationships between schools and families of one's own culture takes time and energy. Forming relationships with families whose values, beliefs, and assumptions are unfamiliar requires, in addition to time and energy, sensitivity, commitment, and persistence" (Edvantia, 2005, p. 2). The National Network for Collaboration (1995) and Comer and colleagues (1996) have developed recommendations for improving partnerships. Some of the recommendations address context and others address process. Combining their recommendations and applying them to family, school, and community while considering diversity, the following suggestions are provided.

Context

- *Assess connectedness.* Explore what kinds of connections exist formally and informally before and during the partnership-building process.
- *Investigate the history of partnerships.* Find out whether the community and other partners have a history of cooperation or competition. Build on strengths.
- *Explore the political climate.* Find out how decisions have been made among the families, schools, and communities in the partnership. Include the varied components of the environment.
- *Be familiar with policies, laws, and regulations.* Many existing policies, laws, and regulations may need to be changed to make the partnership effective. Find out what the current guidelines are. What is the current level of bureaucracy?
- *Catalog your resources.* Make a list of what is available to the partnership in the way of environmental, in-kind, financial, and human resources. Explore ways to increase them.
- *Consider catalysts.* Identify what factors and conditions will support the partnership. This includes how the public views the situation and also relates to the convener who will bring the parties together at the beginning of the process.

Process

- *Build understanding within the community.* Know the people, cultures, and habits of the people involved in the partnership. Learn to understand those groups whose backgrounds differ from your own. Set up opportunities for frequent interaction across the domains.
- *Mobilize the community.* Try to identify the important players and their passions. Explore how resources can be mobilized from a variety of cultural traditions. Share power across the systems.
- *Identify strong leadership.* Partnerships depend on individuals who impact change within their communities. Who will the key players be?
- *Establish clear communication channels.* Address the kind of terminology that will be used and set up an effective process for communication that is culturally appropriate.
- *Set target outcomes and evaluate success.* As noted above, research literature in this area is limited and should be enhanced. It also is important to monitor advancements as a result of the partnership. Relationships with higher education and research institutions can be very helpful.
- *Plan for sustainability.* Systems need to be put in place to allow the initial collaborative efforts to become institutionalized.

References

Anderson-Butcher, D., & Ashton, D. (2004). Innovative models of collaboration to serve children, youths, families, and communities. *Children and Schools, 26*(1), 39–53.

Andrews, A. B. (2002). Children and family life. In N. H. Kaufman & I. Rizzini (Eds.), *Globalization and children: Exploring potentials for enhancing opportunities in the lives of children and youth* (pp. 71–80). New York: Kluwer Academic/ Plenum.

Barbour, C., Barbour, N. H., & Scully, P. A. (2005). *Families, schools, and communities. Building partnerships for educating children* (3rd ed.). Upper Saddle River, NJ: Pearson Education.

Bennett, T. (2006). Future teachers forge family connections. *Young Children, 61*(1), 22–27.

Boethel, M. (2003). *Diversity: School, family, and community connections annual synthesis 2003.* Retrieved May 13, 2006, from http://www.sedl.org/connections/ resources/diversity-synthesis.pdf

Bronfenbrenner, U. (1979). *The ecology of human development.* Cambridge, MA: Harvard University Press.

Bronfenbrenner, U. (1986). Ecology of the family as a context for human development: Research perspectives. *Developmental Psychology, 22,* 723–742.

Bronfenbrenner, U., & Morris, P. (1998). The ecology of developmental processes. In W. Damon (Ed.), *Handbook of child psychology* (Vol. 1, pp. 993–1028). New York: Wiley.

Campus Compact. (2006). Campus Compact. Web site. Retrieved May 12, 2006, from http://www.compact.org

Ceperley, P. E. (2005). *Linking student achievement to school, family, and community involvement—A review of the literature.* Charleston, WV: Appalachian Regional Education Laboratory at Edvantia. Retrieved August 13, 2006, from http://www.edvantia.org/services/pdf/FamilyBrief.pdf

Comer, J. P., Haynes, N. M., & Joyner, E. T. (1996). The school development program. In J. P. Comer, N. M. Haynes, E. T. Joyner, & M. Ben-Avie (Eds.), *Rallying the whole village: The Comer process for reforming education* (pp. 1–27). New York: Teachers College Press.

Cook, T. D., Hunt, H. D., & Murphy, R. F. (1999). Comer's school development program in Chicago: A theory-based evaluation. *American Educational Research Journal, 37,* 535–597.

Coontz, S. (1992). *The way we never were: American families and the nostalgia trap.* New York: Basic Books.

Dai, K. J. (2001). The tradition and change of family education in mainland China. In J. A. Myers-Walls & P. Somlai with R. Rapoport (Eds.), *Families as educators for global citizenship* (pp. 139–157). Aldershot, UK: Ashgate.

Delizonna, L., Alan, I., & Steiner, H. (2006). A case example of a school shooting: Lessons learned in the wake of tragedy. In S. R. Jimerson & M. Furlong (Eds.), *Handbook of school violence and school safety: From research to practice.* (pp. 617–629). Mahwah, NJ: Erlbaum.

Edvantia. (2005). *School improvement specialist training materials: Performance standards, improving schools, and literature review.* Module 3—School-family-community connections. Nashville, TN: Author.

Epstein, J. L., Coates, L., Salinas, K.C., Sanders, M. G., & Simon, B. S. (1997). *School, family, and community partnerships: Your handbook for action.* Thousand Oaks, CA: Corwin Press. Retrieved May 8, 2006, from http://www.csos.jhu.edu/ P2000/sixtypes.htm

Falicov, C. J. (1995). Training to think culturally: A multidimensional comparative framework. *Family Process, 34,* 373–388.

Flanagan, C. A. (2001). Families and globalization: A new social contract and agenda for research. In J. A. Myers-Walls & P. Somlai with R. Rapoport (Eds.), *Families as educators for global citizenship* (pp. 23–40). Aldershot, UK: Ashgate.

Friedland, L. A., & Morimoto, S. (2005). *The changing lifeworld of young people: Risk, résumé-padding, and civic engagement.* Circle Working Paper 40. Retrieved May 13, 2006, from http://www.civicyouth.org/PopUps/WorkingPapers/ WP40Friedland.pdf

Goodman, L. V. (1977). Tending the melting pot. In E. H. Grotberg (Ed.), *200 years of children* (pp. 174–178). DHEW Publication No. (OHD) 77-30103. Washington, DC: U.S. Department of Health, Education, and Welfare.

Handlin, O. (1977). Education and the American society. In E. H. Grotberg (Ed.), *200 years of children* (pp. 125–134). DHEW Publication No. (OHD) 77-30103. Washington, DC: U.S. Department of Health, Education, and Welfare.

Jaffe, P. G., Baker, L. L., & Cunningham, A. J. (2004). *Protecting children from domestic violence: Strategies for community intervention.* New York: Guilford Press.

Jones, G. W., & Moomaw, S. (2003). Who's in the family? In C. Copple (Ed.), *A world of difference: Readings on teaching young children in a diverse society* (p. 74). Washington, DC: National Association for the Education of Young Children.

Martin, N., & Halperin, S. (n.d.). *Whatever it takes: How twelve communities are reconnecting out-of-school youth.* Retrieved May 13, 2006, from http://www .aypf.org/publications/WhateverItTakes.htm

Myers-Walls, J. A., Myers-Bowman, K. S., & Posada, G. (2006). Parenting practices worldwide. In B. Ingoldsby & S. Smith (Eds.), *Families in global and multicultural perspective* (2nd ed., pp. 147–167). Thousand Oaks, CA: Sage.

National Network for Collaboration. (1995). *Collaboration framework—addressing communitiy capacity.* Retrieved May 12, 2006, from http://crs.uvm.edu/nnco/ collab/framework.html

Riggs, N. R., & Greenberg, M. T. (2004). Moderators in the academic development of migrant Latino children attending after-school programs. *Journal of Applied Developmental Psychology, 25*(3), 349–367.

Rogers, R., Light, R., & Curtis, L. (2004). "Anyone can be an expert in something": Exploring the complexity of discourse conflict and alignment for two fifth-grade students. *Journal of Literacy Research, 36*(2), 177–210.

Schorr, L. B. (1989). *Within our reach: Breaking the cycle of disadvantage.* New York: Doubleday.

Smith, C. A., Cudaback, D., Goddard, H. W., & Myers-Walls, J. A. (1994). *The National Extension Parent Education Model final report.* Manhattan: Kansas State Cooperative Extension Service. Retrieved May 12, 2006, from http://www.k-state.edu/wwparent/nepem/nepem.pdf

Thioune, O. (2001). Families as environmental educators in the Sahel. In J. A. Myers-Walls & P. Somlai with R. Rapoport (Eds.), *Families as educators for global citizenship* (pp. 159–163). Aldershot, UK: Ashgate.

U.S. Department of Education. (2004). *Parental involvement: Title I, Part A, nonregulatory guidance.* Retrieved May 13, 2006, from http://www.ed.gov/programs/titleiparta/parentinvguid.doc

U.S. Department of Health and Human Services. (1993). *Evaluating Head Start expansion through performance indicators.* Washington, DC: U.S. Government Printing Office.

Washington, V., & Bailey, U. J. O. (1995). *Project Head Start: Models and strategies for the twenty-first century.* New York: Garland.

Weiss, H., Kreider, H., Lopez, M., & Chatman, C. (Eds.). (2005). *Preparing educators to involve families: From theory to practice.* Thousand Oaks, CA: Sage.

Whitchurch, G. G., & Constantine, L. L. (1993). Systems theory. In P. G. Boss, W. J. Doherty, R. LaRossa, W. R. Schumm, & S. K. Steinmetz (Eds.), *Sourcebook of family theories and methods: A contextual approach* (pp. 325–352). New York: Plenum Press.

White, J. M. & Klein, D. M. (2002). *Family theories: An introduction* (2nd ed.). Thousand Oaks, CA: Sage.

Wright, K., Stegelin, D. A., & Hartle, L. (2007). *Building family, school, and community partnerships* (3rd ed.). Upper Saddle River, NJ: Pearson Education.

Zelniker, T., & Hertz-Lazarowitz, R. (2005). School-family partnership for coexistence (SFPC) in the city of Acre: Promoting Arab and Jewish parents' role as facilitators of children's literacy development and as agents of coexistence. *Language, Culture and Curriculum, 18*(1), 114–138.

Zigler, E., & Muenchow, S. (1992). *Head Start.* New York: Basic Books.

12

Family Life Education

Implications of Cultural Diversity

Deborah B. Gentry

L ena, a capable and insightful undergraduate student, is a teaching assistant for Michael, a family science faculty member at a university in the upper Midwest. On a rotating basis, Michael and a colleague, Julia, have each taught a required undergraduate, topical course that emphasizes cultural diversity among American families. While they have not done so in some time, they have recently initiated a series of discussions between themselves for purposes of informally assessing the course, their teaching of it, and students' reactions to and performance in it. Lena completed the course under Julia's instruction and has been added to the team to offer student insight and feedback as well as assist with course revisions. Lena also hopes to gain valuable experience that will aid her in the design of her own community-based, six-hour family life education program, a requirement of her senior capstone course. The three identify several goals for the reworking of the course, including the design of a workable strategy to minimize student resistance and enhance student engagement. The typical enrollment in a given semester is 35 to 40 students.

Family life education (FLE) is an enterprise that has as

> its primary purpose helping individuals and families learn about human growth, development, and behavior in the family setting and throughout the life cycle.

Learning experiences are aimed at developing the potential of individuals in their present and future roles as family members. The core concept is relationships, through which personality develops, about which individuals make decisions to which they are committed, and in which they develop self-esteem. (Cassidy, 2004, p. F3)

This chapter will elucidate the implications of cultural diversity for the design, delivery, and evaluation or assessment of family life education. Adopting both conflict (see Ingoldsby, Smith, & Miller, 2004) and ecosystem (see Bubolz & Sontag, 1993; Scanzoni, 2004) perspectives that acknowledge the role of differences, I accept variations and differences among families and communities as normal and natural phenomena. Diversity, in and of itself, is neither good nor bad, but how people respond to diverse environments results in outcomes that are more or less constructive or positive. Thus, this chapter focuses on the guiding principles and best practices associated with teaching about cultural and family diversity, teaching audiences of diverse composition, and utilization of diverse teaching techniques and strategies. In addition to their relevance for the standard secondary and postsecondary family science classrooms in the United States, many of the identified principles and practices have relevance also for family life outreach efforts conducted in informal community settings across the nation.

Brief History: The Relationship of FLE and Issues of Diversity

Lewis-Rowley, Brasher, Moss, Duncan, and Stiles (1993) have rendered perhaps the most extensive historical account of family life education. Arcus (1995), Darling (1987), Duncan and Goddard (2005), Gentry (2004), and Powell and Cassidy (2001) also provide other noteworthy accounts Lewis-Rowley et al. identify five time periods over which family life education has grown and developed: coalescence (1776–1860), emergence (1861–1900), crystallization (1901–1920), expansion (1921–1950), and entrenchment (1951–1990). Family science as a field of study and practice originated in the expansion era, though it did not fully emerge until the 1980s (Hollinger, 2003).

"Professionalization" could be an appropriate label for the years since 1990. During these years, the National Council on Family Relations (NCFR) has successfully undertaken a process to certify family life educators as well as programs of study. The Family Science Section of NCFR created a code of ethics for those in the field. Though, at the current time, the U.S. Department of Labor does not formally recognize the occupation of family life educator, NCFR has initiated the process and paperwork to bring about such recognition

(Cassidy, 2004). Family life educators' have also expanded participation in the scholarship of teaching and learning movement.

American communities and the families living within them have become more culturally diverse, particularly during the entrenchment era and, as I am coining it, the professionalization era. According to Umana-Taylor and Wiley (2004), family scholars agree that it is important to address cultural and family diversity within family studies curricula. Yet, there is insufficient knowledge about the degree and manner to which this is done. The revised *Framework for Life-Span Family Life Education,* first created and disseminated by NCFR in 1987, infuses diversity in multiple and various ways (Bredehoft, 2001). Family life educators and academic programs seeking certification must demonstrate that they adequately address the 10 substance areas outlined by the framework, including an appreciation of cultural and family diversity. Numerous college textbooks focusing on diversity have been written and made available for use in family studies courses. Yet, Conway-Turner, Kim, Sherif, and Woolfolk (2001) suggest that educators must thoughtfully review textbooks to ascertain their proper fit with course goals and objectives. Similarly, in light of the rapid proliferation of Web-based resources, instructors must carefully assess the quality and appropriateness of information about family and cultural diversity on the Internet and help their students to do the same.

Michael, Julia, and Lena, the teaching team featured in the vignette that opens this chapter, recognize the wisdom of Banks's statement (1991): "Concepts, content, and teaching strategies cannot be identified and selected until goals [of multicultural curriculum and instruction] are defined" (p. 24). As it is for Banks, a primary goal of the course that Michael, Julia, and Lena teach is to help students to make reflective decisions on issues related to cultural and family diversity and, then, to take personal, social, and civic actions to help solve corresponding problems that exist in our national and global societies. They have jointly confirmed they intend to take a transformation approach to teaching the course with hopes that it will perhaps evolve into a social action approach. According to Banks, these approaches are preferable to either the contributions approach (simply infusing information about ethnic and nontraditional heroes into the standard mainstream curriculum) or the additive approach (characterized by adding a book, a unit, or a course that attends to diversity topics and issues to an existing mainstream curriculum without changing it substantially). In contrast, the transformation approach provides numerous and varied perspectives, frames of reference, and content from different groups in an effort to further students' understanding of the nature, development, and complexity of the United States and the world. Then, the social action approach capitalizes upon what is accomplished during such transformation and provides opportunity for students to make decisions and take actions related to content, issues, or problems they have studied.

With the goals of transformation, and perhaps eventually social action, in mind, the teaching-learning team has revisited their decisions regarding the specific objectives of the family and cultural diversity course and their decisions about the texts and supplementary readings they have been assigning. To help determine the suitability of their current decisions regarding course objectives and readings, they have consulted information compiled by the Ethnic Minority Section of the NCFR, particularly a publication titled *Resource Manual for Teaching about Ethnic Minority Families and Other Diversity Issues* (see NCFR–Ethnic Minority Section, 2004).

While facilitating and enhancing students' cultural competence is often a stated goal found in syllabi prepared for family and cultural diversity courses, Dean (2001) posits that encouraging students to maintain an awareness of their lack of competence is also a worthy goal. Family professionals prepared from this vantage point admit what they don't know and, thus, seek to become better informed by those they serve, the true experts regarding their own cultural values and needs. "There is no thought of competence [on the part of the family professional]—instead one thinks of gaining understanding (always partial) of a phenomenon that is evolving and changing" (p. 624).

Brief Overview: Theoretical Underpinnings and Methods for Studying FLE and Diversity

Foundational Theories, Perspectives, and Frameworks

Family Dynamics

Numerous theoretical perspectives have guided and continue to guide family life educator-scholars, particularly those who focus on issues of diversity, as they design, deliver, and evaluate family studies curriculum and instruction at the postsecondary level. The ecological/systems/ecosystems perspective is one of several that have been particularly influential in providing insights about the dynamics of individual and family functioning in social environments (Burr, Day, & Bahr, 1993; Darling, 1987). To varying degrees, developmental, behavioral, humanistic, cognitive-developmental, social learning, Adlerian, psychoanalytic, structural, feminist, and historical frameworks have provided additional important insights for family life educator-scholars (Gentry, 2004).

Several other theoretical perspectives can be helpful to family life educator-scholars trying to further their understanding of diversity issues. Conflict theory and social exchange theory provide useful lenses for observing and interpreting the dynamics of diverse families as they engage in work and play in the communities within which they live. With the greater focus on family strengths and resilience (see McCubbin, 1995; McCubbin, Thompson, Thompson, & Futrell, 1999), the theory of cultural variance (individuals and families of each and every "social address" illustrate the wide variety of ways daily life can be undertaken that result in positive, yet different, outcomes) now challenges the theory of cultural deviance (individuals and families of minority and nontraditional social addresses are deviant or dysfunctional and, thus, in need of some manner of correction). Finally, as the realities of oppression, discrimination, and injustice have become ever more clear, family life educator-scholars value the insights provided by family stress theory (see Boss, 2002; Burr et al., 2004). Michael, Julia, and Lena, from the vignette, need to clarify the theoretical foundations from which they will individually and jointly view diverse family functioning.

Learning

In a similar vein, Michael, Julia, and Lena might next discuss their preferred theoretical explanations regarding the learning process. In their comprehensive guide to adult learning, Merriam and Caffarella (1999) compare and contrast these theories: behaviorist, cognitivist, humanist, constructivist, and social learning. In brief, behaviorists believe learning is a process of changing behavior, while cognitivists view learning as an internal mental process that emphasizes perception, memory, and insight. For humanists, learning is a personal act to fulfill potential, while learning is a process of constructing meaning from experience according to constructivists. Finally, social learning theorists suggest learning occurs as a result of interaction with and observation of others in a social context. Merriam and Caffarella note that characteristics of adult learners and the ways they engage in learning are different from those of children and youths. While the majority of Julia's and Michael's students are just embarking upon adulthood, these educator-scholars would be wise to consult the work of Knowles (1984a, 1984b), the father of adult learning theory, or andragogy, in an effort to better understand the evolving preferences of their audience. In general, as adult learners mature, they are increasingly goal-oriented, relevancy-oriented, and practical about their learning and prefer to be autonomous or self-directed when engaging in learning activities. Whenever possible, they seek to reflect upon and apply their previous knowledge and experiences under conditions of mutual respect.

Our teaching team should also review the literature on multiple intelligences. In addition to linguistic, logical-mathematical, and spatial abilities, Gardner (1993) identifies intelligence associated with musical ability, kinesthetic ability, personal insight about oneself and others, and ability to make important distinctions in the natural world (among flora and fauna, for example). According to Gardner, a person may be highly competent with regard to one or two intelligences, yet average to dull with regard to the remaining intelligences (cited in Merriam & Caffarella, 1999, p. 178). Salovey and Mayer (1990) and Goleman (1995) theorize that humans also exhibit varying degrees of emotional intelligence, including the abilities to be aware of and manage one's own emotions, to marshal one's emotions in the pursuit of a goal, to recognize and appreciate the emotions expressed by others, and to facilitate the positive interplay of emotions in the context of building fulfilling relationships with other people. Julia, Michael, and Lena might posit that students with competence in personal insight about self and others, as well as competence in logic, would likely perform well in their family and cultural diversity course. Likewise, students possessing and using most or all of the domains of emotional intelligence would successfully accomplish course goals and objectives. The team may want to incorporate exercises that appeal to as many of the intelligences as possible in order to reach their audience.

Humans have preferred styles of processing information and coming to know the world around them (see Marotz-Baden, Osborne, & Hunts, 2000). While each individual tends to have a preferred style, most people adapt to different settings and stimuli such that they can often engage in other styles if need be. When applied to classroom learning, Myers and Briggs's psychological type theory suggests a learner will prefer and perform best when processing information and ideas, as well as interacting with teachers and fellow learners, using one of 16 styles that reflect some degree of extroversion or introversion, sensory or intuitive expertise, analytic thinking or empathetic feeling, and judging or perceiving (see Kroeger & Thuesen, 1988). Teachers bring their preferred styles to the teaching-learning enterprise as well. By comparison, the Gregorc (1982) model of teaching-learning styles consists of just four approaches. Each person, as learner or teacher, will prefer to process and use information in a concrete sequential, an abstract sequential, an abstract random, or a concrete random manner.

Kolb (1984) and McCarthy (1996) advance a third perspective. When presented with information and ideas, Type 1 learners ask "Why?" They seek to connect newly acquired information with various aspects of their lives. Type 2 learners ask "What?" and are particularly intrigued by the facts associated with the information that is presented to them. Type 3 learners are action-oriented. When their question of "How?" is answered, they are immediately ready to put their newfound knowledge to use. Last, Type 4 learners ask "What if?" They are eager to adapt and alter the information given to them in an effort to uncover a new and fresh application. Intertwined with one's preferred style of learning is the use of one's preferred sensory modality. While learners and teachers engage in the teaching-learning process using most, if not all, senses, each person tends to find more comfort and success in doing so in one of these modalities: auditory, visual, or kinetic (Barbe, 1985).

Since self-awareness is critical to effective teaching and learning, Julia, Michael, and Lena plan to facilitate a self-assessment process with their students. Cranton (2000) suggests using published inventories, games and ice-breaker activities, and journaling. Myers-Walls (2000) advises students to reflect on their personal characteristics and the groups to which they belong; on what they truly know and do not know about cultural and family diversity; and on the attitudes, values, and emotions they hold with regard to issues of diversity. As it is often difficult for people to see themselves clearly, it might be helpful for Julia, Michael, and Lena to provide feedback for each other on their tendencies, behaviors, and attitudes. With a better sense of their strengths and limitations as lifelong learners and teachers, they will be better prepared to empower their students to engage in meaningful self-reflection.

Teaching

Generally, in the past, the enterprise of teaching has been described more as an art than a science. Many in the field have said that one is a good teacher because of an inherent talent or aptitude. Boyer (1990) has been among leaders in the field, particularly in higher education, to challenge that supposition and initiate discussion about the distinctions between good teaching, scholarly teaching, and the scholarship of teaching and learning (SoTL). Good teaching, according to McKinney (2003a), facilitates student learning and other desired outcomes that are compatible with the mission, goals, and objectives of an academic unit or institution. Good teaching is noted in student satisfaction ratings, peer observation commentary, and self-reflective portfolios or dossiers. Numerous publications elucidate best practices associated with good teaching, particularly with regard to post-secondary audiences. For instance, Chickering and Gamsom (1991) identify these seven practices as essential to good teaching:

1. Encouraging contact between students and faculty

2. Developing reciprocity and cooperation among students

3. Encouraging active learning

4. Giving prompt feedback

5. Emphasizing time on task

6. Communicating high expectations

7. Respecting diverse talents and ways of learning

Scholarly teaching involves taking a studious or learned approach to designing and delivering instruction. Scholarly teachers are well read and well informed about their subject matter as well as about teaching and learning (McKinney, 2003a). Some scholarly teachers, though not all, may want to engage in SoTL. This requires going beyond scholarly teaching to conducting classroom action research (Cross & Steadman, 1996; Kember et al., 2000; Richlin, 2001).

According to Kreber (2001), effective SoTL includes a public account of some or all of the following aspects of teaching: vision, design, interaction, outcomes, and analysis. It does so in a manner that can be peer reviewed and used by members of one's community. SoTL also meets the following criteria: requires high levels of discipline-related expertise, breaks new ground and is innovative, can be replicated and elaborated upon, can be documented, can be peer reviewed, and has significance or impact. High-quality FLE research involves the same kind of systematic, rigorous investigation that other forms of research exhibit.

During one of their course articulation sessions, Julia, Michael, and Lena address each of the questions posed within Kreber and Cranton's (2000) model of scholarship of teaching. In response to, "Why does it matter what methods, materials, or course design I use?" they agree that they aim to assist their family diversity students in becoming engaged in transformative learning. According to Mezirow and Associates (2000), transformative learning

> refers to the process by which we transform our taken-for-granted frames of reference (meaning perspectives, habits of mind, mind-sets) to make them more inclusive, discriminating, open, emotionally capable of change, and reflective so that they may generate beliefs and opinions that will prove more true and justified to guide action. Transformative learning involves participation in constructive discourse to use the experiences of others to assess reasons justifying these assumptions, and making an action decision based on the resulting insight. (pp. 8–9)

Among family science academicians, experiential learning, active learning, community-based service learning (see Berke, Hamon, & Eby, 2001), and problem-based learning (see Sandifer-Stech & Gerhardt, 2001) approaches are all compatible with Mezirow's ideas about transformative learning.

Once this primary goal of their family and cultural diversity course is established, the next task for Michael, Julia, and Lena is to determine the most suitable method for investigating and resolving the teaching-learning problem they observed when they have taught the course in the past. A barrier of some kind has prevented many of the students from experiencing transformative learning.

Methods

To ensure that SoTL work, including that conducted by family science academicians, receives optimal recognition and merit, the methods of inquiry utilized must be rigorous, well conceived, and properly executed. Carver and Teachman (1995) highlight the variety of methodological options available to researchers, including those pursuing classroom action lines of inquiry. While one can use secondary data sources, or data that have been previously collected by another researcher, researchers most commonly aim to collect primary data of their own. They can generate their data by developing a survey, designing either a classical or a naturalistic experiment, utilizing an ethnographic method of inquiry (e.g., case study, participant observation), or incorporating content analysis. Multiple, varied methods provide more rich and insightful data.

Richlin (2001) suggests scholarly teachers wanting to take their concerns about a particular teaching-learning problem to the next level of inquiry must document a baseline of student learning performance and, then, consult the literature regarding the nature of the problem. For example, Julia, Michael, and Lena could utilize past scores on course examinations as well as answers to particular questions that students have formulated, content analyze any artifacts they have saved that demonstrate the assorted ways students have fulfilled course assignments, critique a videotape of a class session, examine the assessment provided by an objective peer reviewer, or analyze written comments students have provided on course evaluations and oral comments made during exit interviews or focus group sessions (McKinney, 2003b). Once relevant baseline data are compiled, the following series of steps in a process of SoTL inquiry should be undertaken:

- Consult relevant literature.
- Choose and apply an intervention.
- Conduct new systematic, rigorous observation.
- Document observations.

- Analyze results.
- Obtain peer review and feedback.
- Identify key issues.
- Synthesize results.
- Place results into the context of knowledge base.
- Devise a means of reporting findings (e.g., manuscript, paper, poster, or report).
- Submit findings for peer review.
- Disseminate, publish, or present work to a wider audience in hopes of contributing to the knowledge base of the field. (Richlin, 2001)

At this point in the SoTL process, the teaching-learning team members should probably suspend selection of any additional research methods they want to employ until after they have consulted the cultural education literature further and begun to design the teaching-learning intervention(s) they intend to test.

Designing, Implementing, and Assessing a Solution

Having observed a lack of student engagement in the classroom and during other learning activities, Julia, Michael, and Lena review relevant literature on the issue. Now they need to design, implement, and assess an instructional intervention for this teaching-learning problem.

One explanation for this lack of engagement among students enrolled in family and cultural diversity courses is that intensely felt emotions associated with course content create barriers to active learning (Gorski, 1995; Ramos & Blinn-Pike, 1999; Tatum, 1997). Among these potentially problematic emotions are unawareness, fear, and disownership (Gorski) as well as anger and shame (Ramos & Blinn-Pike; Tatum). Some students are intimidated by the realization of the breadth of their unfamiliarity with cultural diversity, prompting them to remain passive. Some students remain quiet for fear that their spoken comments during class might offend the instructor or fellow students, perhaps leading to a heated exchange, a verbal attack in response, or an impression held by others that one is racist, sexist, or prejudiced in some other realm. Other students, prompted by a desire to distance themselves from the realities of prejudice and discrimination, refuse to believe that injustice exists, or at least that it exists at the high levels many purport, or they refuse to believe they contribute in any way to such contemporary injustices, either directly or indirectly. These students may not participate fully in an educational experience that serves to challenge their position.

As a result of real or perceived injustice suffered by themselves or by others close to them, some students may feel a level of anger they believe is inappropriate to express during classroom discussion and, thus, disconnect or disengage. Embarrassment about their social address or cultural group membership, guilt over sometimes receiving unfair privilege or advantage, or humiliation suffered when one's family members and friends act or speak in ways that reveal their prejudices can lead to more global feelings of shame for some students. As a result of deeply felt shame, these students believe they have no right to speak up and, therefore, remain passive and uninvolved in the educational experiences of the course. In addition to anger and disownership or disassociation, there are two other generally unproductive reactions some students display during social justice education (Griffin, 1997): immobilization and conversion. Overloaded by new information and overwhelmed by fresh insight, some students experience a sense of powerlessness in being able to institute any positive change. Other students may instead become such extreme converts to the struggle against various injustices that they begin monitoring and correcting fellow students as they share their viewpoints. They may even become tyrannical in their efforts to shape others' perspectives and monopolize more than their fair share of discussion time.

Continued review of the literature enables Michael, Julia, and Lena to realize the enormous variety of classroom learning activities that could be adopted or adapted for use, many of which need not be completed by students for a grade. Some examples include case studies, debates, field trips, and simulations (Cranton, 2000); reflexive journaling, role-plays, guest speakers, and panels (Adams, Bell, & Griffin, 1997; Allen & Farnsworth, 1993); and storytelling (Rosenblatt, 2001). Games and toys as well as analyses of art, music, television programming, magazines, cartoons, and apparel (Volpe & St. Clair-Christman, 2005) are other possibilities. Educational and feature films and videos are abundantly available (Hamon & Stone, 2005). Poems, plays, novels, short stories, fairy tales, and other pieces literature can be incorporated as well (Kaissi, 2005; Schmitz, Stakeman, & Sisneros, 2001). Regarding the last, O'Brian (2004) discusses the value of and provides helpful hints for conducting literature circles.

While some of these learning activities and teaching strategies are currently being utilized by Julia and Michael, Lena recommends that they be judicious in selecting new interventions. Incorporating too many could overwhelm both the students and instructors as well as render it more difficult to assess the contributions each new approach has to any positive learning outcomes that might result.

Given Lena's enthusiastic support, Michael and Julia consider employing a community mapping, or social mapping, exercise as an intervention. After reviewing multiple resources on the topic (Green, 1999; Knapp, 2003; Robinson, 2005; Robinson, Vineyard, & Reagor, 2004), they realize that there are several elements of the community mapping exercise that will promote student engagement in learning, including discussion. First, students will work in small groups, each having a role as scout, mapper, note-taker, photographer, tabulator, collector, or image maker. Second, students will be physically moving about in various three- to six-block areas of the town or city within which the university is located acquiring information about the assets (e.g., residents, housing, businesses, schools, churches, recreation facilities, libraries and museums, government agencies, social and medical services, transportation thoroughfares, and so on) of the neighborhood and documenting these assets in some fashion (e.g., notes, maps, photos, brochures, newspapers, stone rubbings, flora and fauna, and so on). Third, when students synthesize and report their findings, they will focus on positive assets for individual and community capacity-building, not just on needs and deficiencies. Having students undertake community mapping is not without its challenges. Much preparation on the part of the instructor is needed for the experience to be productive, as well as safe, for the students. Adequate thought must be given to reliable and fair means of assessing and grading the contributions of each student to the work of the group.

When selecting strategies or interventions to help resolve problems with student disengagement in their family diversity course, Julia and Michael recognize their facilitation of learning activities, including discussion, is of utmost importance. Instructors can carefully formulate and reasonably execute the curricular and instructional plans, but if they do so without fully appreciating the nature of their audience, the full potential of their plans may not be reached. Though McDermott's (2001) advice is directed toward family professionals who deliver outreach parenting education, her insights about the varying ways learners might differ from one another are, nonetheless, applicable to audiences of undergraduate students. Learners' views about the primacy of the role of the individual in society, competition, expectations regarding communication, the necessity of taking action to solve a presenting problem, punctuality and time schedules, carrying out work responsibilities and opportunities for play, and family structure and the interdependence of family members are all worthy of inquiry. In family and cultural diversity courses, asking students to submit journals reflecting upon these values could serve as a means of enlightening faculty about the variety of student perspectives.

As Volpe and St. Clair-Christman (2005) identify, those who teach college courses related to family and cultural diversity face an assortment of challenges. They recognize the need to deconstruct myths and stereotypes, yet they also know that doing so involves emotion-laden discussion. They aim to create a classroom climate that is conducive to learning about differences, yet they recognize that all parties present in the classroom have varying perceptions regarding the distribution of power amongst them. They want to help students find personal relevance in what is studied, all the while aiming to not offend any one of them. They also aim to deliver course content in interesting and varied ways that minimize resistance and optimize levels of student engagement in the learning process. Improved cultural competence on the part of their students—the emerging family professionals of tomorrow—is a desired outcome. In the process of teaching such a course, improved cultural competence on the part of the instructor would, of course, be another worthy outcome. According to Barrera and Corso with Macpherson (2003), the degree of cultural competence achieved is based more on perfecting one's ability to craft respectful, reciprocal, and responsive relationships with diverse others than on the extent of information possessed about particular cultures.

For Michael and Julia, their ability to model skilled dialogue, as Barrera and Corso with Macpherson (2003) conceive it, when communicating with the students enrolled in their family and cultural diversity classes is critically important. Three qualities characterize skilled dialogue: respect, reciprocity, and responsiveness. Being respectful entails acknowledging and accepting various boundaries (e.g., physical, emotional, cognitive, or spiritual) that exist between people. Boundaries are "markers that simultaneously connect and distinguish one from others" (p. 43). Should boundaries be crossed without permission, the likely result is distrust, while crossing boundaries with permission likely leaves levels of trust intact. With ample levels of respect present, reciprocity can develop. Reciprocity involves understanding and fully appreciating that every person involved in an occasion for dialogue has experience and perceptions of equal value. While levels of expertise, knowledge, or authority may be different among dialogue participants, "reciprocal interactions provide equal opportunity [for each participant] to contribute and to make choices" (p. 45). One point of view should not dominate, nor should any view be consciously excluded. Being responsive entails "being willing to give up certainty, to not know exactly what to do or what to say" (p. 47). Responsiveness during dialogue with others is demonstrated by a willingness to listen with focused attention, patience, and curiosity (Freedman & Combs, 1996, as cited in Barrera & Corso, 2003, p. 48). A responsive person works to suspend his or her preconceived ideas and judgments in an effort to fully understand and appreciate another person's expressed reality.

An optimal, though time-consuming, approach to modeling the virtues of skilled dialogue for students could be to do so in the context of team teaching. A study of family science educators at the college level conducted by Gentry (1998) indicates a modest number do undertake team teaching with fellow family science faculty members, as well as faculty from other disciplines, with positive outcomes. Though there are costs associated with this approach, the potential benefits to faculty and students are often deemed worth making the sacrifices. One of the benefits is the opportunity for students to observe team teachers listening and responding to one another in the process of presenting course content and carrying out various learning activities. In the context of diversity education, when two team teachers are of differing social addresses or cultural backgrounds, their ability to demonstrate respect, reciprocity, and responsiveness in full view of the students can be of considerable value.

Conclusion

As this chapter draws to a close, the SoTL-related efforts of Julia, Michael, and Lena, introduced in the opening vignette, remain a work in progress. Their review of the literature has rendered them better informed about some likely reasons behind the teaching-learning problem they have observed. Each one has made an effort to better understand his or her own level of cultural competence as well as the initial levels of competence of others around them. They have refreshed their knowledge of relevant theories and methods and spent time rethinking the goals and objectives that have been formulated for the course. While Michael and Julia have considered undertaking teaching their family and cultural diversity course as a team, because such an approach could contribute to enhanced student engagement in learning, particularly during class discussions, they have determined that community mapping is the most suitable teaching strategy to newly incorporate the next time they teach the course. In the days ahead, they will refine the design of the SoTL project they plan to carry out and determine the adequacy of the baseline data they currently have regarding student performance in the course. In anticipation of SoTL results that will be of interest to other diversity educators, Julia, Michael, and Lena have begun identifying a variety of outlets to which they can disseminate their findings (e.g., a campus teaching symposium, national and international conferences that focus entirely or in part upon SoTL, and journals that routinely or occasionally feature SoTL articles).

References

Adams, M., Bell, L. A., & Griffin, P. (Eds.). (1997). *Teaching for diversity and social justice.* New York: Routledge.

Allen, K. R., & Farnsworth, E. B. (1993). Reflexivity in teaching about families. *Family Relations, 42*(3), 351–356.

Arcus, M. E. (1995). Advances in family life education: Past, present, and future. *Family Relations, 44,* 336–344.

Banks, J. A. (1991). *Teaching strategies for ethnic studies* (5th ed.). Boston: Allyn & Bacon.

Barbe, W. B. (1985). *Growing up learning.* Washington, DC: Acropolis Books.

Barrera, I., & Corso, R. M., with Macpherson, D. (2003). *Skilled dialogue: Strategies for responding to cultural diversity in early childhood.* Baltimore, MD: Paul H. Brookes.

Berke, D., Hamon, R., & Eby, J. (Guest Eds.). (2001). Service learning and family science [Special issue]. *Journal of Teaching in Marriage and Family, 1*(3), 1–95.

Boss, P. (2002). *Family stress management: A contextual approach* (2nd ed.). Thousand Oaks, CA: Sage.

Boyer, E. L. (1990). *Scholarship reconsidered: Priorities of the professoriate.* Princeton, NJ: Carnegie Foundation for the Advancement of Teaching.

Bredehoft, D. J. (2001). The Framework for Life Span Family Life Education revisited and revised. *The Family Journal: Counseling and Therapy for Couples and Families, 9*(2), 134–139.

Bubolz, M. M., & Sontag, M. S. (1993). Human ecology theory. In P. G. Boss, W. J. Doherty, R. LaRossa, W. R. Schumm, & S. K. Steinmetz (Eds.), *Sourcebook of family theory and methods* (pp. 419–448). New York: Plenum.

Burr, W. R., Day, R. D., & Bahr, K. S. (1993). *Family science.* Pacific Grove, CA: Brooks/Cole.

Burr, W. R., Klein, S. R., Burr, R. G., Doxey, C., Harker, B., Holman, T. B., et al. (2004). *Re-examining family stress: New theory and research.* Thousand Oaks, CA: Sage.

Carver, K. P., & Teachman, J. D. (1995). The science of family science. In R. D. Day, K. R. Gilbert, B. H. Settles, & W. R. Burr (Eds.), *Research and theory in family science* (pp. 113–127). Pacific Grove, CA: Brooks/Cole.

Cassidy, D. (2004). Challenges in family life education. *NCFR's Family Focus on Family Life Education, Issue FF22,* 1 & 3.

Chickering, A. W., & Gamson, Z. F. (1991). *Applying the seven principles for good practice in undergraduate education.* San Francisco: Jossey-Bass.

Conway-Turner, K., Kim, S., Sherif, B., & Woolfolk, T. (2001). Diversity in families: Exploration in effective pedagogy. *Journal of Teaching in Marriage and Family, 1*(1), 15–26.

Cranton, P. (2000). Individual differences and transformative learning. In J. Mezirow & Associates (Eds.), *Learning as transformation: Critical perspectives on a theory in progress* (pp. 181–204). San Francisco: Jossey-Bass.

Cross, K. P., & Steadman, M. H. (1996). *Classroom research: Implementing the scholarship of teaching.* San Francisco: Jossey-Bass.

Darling, C. A. (1987). Family life education. In M. B. Sussman & S. K. Steinmetz (Eds.), *Handbook of marriage and family* (pp. 815–833). New York: Plenum Press.

Dean, R. C. (2001). The myth of cross-cultural competence. *Families in Society: The Journal of Contemporary Human Services, 82*(6), 623–630.

Duncan, S. F., & Goddard, H. W. (2005). *Family life education: Principles and practices for effective outreach*. Thousand Oaks, CA: Sage.

Gardner, H. (1993). *Multiple intelligence: The theory in practice*. New York: Basic Books.

Gentry, D. (1998). Family science educators' perceptions of and experiences with interdisciplinary team teaching. *Family Science Review, 11*(1), 33–47.

Gentry, D. (2004). Contemporary family life education: Thirty years of challenge and practice. In M. Coleman & L. H. Ganong (Eds.), *Handbook of contemporary families: Considering the past, contemplating the future* (pp. 538–554). Thousand Oaks, CA: Sage.

Goleman, D. (1995). *Emotional intelligence: Why it can matter more than IQ*. New York: Bantam Books.

Gorski, P. (1995). *The language of closet racism: An illustration*. Retrieved June 28, 2005, from http://www.edchange.org/multicultural/papers/langofracism2.html

Green, J. W. (1999). *Cultural awareness in the human services: A multi-ethnic approach* (3rd ed.). Boston: Allyn & Bacon.

Gregorc, A. F. (1982). *An adult's guide to style*. Columbia, CT: Author. (Available from Learning Styles Unlimited, Inc. 1911 S.W. Campus Drive, Suite 370, Federal Way, WA 98023)

Griffin, P. (1997). Facilitating social justice education courses. In M. Adams, L. A. Bell, & P. Griffin (Eds.), *Teaching for diversity and social justice* (pp. 279–298). New York: Routledge.

Hamon, R., & Stone, S. R. (2005, June). *Using feature films to integrate family diversity in the ten family life education substance areas*. Paper presented at the Family Science Association's annual Teaching Family Science Conference, Strasburg, PA.

Hollinger, M. A. (2003). Family science. In J. J. Ponzetti, R. R. Hamon, Y. Kellar-Guenther, P. K. Kerig, T. L. Scales, & J. M. White (Eds.), *International encyclopedia of marriage and family* (2nd ed., pp. 629–635). New York: Macmillan Reference.

Ingoldsby, B. B., Smith, S. R., & Miller, J. E. (2004). *Exploring family theories*. Los Angeles: Roxbury.

Kaissi, C. (2005, June). *The relevance of literature*. Paper presented at the Family Science Association's annual Teaching Family Science Conference, Strasburg, PA.

Kember, D., Ha, T. S., Lam, B., Lee, A., Ng, S., & Yan, L. (2000). *Action learning and action research: Improving the quality of teaching and learning*. London: Kogan Page.

Knapp, C. (2003). *Making community connections: The Orton Community Mapping Program*. Redlands, CA: ESRI Press.

Knowles, M. S. (1984a). *The adult learner: A neglected species* (3rd ed.). Houston, TX: Gulf.

Knowles, M. S. (1984b). *Andragogy in action: Applying modern principles of adult learning*. San Francisco: Jossey-Bass.

Kolb, D. A. (1984). *Experiential learning*. Englewood Cliffs, NJ: Prentice Hall.

Kreber, C. (2001). Conceptualizing the scholarship of teaching and identifying unresolved issues. In C. Kreber (Ed.), *Scholarship revisited: Perspectives on the scholarship of teaching* (pp. 1–18). San Francisco: Jossey-Bass.

Kreber, C., & Cranton, P. A. (2000). Exploring the scholarship of teaching. *Journal of Higher Education, 71*(4), 476–495.

Kroeger, O., & Thuesen, J. M. (1988). *Type talk: The 16 personality types that determine how we live, love, and work.* New York: Delta/Tilden Press.

Lewis-Rowley, M., Brasher, R. E., Moss, J. J., Duncan, S. F., & Stiles, R. J. (1993). The evolution of education for family life. In M. E. Arcus, J. D. Schvaneveldt, & J. J. Moss (Eds.), *Handbook of family life education* (Vol. 1, pp. 26–50). Newbury Park, CA: Sage.

Marotz-Baden, R., Osborne, S., & Hunts, H. (2000). Teaching and learning styles: Implications for more effective pedagogy. *Family Science Review, 13*(1/2), 44–59.

McCarthy, B. (1996). *About learning.* Schaumburg, IL: Excel.

McCubbin, H. (1995). *Resiliency in ethnic families under stress: Theory, reality, and research.* Madison: University of Wisconsin Press.

McCubbin, H., Thompson, E. A., Thompson, A. I., & Futrell, J. A. (1999). *The dynamics of resilient families.* Thousand Oaks, CA: Sage.

McDermott, D. (2001). Parenting and ethnicity. In M. J. Fine & S. W. Lee (Eds.), *Handbook of diversity in parent education: The changing faces of parent and parent education* (pp. 73–96). San Diego, CA: Academic Press.

McKinney, K. (2003a). *What is the scholarship of teaching and learning (SoTL) in higher education?* Retrieved June 28, 2005, from http://www.cat.ilstu.edu/pdf/definesotl.pdf

McKinney, K. (2003b). *Research methods for doing the scholarship of teaching and learning.* Retrieved June 30, 2005, from http://www.cat.ilstu.edu/pdf/sotl_research.pdf

Merriam, S. B., & Caffarella, R. S. (1999). *Learning in adulthood: A comprehensive guide* (2nd ed.). San Francisco: Jossey-Bass.

Mezirow, J. & Associates. (Eds.). (2000). *Learning as transformation.* San Francisco: Jossey-Bass.

Myers-Walls, J. A. (2000). Family diversity and family life education. In D. H. Demo, K. R. Allen, & M. A. Fine (Eds.), *Handbook of family diversity* (pp. 359–379). New York: Oxford University Press.

NCFR–Ethnic Minority Section. (2004). *Resource manual for teaching about ethnic minority families and other diversity issues.* Retrieved June 28, 2005, from http://www.asn.csus.edu/em-ncfr/down99/manualintro.htm

O'Brian, M. (2004). Using the concept of literature circles in a college course. *Journal of Teaching in Marriage and Family, 4*(1), 217–224.

Powell, L., & Cassidy, D. (2001). *Family life education: An introduction.* Mountain View, CA: Mayfield.

Ramos, K. D., & Blinn-Pike, L. (1999). College students' feelings about diversity: Using emotions to enhance learning in a multicultural family science course. *Family Science Review, 12*(4), 220–236.

Richlin, L. (2001). Scholarly teaching and the scholarship of teaching. In C. Kreber (Ed.), *Scholarship revisited: Perspectives on the scholarship of teaching* (pp. 57–68). San Francisco: Jossey-Bass.

Robinson, C. M. (2005, June). *Teaching family resource management*. Paper presented at the Family Science Association's annual Teaching Family Science Conference, Strasburg, PA.

Robinson, C. M., Vineyard, M. L., & Reagor, J. D. (2004). Using community mapping in human ecology. *Journal of Family and Consumer Sciences, 96*(4), 52–54.

Rosenblatt, P. C. (2001). Teaching undergraduate family diversity courses. *Journal of Teaching in Marriage and Family: Innovations in Family Science Education, 1*(1), 1–14.

Salovey, P., & Mayer, J. D. (1990). Emotional intelligence. *Imagination, Cognition and Personality, 9*(3), 185–211.

Sandifer-Stech, D. M., & Gerhardt, C. E. (2001). Real world roles: Problem-based learning in undergraduate family studies courses. *Journal of Teaching in Marriage and Family: Innovations in Family Science Education, 1*(2), 1–13.

Scanzoni, J. (2004). Household diversity: The starting point for healthy families in the new century. In M. Coleman & L. H. Ganong (Eds.), *Handbook of contemporary families: Considering the past, contemplating the future* (pp. 3–22). Thousand Oaks, CA: Sage.

Schmitz, C. L., Stakeman, C., & Sisneros, J. (2001). Educating professionals for practice in a multicultural society: Understanding oppression and valuing diversity. *Families in Society: The Journal of Contemporary Human Services, 82*(6), 612–622.

Tatum, B. D. (1997). *"Why are all the Black kids sitting together in the cafeteria?" And other conversations about race*. New York: Basic Books.

Umana-Taylor, A. J., & Wiley, A. R. (2004). Family diversity in the classroom: A review of existing strategies. *Journal of Teaching in Marriage and Family, 4*(1), 127–143.

Volpe, J. D. E., & St. Clair-Christman, J. (2005, June). *Working from students' strengths and interests to increase engagement in discussion about diversity*. Paper presented at the Family Science Association's annual Teaching Family Science Conference, Strasburg, PA.

13

The Compelling Realities of Diversity, Policies, and Laws

Tammy L. Henderson

Honoring and acknowledging family diversity, sometimes referred to as *multiculturalism* or *cultural competency*, requires a distinct understanding of laws that either explicitly or implicitly shapes human development (for example, see Henderson & Moran, 2001; McWey, Henderson, & Tice, 2006). Diversity might, in fact, compound the role of government. In this chapter, I explain the relationship of diversity and laws by providing readers with a broad historical review of judicial rulings and legislative acts that represent the government's response to the diverse needs of citizens. I highlight the challenges faced by policy makers and citizens as they struggle to move American democracy toward a position of equity and justice. Although this chapter cannot by its very nature represent or address the multifaceted experiences of all diverse peoples, I have worked diligently to ensure that it treats such groups with respect and honor, and that it presents those facts as space permits.

I provide a few reminders and a legal framework to set the context for this chapter. First, diversity is not a modern conception; on the contrary, it has always existed and in fact began (in terms of North America) with the American Indians. Robert Jarvenpa (1985) stated that diversity among "Indian people in North America probably surpassed that of Renaissance

Europe" (p. 29). Today, despite a general loss of culture resulting from such contributing factors as general oppression and acculturation into larger White society, American Indians have managed to preserve at least 45 original languages, such as Cherokee, Creek, Crow, and Navajo (Olson, 1994). Some American Indians maintain culture-based views regarding tolerance and interdependence (John, 1998), generally condemn greed and competition, and seek to preserve unity with the environment (Olson, 1994).

Second, Blacks have treaded several pathways to and within this country, paths that likewise have affected family diversity. Blacks in the United States have included free persons; indentured servants; immigrants from Ghana, Nigeria, Haiti, Jamaica, Trinidad, and Barbados; refugees from Ethiopia, Somalia, Sudan, and Liberia; and slaves from African countries, the Caribbean, the West Indies, and elsewhere (Berlin, 1998; Commission on Civil Rights, 1999). Despite positive and negative realities, Black families have remained resilient, maintaining adaptive familial and fictive systems (Singh, Williams, & Singh, 1998; Stack & Burton, 1993; Sudarkasa, 1988).

Third, European immigrants represent a nonhomogenous group who relocated to the United States to practice religious freedom, improve the quality of their lives, and seek economic self-sufficiency. European immigrants— free persons or indentured servants—exhibited divergent immigration and language patterns, religious precepts, and national origins (Olson, 1994). For example, before 1790, U.S. immigrants arrived from Africa, England, Ulster (Scots-Irish), Germany, Scotland, Ireland, Netherlands, and Wales (*Immigration to the United States*, 2005). Africa, England, Ulster (Scots-Irish), and Germany provided the largest number of immigrants, and most slaves came from Africa.

This mere snapshot of European immigrants fails to provide a complete picture. For example, immigrants did not reside in one location, but developed ethnic communities across the country. Ethnic diversity emerged in different regions: Puritans moved into the New England area, while the Dutch settled in "New Netherlands" (now New York and New Jersey) and the Quakers in Pennsylvania, New Jersey, and Delaware. German and Scots-Irish immigrants moved to Pennsylvania; yet, the Scots-Irish also settled in regions of Appalachia and the West. Ethnic diversity expanded so rapidly that by 1790, more than 3.1 million European immigrants and 800,000 African slaves resided on the continent.

As European immigrants practiced geographic segregation and social distancing, ethnic diversity, like racial diversity, posed challenges to their daily lives (Parillo, 1994). Tensions existed between English Anglicans and Scots-Irish Presbyterians. Quakers and Germans established their own colleges to promote religious and cultural segregation. Discriminatory practices were enacted against Catholics and Jews; they were sometimes denied the right to immigrate or vote. Therefore, the use of the inclusive term *Whites* to describe European immigrants blurs the realities of the ethnic, cultural, religious, and familial diversity that existed, and continues to exist, among them. Although the literature provides conflicting reports (Alba, Lutz, & Vesselinov, 2001), European immigrants experienced unequal treatment. Yet, they secured the political authority by holding a shared sense of nationalism, putting aside their differences. Common interests, such as religious and economic freedom, bound them. They established a new government that began in 1776 with the Declaration of Independence, focused on nationalism or common interests, and used immigration and naturalization laws to protect their interests and to promote nationalism (Ngai, 1999; Olson, 1994).

A Response to Diversity: Laws and Policies

Legal documents and laws that shape our sense of national identity, such as the Declaration of Independence and the U.S. Constitution, establish justice, internal harmony, individual rights, and the common good as important American values. Regardless, the existence of these key principles is fluid or remains unrealized. Citizens and policy makers must always challenge the moral and ethical fabric of our laws and policies (Carter, 2005; Coburn, 2003). Collectively, laws and policies demonstrate the tension faced by policy makers who must perform two simultaneous tasks: protect the individual rights of citizens against unwarranted government intrusion and balance those rights against the government's interest in protecting all citizens.

Setting the Stage: Citizen's Familial and Individual Rights

The government or state maintains a *compelling interest* in protecting the overall well-being of all citizens, an interest it expresses in the form of laws (Harvard Law Review [HLR], 1980; Mnookin & Weisburg, 2005). When a citizen claims that a law unjustly intrudes upon a constitutionally protected right, the court weighs the government's interests in protecting the well-being of all citizens against the individual rights of one citizen (or group), a situation that actually parallels *equity* rather than *equality*. In determining their response, courts use different legal tests, such as a *rational basis test, immediate scrutiny,* and *strict scrutiny,* respectively the lowest to the highest forms of judicial review. Depending on the right in question, *the best interests of the child* or *clear and convincing evidence* are other legal tests used in family law decisions. *Guilt beyond a reasonable doubt* is used to protect the interests of potential criminals, but this level of scrutiny does not govern legal decisions regarding familial concerns.

To perform its role, the government is permitted to use its police powers to regulate behaviors designed to protect the safety, health, and overall well-being of citizens. It also may exercise its *parens patriae* powers, a rule of law that allows the government to function as the ultimate parent and protect vulnerable citizens, such as children, wards of the state, and disabled persons. To provide a clearer understanding about the relationship of governmental regulations, government roles, and family diversity, in this section of the chapter, I briefly discuss fundamental rights, liberty interests, privacy rights, and protection against racial and gender discrimination, among others.

Fundamental Rights

A *fundamental right* encompasses both constitutional rights and natural human rights (Black, Nolan, & Nolan-Haley, 1991) and other privacy rights implicitly or explicitly guaranteed in the federal or state constitutions, such as freedom of speech (HLR, 1980). Moreover, courts have recognized as fundamental an individual's rights to marriage, procreation, contraception, abortion, family relations, and childrearing. When a right is considered fundamental, the government must have a compelling reason to intrude upon it. In an effort to protect all citizens, some laws do place limits on citizen's rights. Because the government has an interest in protecting all citizens against illiteracy and an outbreak of smallpox, laws requiring universal education (*Pierce v. Society of Sisters,* 1925; *Wisconsin v. Yoder,* 1972) and vaccinations (*Jacobson v. Massachusetts,* 1905) are examples of mandates that place limits on personal liberties and fundamental rights.

This does not mean, however, that such laws have not met with challenges. With regard to universal education, for example, Oregon's Compulsory Education Act of 1922 obliged parents or guardians to send children between eight and sixteen years of age to public schools (*Pierce v. Society of Sisters,* 1925). The Society of Sisters, a corporation that cared for orphans, taught youth, and created and sustained schools and other academic institutions, challenged the state of Oregon on this point of law. They argued that it violated the liberty of parents to direct the education of their children and the right of schools and teachers to effectively conduct business or engage in their profession. The U.S. Supreme Court determined that the law indeed violated "the fundamental liberty" of parents, forcing them to accept only the instruction of teachers in public schools, and decided that states could not use their compulsory education laws to prevent children from attending private or religious schools. The fundamental liberty of parents—and the corporation—was upheld.

Prince v. Massachusetts (1944) provides a contrary example. Three grievances involving child labor laws were filed against the guardian of a nine-year-old girl: (1) failing to disclose her child's identity and age to an officer responsible for enforcing child labor laws; (2) giving the child religious materials to sell in an open, public area, which was against the law; and (3) as the child's legal guardian, authorizing the child to work contrary to law. The woman and her husband were Jehovah's Witnesses and ordained ministers who regularly gave their children the task of distributing religious material. Although the woman claimed that the state's child labor laws violated her equal protection and religious rights, the U.S. Supreme Court determined that the welfare of the child was a compelling reason for intruding upon those rights.

Privacy Rights

Citizens also have the right to personal privacy or a guaranteed zone of privacy (*Carey v. Population Services International,* 1977). Although privacy rights are not directly specified in the U.S. Constitution, they are constructed or interpreted within the confines of the First, Fourth, and Fifth Amendments and the penumbras of the Bill of Rights and are reserved to citizens under the Ninth Amendment (for example, see *Griswold v. Connecticut,* 1965). Procreation, abortion, and contraception compose one order of privacy rights (HLR, 1980). For instance, justices have protected procreation rights for both married and unmarried adults (*Griswold*). In *Eisenstadt v. Baird* (1972), justices struck down a Massachusetts law that prohibited the dispersing of contraception to unmarried citizens, arguing that individuals had the natural right to reproduce or not, as they so chose. Moreover, in *Roe v. Wade* (1973), a case that carefully weighed the life of the child against the health and life of the woman, justices concluded that women have the right to an abortion in the first trimester of a pregnancy.

Liberty Interests

Citizens also have liberty interests, which under the Fourteenth Amendment are deemed fundamental or implicitly controlled. Parents' desire for and right to the companionship, care, custody, and management of their children is highly guarded (e.g., *Stanley v. Illinois,* 1972), requiring a compelling reason to permit governmental intrusion (HLR, 1980; Skinner &

Kohler, 2002). Regardless of that stricture, however, such rights are not absolute (HLR, 1980). While some U.S. Supreme Court decisions have protected parents' right to teach their children a foreign language or to educate their child in a private school, others have prevailed over parental "rights." On March 15, 1902, for example, Cambridge, Massachusetts, resident Reverend Henning Jacobson, who during a smallpox epidemic refused to be vaccinated, was charged, convicted, and fined $5. His conviction later was upheld by the lower courts of Massachusetts and by the U.S. Supreme Court. The latter body, in *Jacobson v. Massachusetts* (1905), rejected the argument that mandatory vaccination violated an individual's due process and equal protection rights and instead determined that states could in fact limit the liberties of citizens to protect public health.

Personal and Family Relationships

Citizens' liberty interests and fundamental rights also incorporate personal and family relations and associations (Bell, 1992; *Loving v. Virginia,* 1967; *Moore v. the City of East Cleveland,* 1977). Take, for example, the case of Richard and Mildred Loving, who were charged with violating a Virginia law prohibiting interracial marriage. The U.S. Supreme Court concluded that this law violated marital autonomy, equal protection, and due process rights based on race. In a statement that perfectly captures the essence of personal privacy as it relates to marriage, personal association, and race, Chief Justice Earl Warren concluded, "Under the Constitution the freedom to marry, or not to marry, a person of another race resides with the individual and cannot be infringed [upon] by the state" (*Loving,* p. 11).

As modern conceptions of the traditional nuclear family have evolved, so have the Court's decisions regarding familial rights. For example, in *Moore v. the City of East Cleveland* (1977), it determined that only those extended families functioning like traditional ones deserved legal protection. *Troxel v. Granville* (2000) demonstrated those limitations when paternal grandparents sought additional visitation rights against the objections of the biological mother and stepfather—the adoptive parent. Recognizing that visitation cases use a different, less rigorous legal standard than do custody cases (Avin, 1994; Bohl, 1996), it was reasoned that giving third parties— that is, anyone but parents—visitation rights because doing so served the best interests of the child made the state's law too broad. The Court did not address the constitutionality of grandparent visitation laws beyond the state of Washington, a fact that gives states the authority to manage third-party visitation decisions. Given these facts, it is not surprising that between 1986 and 2001, grandparents were awarded visitation in 65 of 178 cases

(36.5 percent); their success was largely based on rulings that determined visitation served the best interests of the child (54 of 65 cases, or 86.2 percent) (Henderson, 2005).

Today, marriage initiatives, covenant marriages, and same-sex unions serve as the focus of political debate, raising persistent questions about fundamental rights, liberty interests, and the complexities of contemporary family life. If every citizen possesses fundamental rights and liberty interests related to parenting, marriage, and family, then it is not surprising that lesbian and gay adults continue to seek legal participation and recognition. The relationship of sexual orientation, the right to family, and parental autonomy has polarized this nation. Based on religious and political ideologies that only two heterosexual parents with children or single biological parents have a constitutional right to parent and marry (Skinner & Kohler, 2002; Younger, 1996), some groups would deny the same rights to lesbian and gay adults. Other groups argue just as vociferously for the ability to exercise marital and parenting rights, regardless of the individuals' sexual orientation.

In 2000, Vermont enacted landmark legislation that not only recognized civil unions between same-sex individuals but also granted such partners virtually all the benefits, protections, and responsibilities of traditional married couples. Similarly, the Massachusetts Supreme Judicial Court concluded that the state constitution guarantees equal marriage rights for same-sex couples (National Conference of State Legislatures, 2005). Laws, however, that allow same-sex citizens to exercise their fundamental right to marriage have met legal opposition, such as with the overturning of Hawaii's same-sex marriage law (*Hawaii v. Mallan*, 1998).

Race, Ethnicity, Gender, and Disability

The government also maintains an interest in the survival of its citizens (HLR, 1980). In 1865, the Thirteenth Amendment was enacted as an initial step in a long legal process designed to abolish slavery, demonstrating the struggle toward a position of hope for a future that would embrace democracy and justice (Harding, 1981). Yet, like most elements of a process, democracy and justice prove ever-evolving. This must be so, for our interpretations of basic facets of citizenship, family, and everyday life continue to change.

With the end of slavery in 1865 and legal recognition of Blacks as citizens in 1868, some progress was made toward democracy and justice. Blacks, however, were not the only group to be affected by the changes occurring in the growing United States. Just prior to these compelling legal decisions, the Treaty of Guadalupe Hidalgo (1848) outlined the end of the Mexican-American

War. This treaty not only forcibly gave the United States the territory that is today Texas, Colorado, Arizona, New Mexico, and Wyoming, but it also automatically conferred citizenship on all residents of this area who remained there or did not proclaim Mexican citizenship within one year (U.S. General Accounting Office, 2001). On the surface, citizenship appeared to be the primary focus of this decision, but in truth, race was at the core of the Treaty of Guadalupe Hidalgo (Ngai, 1999). Demonstrating the way in which race matters, in the 1897 decision *In re Rodriguez,* the court denied citizenship to petitioner Ricardo Rodriguez due to two factors: his "color" and illiteracy. As the decision notes,

> The applicant, a citizen by birth of the republic of Mexico, desires to avail himself of the inherent right of expatriation, and to invest himself with the rights and privileges pertaining to citizenship of our country. . . . To the question, why may not he be naturalized under the laws of congress? It is replied that by section 2169 of the Revised Statutes it is provided: "The provisions of this title shall apply to aliens (being free white persons, and to aliens) of African nativity, and to persons of African descent." The contention is that, by the letter of the statute, a Mexican citizen, answering to the description of the applicant, is, because of his color, denied the right to become a citizen of the United States by naturalization; and, in support of this view, the following authorities are relied upon: In *re Ah Yup* (decided by Judge Sawyer in 1878) . . ., where the learned chancellor expresses a doubt in these words:
> "Perhaps there might be difficulties also as to the copper-colored natives of America, or the yellow or tawny races of Asiatics, and it may well be doubted whether any of them are white persons, within the purview of the law." (*In re Rodriguez,* 1897, p. 1)

As this decision notes, the court bestowed citizenship upon Whites and Blacks, but was unwilling to do the same for a Mexican, a member of the "copper-colored native or tawny races" who were not White. Regardless, progress toward justice did not stagnate: The enactment of the Nineteenth Amendment (1920) established the right to vote, a privilege of citizenship, regardless of gender.

Policy makers have also attempted to redress discrimination against American Indians. For example, the Indian Reorganization Act of 1934 was designed to redress issues of economic and tribal autonomy. Under this law, American Indians are able to draft their own constitutions, assume ownership of all reservation lands, secure all surplus land reverted automatically to the tribe, and promote their groups to develop businesses and other forms of incorporations for the purpose of managing reservation resources (Kehoe, 1981; Olson, 1994). The federal government budgeted $10 million to foster tribal self-sufficiency and $2 million each year for the purchase of land. Upon the implementation of this law, 550,000 Native Americans resided on government reservations; they were financially dependent on but culturally free of European society (Olson, 1994). By 1990, only 900,000 American Indians resided on reservations; most had moved to urban areas.

The nation's consciousness about other vital Fourteenth Amendment rights was slightly transformed in the 1950s and 1960s, although its policies did not fully accomplish their goals. On May 17, 1954, the U.S. Supreme Court handed down its groundbreaking decision in *Brown v. Board of Education,* which determined that segregated educational facilities were innately unequal. Despite the theoretical premise of *Brown,* however, historically Black colleges and universities (HBCUs) still do not receive the same state appropriations as predominately White colleges and universities (PWCUs). For example, in Florida, PWCUs receive 53 percent of their revenues from the state; HBCUs, only 42 percent. Similarly, in Texas PWCUs receive 51 percent while HBCUs receive just 41 percent. Although Sav (1997) points out that when state contributions are lacking, the federal government steps in to provide assistance—7 of 15 states surveyed for this study exhibited lower appropriations for HBCUs.

How have all of these issues converged for us as a nation? Beginning as early as the late 1940s, the Civil Rights Movement (CRM) kindled awareness of nationalism and attempted to forge a collective consciousness in an attempt to gain justice for diverse groups, including Blacks. The Civil Rights Act of 1964 involved several laws that prohibited employment discrimination, outlawed discrimination related to public facilities, established fair housing laws, and led to school desegregation. Discussions about the CRM often focus solely on Blacks, ignoring how these decisions developed the constitutional foundation that protects other diverse communities, such as those of women, American Indians, Mexican Americans, and others. The CRM actually was more cross-cultural in nature than most Americans realize. For example, American Indians organized and implemented pan-Indian associations, such as the American Indian Movement (AIM), to promote civil rights, economic opportunities, and cultural autonomy (Kehoe, 1981; Olson, 1994). As a result, Indians began actively to revise negative cultural stereotypes that had been entrenched in American history since the days of Buffalo Bill Cody's Wild West Shows. *Bury My Heart at Wounded Knee* (Brown, 1970) and *Custer Died for Your Sins* helped counter stereotypes (Deloria, 1969). Other cultural groups followed suit, each attempting to revise or rewrite negative cultural constructions.

While diversity plays a crucial role in constructions of family law, it should be considered virtually indivisible from issues related to gender.

Various policies have attempted over time to redress gender-based inequities with varying degrees of success. For instance, while the Nineteenth Amendment extended voting rights to women, even 1963's Equal Pay Act has not been able to normalize pay across gender lines. In 2004, the median earnings of women who worked full time were just 77 percent of men's median earnings; this gap is the same as the wage gap when measured in 2002 (Rose & Hartman, 2004). Such data demonstrate fundamental flaws in the philosophical premise of the Equal Pay Act, one of which is that the gender gap exists for a number of reasons, such as women holding caregiving jobs that pay relatively low wages.

As a nation, we have made many attempts to enact justice based on issues of race, ethnicity, and gender, moving the civil rights era into the 1970s. More recently, we have focused our efforts on laws to protect the disabled, beginning with 1973's Rehabilitation Act, which prohibits employers who are federal contractors or subcontractors from discriminating against disabled citizens. The Americans with Disabilities Act was passed in 1990, barring employers from discriminating against disabled citizens and providing civil rights protection to individuals based on race, color, sex, national origin, age, and religion. It also guarantees equal opportunity for disabled individuals in public accommodations, employment, transportation, government services, and telecommunications.

Children's Rights

The government may invoke its *parens patriae* or its police powers to protect the interests of its citizens (HLR, 1980). For children, the government serves as the ultimate parent and protector and can use the best interests of the child standard to protect children from unfit parents or other threats of harm (HLR, 1980; Mnookin & Weisburg, 2005). For example, in *Jefferson v. Griffin* (1981), the government invoked its *parens patriae* powers when, because of her religious beliefs, a pregnant woman refused to undergo a Caesarian section and blood transfusion, both procedures designed to save the life of her unborn child. Because her child was entitled to protection by the government in its capacity as *parens patriae*, justices determined that the mother could not refuse the Caesarian section. Although this action directly conflicted with the parent's religious convictions, the government used its parental powers to take protective custody of the child.

Children's rights, though unequal to those of adults, have not remained stagnant. The nation has struggled with the conception of justice across the human life span, recognizing children's right to religion, procedural due process rights, the right to be heard, and the right of free speech. *Prince v. Massachusetts* (1944), for example, established children's right to exercise their religious beliefs. During the CRM, *In re Gault* (1967) further established the rights of children with regard to due process. This case involved the arrest of a minor child (for improper telephone usage) without an adult or other legal representation present. The child did not receive notification about the date of his hearing. The U.S. Superior Court held that children have some guaranteed procedural due process rights, such as the right to notice of charges, counsel, confrontation, and cross-examination.

In the dissent to *Wisconsin v. Yoder* (1972), justices established children's right to be heard, pointing out that their liberty interests in attending school may override their parents' right to religious freedom. *Tinker et al. v. Des Moines Independent Community School District* (1969) shaped children's right to free speech, such as (in this case) the wearing of armbands to protest the Vietnam War. The Court reasoned that the armbands were neither disruptive nor aggressive; therefore, the students' action did not represent a group demonstration that hindered the order or economics of the school. The profound message rendered by the Court was, "Students in the public schools do not shed their constitutional rights of freedom of speech or expression at the schoolhouse gate" (*Tinker,* p. 3, 1969).

"Racial Disproportionality"

Using its *parens patriae* powers, then, the government is responsible for protecting vulnerable citizens, including children. Yet the foster care system continues to face social justice challenges, such as "racial disproportionality" (Courtney & Skyles, 2003; Skyles, 2002), which demonstrates the government's inability to act as an effective *parent*. "Disproportionality" refers to the overrepresentation of children or families of some racial and ethnic groups in various child welfare services populations; their numbers are disproportionate when compared to the numbers of the general family or child population (Courtney & Skyles, 2003).

How can children or families who enter the welfare system be assured of justice, given the broad legal protections given to parents? Typically, child maltreatment and parental unfitness have been the only compelling reasons for the government to interfere with the rights of parents. Yet, the current foster care law, the Adoption and Safe Families Act (ASFA, 1997), has relaxed the protections given to parents in order to protect the interests of children. ASFA promotes adoption by nonrelatives, with only 18 states having relative care as an option. This law represents a significant shift away from family preservation and instead focuses on termination of parental rights in cases where identified problems are not remedied within a year. The foster care plan may require parents to perform a set of assigned tasks, such as holding a job, going to parenting classes, seeking counseling, and visiting their child. If parents fail to comply with these requirements, the child could remain in the state's custody, and the government could initiate the adoption process (Roberts, 2000, 2002).

Here are the facts. Black, Native American, and Latino children are overrepresented in the national foster care population (Skyles, 2002), constituting racial disproportionality. Native American children make up 1 percent of the nation's children but compose 2 percent of the foster care population (Administration for Children, Youth, and Families, 2003). Black children represent 15 percent of the nation's youth, but make up almost 38 percent of the nation's foster care population. These numbers give some evidence that race, ethnicity, and class shape the experiences of children and families from diverse backgrounds. Based on 2001 figures, while children of color composed only 3 out of 10 children in the country, they accounted for nearly 65 percent of the 542,000 children in foster care.

Conclusion

Given the unique social addresses of our citizenry, our need to honor and acknowledge family diversity is inevitable. Family diversity long has been influenced by laws and legal decisions, which demonstrates how this country labels individuals and families with some families being denied the right to exercise some rights or to participate in our democratic society. Laws were used to privilege one group over another; and laws were enacted to ensure that all people—including diverse groups—have the opportunity to enjoy fundamental rights, liberty interests, and individual rights. Laws were enacted to abolish slavery, grant voting rights to women and Blacks, and promote equal protection under the law. In the 1960s, the fight for democracy reached a new level, as citizens collaborated to promote the good of marginalized groups, and nationalism cut across all social addresses. We must not be content with the accomplishments of democracy, but must celebrate the ways in which this nation struggles to ensure that all citizens share the principles of democracy. Today, as in the past, this nation must continually work to protect the fundamental rights of all citizens, seek to ensure equal education for all, and protect the rights of parents, children, grandparents, and the disabled.

The USA Patriot Act (2001), for example, was established to protect citizens from domestic or international terrorism. Critics have argued that it also infringes on citizens' First, Fourth, Fifth, Sixth, Eighth, and Fourteenth

Amendment rights, permitting the government to conduct secret searches and wiretaps, place individuals and businesses under surveillance, secretly monitor telephone conversations, and more (Whitehead & Aden, 2002). Likewise, laws enacted during the CRM required privileged citizens to allow some infringement on their rights and power to allow others to participate in a democratic society. Thus, to balance individual rights against the interests of all citizens, the government must walk a fine line.

When considering the topic of diversity, readers should remember the words of Marianne Williamson:

> Atonement is the release from fear, not a dive deeper into it. It is a corrective device, not a punishment, to admit the exact nature of our wrongs and to do our best to make them right. Atonement is essential to the healing of the United States, because there will be no new America until we have done everything possible to right the wrongs of the old one. (1997, p. 90)

Opportunities and challenges related to family diversity and laws are guaranteed in our founding documents and evident in the way this country continues in its struggle to protect and balance individual rights against the common good. Nevertheless, we must not be satisfied until equal protection under the law is a reality, a development that would show the world that the United States has the capacity to honor diversity and still maintain nationalism. In order to protect the common good, we must permit some intrusion by the government on our individual rights, personal liberties, religious freedoms, and fundamental rights. Still, we must determine how much of our individual rights we can afford to relinquish in the process.

References

Administration for Children, Youth, and Families. (2003, March). *The AFCARS Report: Preliminary FY 2001 estimates as of March 2003*. Retrieved October 8, 2003, from http://www.acf.hhs.gov/programs/cb/publications/afcars/report8.pdf

Adoption and Safe Families Act, Pub. L. 105-89 (1997).

Alba, R., Lutz, A., & Vesselinov, E. (2001). How enduring were the inequalities among European immigrant groups in the United States? *Demography, 38*, 349–356.

Americans with Disabilities Act, 42 U.S.C. 12101 et seq. (1990). Retrieved June 6, 2005, from http://www.usdoj.gov/crt/ada/statute.html

Avin, J. E. (1994). Grandparent visitation: The one and only standard—Best interests of the child. *University of Baltimore Law Review, 2* [Electronic version]. Retrieved December 8, 1998, from http://web.lexis-nexis.com

Bell, D. (1992). *Race, racism, and American law*. New York: Aspen Law and Business.

Berlin, I. (1998). *Many thousands gone: The first two centuries of slavery in America*. Cambridge, MA: Belknap Press of Harvard University.

Black, H. C., Nolan, J. R., & Nolan-Haley, J. M. (1991). *Black's law dictionary*. St. Paul. MN: West.

Bohl, J. C. (1996). The unprecedented intrusion: A survey and analysis of selected grandparent visitation cases. *Oklahoma Law Review, 33* [Electronic version]. Retrieved December 4, 1998, from http://web.lexis-nexis.com

Brown, D. (1970). *Bury my heart at Wounded Knee: An Indian history of the American West*. New York: Henry Holt.

Brown v. Board of Education, 347 U.S. 483 (1954).

Carey v. Population Services International, 431 U.S. 678 (1977).

Carter, J. (2005). *Our endangered values: America's moral crisis*. New York: Simon & Schuster.

Civil Rights Act of 1964, Pub. L. 88–352, H.R. 7152. (1964). Retrieved June 5, 2005 from http://usinfo.state.gov/usa/infousa/laws/majorlaw/civilr19.htm

Coburn, T. H. (2003). *Breach of trust: How Washington turns outsiders into insiders*. Nashville, TN: WND Books.

Commission on Civil Rights. (1999). *The health care challenge: Acknowledging disparity, confronting discrimination, and ensuring equality: Vol. I. The role of governmental and private health care programs and initiatives*. Washington, DC: Author.

Courtney, M., & Skyles, A. (2003). Racial disproportionality in the child welfare system. *Children and Youth Services, 25*(5), 355–358.

Deloria, C., Jr. (1969). *Custer died for your sins*. New York: Macmillan.

Eisenstadt v. Baird, 405 U.S. 438; 92 S. Ct. 1029; 1972 U.S. LEXIS 145; 31 L. Ed. 2d 349 (29 June 1999). http://web.lexis-nexis.com

Equal Pay Act of 1963, Pub. L. 88-38. (1963). Retrieved June 6, 2005, from http://www.eeoc.gov/policy/epa.html

Griswold v. Connecticut, 381 U.S. 479 (1965).

Harding, V. (1981). *There is a river: The Black struggle for freedom in America*. Orlando, FL: Harcourt Brace.

Harvard Law Review. (1980). *Developments in the law: The Constitution and the family*. Boston: Author.

Hawaii v. Mallan, 86 Haw. 440; 950 P.2d 178; 1998 Haw. LEXIS 6. Retrieved June 1, 2005, from http://web.lexis-nexis.com

Henderson, T. L. (2005). Grandparent visitation rights: Circumstances of their success. *Journal of Family Issues, 26*, 107–137.

Henderson, T. L., & Moran, P. B. (2001). Grandparent visitation rights: Testing the parameters of parental rights. *Journal of Family Issues, 22*, 619–638.

Immigration to the United States. (2005). Retrieved April 25, 2005, from http://en.wikipedia.org/w/index.php?title=Immigration_to_the_United_States&printable=yes

In re Gault, 387 U.S. 1 (1967).

242 Contextual Issues and Culturally Diverse Families

In re Rodriguez, 81 F. 337; 1897 U.S. Dist. LEXIS 50 (1897).

Indian Reorganization Act of 1934, 25 USC Sec. 461 (1934).

Jacobson v. Massachusetts, 197 U.S. 11 (1905).

Jarvenpa, R. (1985). The political economy and political ethnicity of American Indian adaptations and identities. *Ethnic and Racial Studies, 8*(1), 29–48.

Jefferson v. Griffin, 247 GA 86, 274 S. E. 2d 457 (1981).

John, R. (1998). Native American Families. In C. H. Mindel, R. W. Habenstein, & R. Wright, Jr. (Eds.), *Ethnic families in America: Patterns and variation* (4th ed., pp. 382–421). Upper Saddle River, NJ: Prentice Hall.

Kehoe, A. B. (1981). *North American Indians: A comprehensive account.* Englewood Cliffs, NJ: Prentice Hall.

Loving v. Virginia, 388 U.S. 1; 87 S. Ct. 1817; 1967 U.S. LEXIS 1082; 18 L. Ed. 2d 1010.

McWey, L. M., Henderson, T. L., & Tice, S. (2006). Mental health needs of families involved in the foster care system. *Journal of Marriage and Family Therapy, 32,* 195–214.

Mnookin, R. H., & Weisburg, D. K. (2005). *Child, family, and state: Problems and materials on children and law* (5th ed.). Boston: Little, Brown.

Moore v. the City of East Cleveland, 431 U.S. 494; 97 S. Ct. 1932; 1977 U.S. LEXIS 17; 52 L. Ed. 2d 531.

National Conference of State Legislatures. (2005). *Timeline—Same sex marriage.* Retrieved June 6, 2005, from http://www.ncsl.org/programs/cyf/samesextime .htm#2004

Ngai, M. M. (1999). The architecture of race in American immigration law: A reexamination of the Immigration Act of 1924. *Journal of American History, 86* [Electronic version]. Retrieved June 2, 2005, from http://history.uchicago.edu/ faculty/MaeNgai/ngai.html

Olson, J. S. (1994). *The ethnic dimension in American history* (2nd ed.). New York: St. Martin's Press.

Parillo, V. N. (1994). Diversity in America: A sociohistorical analysis. *Sociological Forum, 9,* 523–545.

Pierce v. Society of Sisters, 268 U.S. 510; 45 S. Ct. 571; 1925 U.S. LEXIS 589; 69 L. Ed. 1070; 39 A.L.R. 468.

Prince v. Massachusetts, 321 U.S. 158 (1944).

Rehabilitation Act of 1973, Pub. L. 93-112 93rd Congress, H.R. 8070 (1973).

Roberts, D. E. (2000). *Is there justice in children's rights? The critique of federal family preservation policy.* Retrieved September 30, 2002, from http://www.law .upenn.edu/conlaw/vol2/num1/roberts_ct.html

Roberts, D. E. (2002). *Shattered bonds: The color of child welfare.* New York: Basic Books.

Roe v. Wade, 410 U.S. 113 (1973).

Rose, S. J., & Hartman, H. I. (2004). *Still a man's labor market: The long-term earnings gaps.* Washington, DC: Institute for Women's Policy Research.

Sav, G. T. (1997). Separate and unequal: State financing of historically black colleges and universities. *Journal of Blacks in Higher Education* [Electronic version]. Retrieved June 17, 2004, from http://www.jstor.org

Singh, B., Williams, J., & Singh, B. (1998). An examination of extended family residence sharing predispositions in the United States: 1973–1989. *Marriage and the Family Review, 27,* 131–143.

Skinner, D. A., & Kohler, J. K. (2002). Parental rights in diverse family contexts: Current legal developments. *Family Relations, 51,* 291–300.

Skyles, A. (2002, November). *Racial disproportionality in the U.S. child welfare system: Intersection of law, family, and race.* Special session given at annual conference of the National Council on Family Relations, Vancouver, British Columbia.

Stack, C. B., & Burton, L. M. (1993). Kinscripts. *Journal of Comparative Family Studies, 24,* 157–170.

Stanley v. Illinois, 405 U.S. 645; 92 S. Ct. 1208; 1972 U.S. LEXIS 70; 31 L. Ed. 2d 551.

Sudarkasa, N. (1988). Interpreting the African heritage in Afro-American family organization. In H. P. McAdoo (Ed.), *Black families* (2nd ed., pp. 27–43). Newbury Park, CA: Sage.

Tinker et al. v. Des Moines Independent Community School District, 393 U.S. 503; 89 S. Ct. 733; 1969 U.S. LEXIS 2443; 21 L. Ed. 2d 731; 49 Ohio Op. 2d 222.

Treaty of Guadalupe-Hidalgo, U.S.-Mex., Feb 2, 1848, Perfected Treaties, 1778-1945; Record Group 11; General Records of the United States Government, 1778-1992; National Archives. Retrieved August 7, 2006, from http://www.our documents.gov/doc.php?flash=true&doc=26

Troxel v. Granville, 120 S. Ct. 2054; 2000 U.S. LEXIS 3767; 147 L. Ed. 2d 49; 68 U.S. L.W. 4458 2000 Cal. Daily Op. Services 4345; 2000 Daily Journal DAR 5831; 13 Fla. Law W. Fed. S. 365.

USA Patriot Act, H.R. 3162 (2001). Retrieved June 5, 2005, from http://www .fincen.gov/hr3162.pdf

U.S. General Accounting Office. (2001). *Treaty of Guadalupe Hidalgo: Definition and List of Community Land Grants in New Mexico* (Exposure draft). GAO-01-330. Washington, DC: Author.

Whitehead, J. W., & Aden, S. H. (2002). Forfeiting enduring freedom for homeland security: A constitutional analysis of the USA Patriot Act and the Justice Department's terrorism initiatives. *The American University Law Review* [Electronic version]. Retrieved August 18, 2005, from http://web.lexis-nexis.com

Williamson, M. (1997). *Healing the soul of America: Reclaiming our voices as spiritual citizens.* New York: Touchstone.

Wisconsin v. Yoder, 406 U.S. 205 (1972).

Younger, J. T. (1996). Responsible parents and good children. *Law and Inequity, 14,* 489–520.

14

Ethical Reflections for a Globalized Family Curriculum

A Developmental Paradigm

Mary Ann Hollinger

For several decades the discipline of family science has worked to extricate itself from its Western, and most notably, American moorings. By the dawn of the twenty-first century, many departments had made significant strides toward infusing their curricular offerings with enhanced appreciation for culturally diverse families (Smith & Ingoldsby, 1992). A growing collection of resources helped enhance these curricular offerings (Fine, 1993; Hamon & Ingoldsby, 2003; Hutter, 2004; Leeder, 2004). Support for this trend was further galvanized by the 1994 United Nations International Year of the Family (Altergott, 1993) and its 2004 International Year of the Family successor (Benjamin, 2003; Fitzpatrick, 2005). Even those departments initially lagging behind are now making concerted efforts to internationalize their curricula, faculty, and research agendas.

As a result, students in family science classes are being confronted with an ever-broadening kaleidoscope of traditional family practices they occasionally describe as "strange," "bizarre," even "incomprehensible." Initial classroom response to a more globalized curriculum can range from shock and disdain to outright ridicule. Well-intentioned faculty are sometimes left with a nagging suspicion that this enhanced knowledge base has in some cases resulted in less rather than greater cultural sensitivity.

What concrete steps might be taken to address this challenging dilemma? Is it possible for students to be freed from the grip of their own cultures without becoming stranded in a nebulous amoral quagmire? And what exactly is the objective for faculty? Is the pedagogical goal to simply neutralize students' visceral reactions based on their sometimes limited experience and ethnocentrism, or can there be a larger vision of guiding future family scientists along a trajectory from ethnocentric thinking toward constructive ethical reflection and responsible social action?

If so, this process is not likely to happen by chance. If the discipline of family science is truly committed to a more thoroughgoing internationalization, it is imperative to cultivate reflective and analytical skills in nuancing cross-cultural family ambiguities and complexities. This chapter proposes a developmental paradigm for launching a more robust understanding of and appreciation for complex family issues.

Theoretical Framework

Cultivating a global worldview with its corollary appreciation for culturally diverse families is a lifelong process. The most seasoned of diplomats, anthropologists, and development workers are often caught by surprise at the stubborn persistence of their own ethnocentric beliefs and judgments. Even after such individuals have rationally and cognitively rejected their own judgmental thinking, they may still find themselves repelled when encountering certain traditional family practices. When learning, for example, of practices like child marriage, arranged marriage, polygamy, the levirate, infant swaddling, child fosterage, sibling caretaking, cosleeping patterns among extended family members, ritual circumcision, and ancestor worship, it is easy for westerners to dismiss them out of hand. Indeed, few of us ever fully transcend the delimiting vision of our own cultures.

If seasoned professionals struggle to reconcile these issues, it is easy to understand why students would have at least as much difficulty. Change is not likely to happen overnight, and not without some intentionality. For this reason, it might be helpful to visualize the journey toward greater cultural competence and sensitivity as a developmental process (Bennett, 1993; DeSensi, 1994; Mahoney & Schamber, 2004).

The idea of employing a developmental construct is not alien territory to family scientists. There is a long tradition of conceptualizing family life cycle changes or "family careers" (Aldous, 1978) in developmental terms (Duvall, 1957; White, 1991). Despite its limitations, family development theory continues to find application to a variety of cultural contexts including those of German, Indian, and Eastern European families (White, 2003).

In addition to family development theory, family science also focuses on the life course development of the human person from birth to death. Indeed one of the substance areas required for official certification as a family life educator (CFLE) is called "Human Growth and Development Over the Life Span" (Bredehoft & Walcheski, 2005; Powell & Cassidy, 2001). More recently there have been creative attempts to integrate the human life course perspective with family development theory (Aldous, 1990; Bengston & Allen, 1993). White (2003) predicts the synergy between individual development and family development theories may reach new levels of integration and application in the years ahead.

As demonstrated above, there is a long tradition of employing developmental paradigms in the field of family science. It would appear a developmental model is particularly well suited to describe the progress one might make along a personal trajectory from ethnocentrism toward greater openness and ultimately informed critical reflection and social engagement (see Figure 14.1). It is hoped that such a journey will ultimately temper the knee-jerk reactions and cavalier judgments regarding unfamiliar family practices that students and professionals alike are sometimes prone to make.

Developmental Stages

Stage 1: Recognizing and Claiming One's Own Ethnocentrism

Ethnocentrism is the tendency to evaluate and judge other cultures with the standards of one's own (Leeder, 2004; Strong, DeVault, & Cohen, 2005). From this perspective, "The local is viewed as universal, the relative as absolute, and the complex as simple" (Kauffman, Martin, & Weaver, 1992, p. 140). In its extreme form, jingoism, people truly believe their own culture to be superior over others. Media coverage of the 1996 Olympic Games in Atlanta might illustrate this ethnocentric bias:

> At those games the United States did quite well, garnering many medals. Other countries did equally well. However, if one watched only U.S. television, including CNN, one would think that only the United States had been so successful. The media featured mainly U.S. athletes, and showed only events in which the

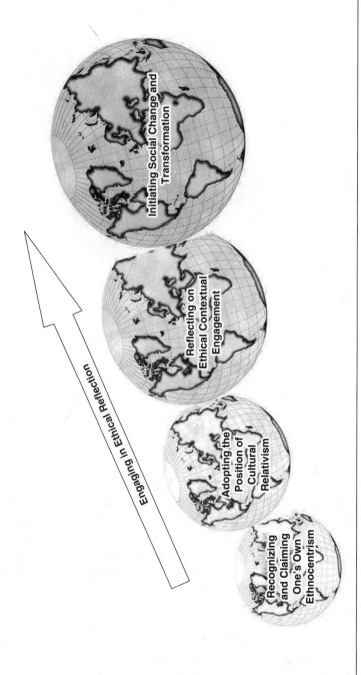

Figure 14.1 Developmental Model for Ethical Reflection

United States triumphed. This is an example of jingoism, which led to embarrassment on the part of those who have a more global perspective. (Leeder,
2004, p. 18)

Ethnocentric impulses turn even darker when held hostage to fear of those
that are different and unknown. In her book on *Families in Cultural Context,*
DeGenova (1997) observes that

> to minimize these uncomfortable feelings, many people want to be associated
> only with others similar to themselves in color, belief, or language. Even among
> people who look like them, act like them, and dress like them, if they don't
> know anyone in the new group from previous experience, they are distinctly
> uncomfortable. So adamant are some people in their desire to be with their own
> kind that tribal genocide, ethnic cleansing, and civil wars are now a way of life
> in many countries. (p. 2)

It was partly from the ashes of such experience that Leeder (2004) was
inspired to write her book on *The Family in Global Perspective.* As she
describes it,

> I have written this book as a labor of love. As I said earlier, my father was a
> Holocaust refugee, and I am of the post-Holocaust generation. The Holocaust
> occurred because of racism and an exaggerated idea about the evils of differ-
> ence. I believe that it is imperative that we, as citizens of the world, understand
> others so that there will not be another Holocaust. (p. 272)

One might ask why ethnocentrism is so pervasive. Greeley (1969) suggests
that "family, land and common cultural heritage have always been terribly
important to human beings, and suspicion of anyone who is strange or different seems also deeply rooted in the human experience" (p. 21). But while this
propensity toward ethnocentric thinking is seen in all world cultures, it is
uniquely expressed among Americans. Perhaps it is rooted in our legacy of manifest destiny or more recently our economic prosperity, but for whatever reason,
it is a trap into which many Americans unwittingly fall. Waiarda (1985)
laments that this "deeply ingrained American ethnocentrism [creates] an inability to understand the Third World on its own terms, an insistence on viewing it
through the lens of our own Western experience, and the condescending and
patronizing attitudes that such ethnocentrism implies" (1985, p. 1).

The critical importance of addressing issues of ethnocentrism was brought
home to me some years ago while teaching a course on cross-cultural
childrearing. During the second week of class we were discussing the
comparative family contexts in which children are raised and nurtured. To

help visualize the experience of growing up in an extended versus a nuclear family, I showed a short clip from the video *Not Without My Daughter* (Ufland & Ufland, 1991).

The narrative unfolds with a successful Iranian doctor interacting in a small nuclear family setting in Michigan with his American-born wife, child, and in-laws. Juxtaposed against this tranquil, intimate setting, the viewer then follows the Mahmoody family as they return home to Iran and are greeted at the airport by a boisterous throng of extended family members. The tiny nuclear family is enveloped and whisked away in an extended family motorcade. Upon arrival home, they step out of the car in a welcoming ritual over the carcass of a freshly slaughtered lamb. Despite the fact that the class roster included two veiled women from Saudi Arabia and an American student with an Iranian husband, a portion of the class snickered throughout the video clip at the traditional Islamic dress and the passionate, demonstrative airport greeting. Likewise, there was much audible gagging at the sight of the slaughtered lamb in the welcome-home ritual. Needless to say, students from the Persian Gulf region were sliding pretty low in their seats by this time. They were visibly shaken by the ridicule of their home cultures, and by the lack of sensitivity on the part of some students toward their sense of isolation and exclusion.

If our long-range goal is building the capacity for objective and critical reflection, we need to begin by recognizing the pervasiveness of our own ethnocentric thinking. It may be too threatening to start by positioning the laser beam directly on one's own most private thoughts, affections, and prejudices. Instead, an initial strategy might be identifying ethnocentric thinking woven throughout academic literature and the popular press (Paul, 1992). For example, what does a closer examination of our textbooks reveal? Is a Eurocentric bias subtly perpetuated? Some texts still draw heavily on maps and terminology dating back to the colonial era when the British Empire was viewed as the geographic and political center of the universe. With Britain as the reference point, the Holy Land was viewed as the "Near East," Persia as the "Middle East," and India and China the "Far East" (Hernandez, 1989).

One might also make note of lapses into ethnocentric thinking exhibited by even the most respected journalists. Typical examples include the following:

1. *Time* magazine once featured a special inset announcing the upcoming marriage of Benazir Bhutto, then prime minister of Pakistan. After explaining this was an arranged marriage, the *Time* writer added, "The wedding will probably not take place until winter, by which time her followers—and

Benazir—should have grown accustomed to the idea" ("Getting to Know You," 1987, p. 23). In actuality, it was not Bhutto and her devoutly Muslim followers that had to "get used to" the idea of arranged marriage, but rather the ethnocentric Western journalist.

2. A similarly jaded view of arranged marriage was conveyed by a front-page article in the *Washington Post* (Coll, 1994). The article described an enterprising young Indian businessman, Jatin Mehta, who heads an international diamond cartel. Mehta had announced plans to market his diamonds to the 400 million–plus Indian women.

The *Post* writer mused that Mehta would have his work cut out for him trying to persuade these millions of women that diamonds are their best friend. The task would be especially daunting since, as the writer noted, many of these women were "trapped by lonely, arranged marriages and feudal family values" (p. A1).

I watched for letters of protest from the Indian community, but saw none. It is likely that the nonconfrontational approach of many Asian cultures would make it difficult to publicly protest biased journalism by a major media outlet. But one might safely assume that there were more than a few readers who were hurt and offended by such pejorative language.

3. Not only can Americans be quite ethnocentric in their view of other cultures, they can also be guilty of regional ethnocentrism, as well. The *Washington Post* recounted the story of an Indiana University student who is a prime example of ethnocentrism run amok. The student, a native New Yorker, had never been west of the Hudson River prior to landing in Bloomington, Indiana. According to a classmate,

> This woman never bought the local newspaper because she never had to. Her mother Federal Expressed her the *New York Times* every single day, including Sundays, for four solid years. Also Fed Ex-ed her bagels and lox once a week, minimum. The one that really got to me was the weekly shipment of two gallons of Evian water. As if they don't sell that blessed fluid in the Midwestern provinces!" the classmate quipped. (Levey, 1994, p. D20)

Sleuth work for illustrations of ethnocentrism can become addictive! Just as sensitivity to inclusive language has solidified over the past several decades, so our radar screens can be sharpened to instances of ethnocentric thinking. By the end of the semester, they should fairly leap out at us from the page.

As sensitivity to ethnocentric attitudes and behaviors exhibited by others is heightened, we are better equipped to confront the possibility that we, too, might be guilty of ethnocentric thinking. Through critical self-reflection we come face to face with our own denial, painfully aware of those instances where we arbitrarily judge others by the standards of our own culture.

The capacity to recognize and claim one's own ethnocentrism is of critical importance to emerging family science researchers, educators, and practitioners. It is far easier to assume that family practices with which we are most familiar are somehow "innate" to all people (DeGenova, 1997, p. 8). Holding fast to ethnocentrism is "entirely inconsistent" with an ability to offer holistic care for children and families of diverse cultures (Husband, 2000, p. 58). It also impedes the practitioner's ability to gain appreciation for and deep knowledge of other cultures (Leininger, 1995), for it leads us "to believe we have nothing to learn from places or people unlike ourselves, particularly people who might be materially less well-off" (Leeder, 2004, p. 18).

Stage 2: Adopting the Position of Cultural Relativism

As we begin to distance ourselves from our own lived experience, we are more open to viewing the world through the lens of "the other." In the process we recognize the limitations of judging other cultures by the standards of our own. We are eventually persuaded, to paraphrase an old proverb, that "anyone who knows only one culture, knows no culture" (Augsburger, 1986, p. 18). To a certain extent, this stage involves "deconstructing the myths of American culture," as one college student freshly returned from studying abroad put it (Kauffman et al., 1992, p. 110).

Inherent in the notion of cultural relativism is the willingness to study and learn from other cultures. This challenge may be more daunting for middle- and upper-class Americans who, from an international perspective, come from backgrounds of enormous privilege and learned entitlement (Marks, 2000). Cultural relativism argues for deep engagement with and meaningful dialogue between cultures:

> This is not the easy cosmopolitanism that implies enormous privilege—the capacity, for example, to spend three days in the Bali Hilton. It's a deeper form of knowing that entails some recognition that I am one among others. I am not the center of the universe. (Rosaldo, 2000, p. 5)

In Stage 2, cultural relativism, the family scientist temporarily suspends ethical and moral judgments. It is essential to "bracket one's own values and control one's spontaneous reactions to a number of exotic phenomena"

(*Cultural Relativism,* 2005, p. 1). If one ceases to operate from the assumption that one's own culture is normative for all others, family practices that originally seemed absurd or irrational can begin to make sense when situated in their larger, natural context.

Cultivating Empathetic Understanding

Among other things, cultural relativism involves stepping inside the shoes of individuals in another culture in order to gain a more empathetic understanding of the culture (Bennett, 1993; Leeder, 2004). In the process, a serious effort is made to imagine or comprehend the other's world without imposing one's values upon it. At its best, "intellectual empathy" (Paul, 1992, p. 153) presupposes a fairly high degree of intercultural knowledge and sensitivity (Kauffmann, Martin, & Weaver, 1992).

Leeder (2004) employed the lens of cultural relativism to shed light on the traditional practice of child marriage. She notes that even though child marriage was outlawed in India through the Child Marriage Restraint Act in 1978, as late as 1996 over half of all females surveyed in Rajasthan were married by age 18. In this province, it was not uncommon for brides to go to the altar as young as four years of age. Leeder cautions that

> since such a union is not about love, it is interesting to ponder the causes. Once again it is important to look at history rather than to judge by Western standards. Remember to employ cultural relativity, rather than ethnocentrism, in thinking about this. (p. 184)

She continues by describing the link between child marriage and economic deprivation. For poor families, arranging an early marriage helps lighten the crushing load of poverty. As such, it is not irrational for families to marry off their toddler daughters in order to shorten the number of years required to support them. It is further believed in this culture that early marriage will protect their daughters from sexual exploitation, since many men in the region believe that "having sex with a 'fresh' girl can cure syphilis, gonorrhea, and even the virus that causes AIDS" (Burns, 1998). Leeder (2004) models a serious attempt to understand traditional family practices through the eyes of Rajasthani culture.

The traditional practice of polygamy might also be explored through the lens of cultural relativism or intellectual empathy. When westerners are asked their views on polygamy, they typically think of one thing: sex. Why else would a person be motivated to consider such a relationship?

Polygamists must have voracious sexual appetites. One woman for each man is just not enough for these sexual perverts! It takes so little effort to judge a practice like polygamy from the norms and values of our own culture. However, it is only when stepping inside, say, a West African worldview, that one comes to appreciate the roles and purposes polygamy serves in providing economic stability for the family and security for widows in their old age (Hillman, 1975).

Acknowledging Integrative Aspects of Culture

In addition to creating intellectual empathy in Stage 2, we also grow to appreciate the integrative aspects of a culture. This approach assumes a fundamental respect for the "integrity" of all world cultures (Bennett, 1993, p. 31). Cultures come to be viewed in holistic, rather than fragmented, terms (Partington, 1987). Anthropologist Ruth Benedict (1934) argued that there is a natural "fit" or complementarity between the various components of culture. Each culture has its own unique patterning or configuration. From this perspective, family practices like bride-price payments or the levirate are not just random ideas or novel experiments. Their meaning and function are intimately tied to the norms, values, beliefs, and worldview of the cultures in which they are embedded. Through this lens one can more readily see the social, economic, or ritualistic purposes served by otherwise baffling family customs.

As we progress through Stage 2, it is hoped that we will begin migrating from ethnocentrism toward a cultural relativism that enables us to evaluate a culture on its own terms (Rosado, 1994). Cultural relativism as understood here is not to be confused with moral relativism. The point is not to see how desensitized we can become to such practices as infanticide, sex-selective abortions, wife-beating, and genital mutilation. Rather it is to more fully appreciate the functions and purposes served by traditional family practices before judging and critiquing them.

Stage 3: Ethical Reflection and Engagement

The cultural relativism of Stage 2 is not our final destination. By expanding appreciation and respect for other cultures in this stage, we are better prepared to engage in thoughtful ethical reflection. It is here that "selective adoption" is employed, whereby certain practices are appreciated and valued while others are rejected (Pusch, 1979, p. 19). Here we actively affirm what is worthwhile and valuable while recognizing our own responsibilities in a pluralistic world (Kauffmann et al., 1992). There is a curious paradox here, because in higher education today, "pluralism" is a cherished value. There is much ambivalence about sounding judgmental of other ways of life. To run that risk sounds neither enlightened nor politically correct.

Several years ago *U.S. News and World Report* (Leo, 2002) featured an article entitled, "Professors Who See No Evil." It described the findings of a national poll in which 73 percent of college seniors claimed their professors did not believe in right and wrong. Morality was seen simply a matter of personal preference and cultural diversity. Within this context, 10 percent to 20 percent of students in one study indicated they

> could not bring themselves to criticize the Nazi extermination of Europe's Jews. Some students expressed personal distaste for what the Nazis did. But they were not willing to say that the Nazis were wrong, since no culture can be judged from the outside and no individual can challenge the moral worldview of another. College students are rarely taught this directly, but they absorb it as part of the multiculturally tolerant, nonjudgmental campus culture. Deferring to the moral compass of mass murderers is a drastic step, even for collegians steeped in moral relativism. (p. 14)

Applebaum (1996) discusses this unsettling phenomenon at some length. She observes that while multiculturalism has heightened public sensitivity toward ethnocentrism, it has at the same time led to a form of "moral paralysis" (p. 185). People of goodwill are so fearful of making ethnocentric and racist-sounding judgments that they sometimes "decide not to risk judging at all" (Walking, 1980, p. 89).

Out of this relativistic milieu has come a clarion call for more intentional ethical reflection in higher education. Some have written disparagingly of the so-called Trivial Pursuit theory of knowledge, which fills students' brains with arcane bits of information but does little more with them. Projects like Princeton University's Center for Human Values were designed to correct this perceived deficit in higher education. In a monograph commissioned for the center's inauguration, the director wrote,

> The ethical issues of our time pose a challenge to any university committed to an educational mission that encompasses more than the development and dissemination of empirical knowledge and technical skills. Can people who differ in their moral perspectives nonetheless reason together in ways that are productive of greater ethical understanding? The University Center faces up to this challenge by supporting a university education that is centrally concerned with examining ethical values, the various standards according to which individuals make significant choices and evaluate their own as well as other ways of life. (Taylor, 1992, p. ix)

Stanford University responded to a similar challenge by hosting a teach-in on moral relativism and absolutism as part of their new "ethics across the curriculum initiative" (O'Toole, 1999, p. 1). According to a participant, faculty lamented "how omnipresent ethical relativism is among students and that [they as] faculty don't know what to do when they hear students treat everything as a matter of personal opinion" (p. 2). Faculty feared appearing dogmatic and narrow-minded, yet they also did not want "to leave students with the impression that all opinions are equally valid and that there are no systematic ways of thinking about ethical issues" (p. 2).

A similar interest in ethical reflection has filtered down to the social sciences. *The Chronicle of Higher Education* featured an article on the "Revival of Moral Inquiry in the Social Sciences" in which Wolfe (1999) argues there is no inherent conflict between a scholar's commitment to objectivity and the possession of strong moral convictions:

> Good social science does not require complete detachment and neutrality—just objectivity. Objectivity does not mean that one has no personal views about the world. It means, instead, that one demonstrates a willingness to recognize the viability and integrity of positions other than one's own." (p. B5)

Not only is ethics now of keen interest to social scientists generally, but it has percolated down to the field of family science in particular (Brock, 1993). In 1998 the discipline formally adopted a code of professional ethics (Adams, Dollahite, Gilbert, & Keim, 2001), and since then it has identified ethics as one of 10 areas of demonstrated expertise required for certification as a Family Life Educator (Bredehoft & Walcheski, 2005; Powell & Cassidy, 2001). Many family science departments offer at least one course in ethics related to the discipline.

One explanation for this groundswell of interest in ethics is that the "Trivial Pursuit" of empirical knowledge tends to oversimplify complex issues and strip them of their controversial and ambiguous elements (McPeck, 1990). At times students themselves complain that the learning process is aborted. Exotic new worlds are opened up to them, yet they feel inadequate to process this information on their own. They want to be open-minded and receptive to new ideas, yet they sense a vague disease over the pain, injustice, and oppression that is implied by some of these customs.

In fact there *are* some pretty sobering, and at times horrific, traditions practiced by well-meaning family members around the world.

- In some cultures, when twins are born, one of them is or both of them are routinely killed (Queen, Habenstein, & Quadagno, 1985).
- In Ivory Coast, Down syndrome babies are sometimes gently laid by their mothers back into the lagoon or river whence they are believed to have come so

they have a chance to "come out right the next time" (Krabill, personal communication, March 8, 1994).

- Scarification is practiced in Nigeria, where babies were traditionally cut with deep tribal markings on their face and torso to identify them with their family and lineage (Ecker, 1994).

- Nearly 100 percent of all young girls in Somalia are subjected to a painful circumcision ritual often performed without anesthesia (Headley & Dorkenoo, 1992).

- Honor killings are performed in parts of South Asia and the Middle East, whereby men seek to protect the honor of their families by killing or physically punishing their daughters and sisters for their sexual indiscretions (Muslim Women's League, 1999).

- Brides in India are sometimes burned alive if their families cannot deliver dowry payments in timely fashion, while other Indian families live in abject poverty as they struggle to pay back dowry debts into the third and fourth generations ("India: Till Death," 1990).

Somehow it seems irresponsible to drop information like this in students' laps and walk away. After all the soul searching to peel away judgmental attitudes and layers of resistance, what then?

Martha Nussbaum (2000), professor of ethics and law at the University of Chicago, has wrestled deeply with this issue. In her book *Women and Human Development,* she concludes,

> In light of the fact that some traditional practices are harmful and evil, and some actively hostile to other elements of a diverse culture, we are forced by our interest in diversity itself to develop a set of criteria against which to assess the practices we find, asking which are acceptable and worth preserving, and which are not. (p. 59)

The following ethical frameworks may be useful in this process of assessing global family practices. Each has relevance for Stage 3, ethical reflection, and each will be followed by a practical illustration from the field of family science.

Consequentialist Ethics

The first is the consequentialist approach, in which ethical reasoning is based on the consequences of human actions (Thiroux, 1990). In addition to ethical egoism, a key variation of consequentialism is utilitarianism (Hollinger, 2002). Here one asks, "What is the greatest good for the greatest number of people?" A related question might focus on the issue of relative risk. What implication, for example, does a practice like female genital mutilation have for mortality and morbidity? Can one quantify the economic and social consequences of this practice?

In fact, it does appear that a practice like female circumcision is not just an unappealing birth or puberty ritual. Research in countries like Kenya indicates that more than 80 percent of all circumcised women report having had at least one related medical complication including hemorrhaging, infection, scarring, psychological problems, or painful intercourse (Leeder, 2004; Okie, 1993). Additional complications identified by the Institute for Development Training include infertility, chronic pelvic pain, menstrual difficulties, recurrent urinary tract infection, and loss of tissue elasticity during childbirth (*Health Effects,* 1986). In economic terms, there is a staggering medical cost associated with these otherwise preventable health conditions.

Consequentialist ethics can also be used to evaluate child marriage. On the one hand, child marriage is clearly compatible with the worldviews of particular subcultures in the Indian subcontinent, where it is "vigorously defended in both religious and cultural terms" (Nussbaum, 2000). On the other hand, child marriage can be shown to have serious economic and social consequences for society. For one, early unions are associated with low rates of female literacy. In one region where child marriage is practiced, only 18 percent of the 5,000 women studied were literate (Leeder, 2004). Families were large and in generally poorer health than families in other parts of India. Infant mortality rates were high with 176 of every 1,000 live births ending in death by age five. Of the remaining children under four years of age, 63 percent were found to be malnourished (Leeder, 2004).

One might also apply consequentialist ethics to the traditions of dowry and bride-price. With the practice of dowry, money or property (cattle, land, jewelry, utensils, furniture, even VCR and DVD players) pass from the bride's family to the groom's as part of an arranged marriage (Strong et al., 2005). Srinivasan and Lee (2004) conducted a fascinating study of the dowry system in the northern province of Bihar, India. Using a consequentialist approach, the authors identified a number of negative consequences that can result from the practice including financial ruin for the bride's parents, wife battering, bride burnings, female feticide (abortion of female fetuses), and infanticide. Despite these potential negative consequences, the practice appears to be flourishing. In an intriguing twist of fate, the very modernism that critiques the dowry system on the one hand may be perpetuating it on the other. The authors suggest that one reason its practice may be resistant to change is "because its social and economic consequences carry tangible benefits in an increasingly materialistic culture" (p. 1108).

A final application of consequentialist ethics might be to the issue of sex-selective abortions. In countries like India there is a deeply entrenched cultural and worldview preference for male sons. The traditional killing of female infants through poisoning or exposure ("Asia: Discarding Daughters," 1990) has been replaced by sex-selective abortions (Leeder, 2004). With the aid of modern technology, pregnant women can now find out early on whether they are carrying a female fetus and terminate their pregnancy accordingly. This application of modern technology does not come without social and economic consequences. For example, a study in one hospital found that of the 700 amniocenteses, 430 out of 450 female fetuses were aborted, yet all male fetuses were carried to full term (Miller, 1987). The long-term impact in the region of such a dramatic gender imbalance could have dire social and economic consequences (Glenn, 2004). However, in describing these consequences, Leeder (2004) still "urges the suspension of any ethnocentric value judgments" (p. 247). She acknowledges, "It is true that these figures are disturbing and certainly are contrary to Western-based humanistic values," but she urges the reader "to keep a view that is culturally relative" (p. 248).

Consequentialist ethics, then, provides a tangible framework for evaluating the potential positive or negative impact of particular family practices. These may be related to social, mental health, economic, political, educational, or health-related criteria.

Deontological Ethics

A second tool for moral inquiry and reflection is that of deontological ethics. Here one focuses on inherent duties and obligations that are expressed in moral principles and rules (Thiroux, 1990). These are *non*consequentialist in that they are viewed as inherently right regardless of the consequences. Such principles and rules are traditionally derived from three sources: reason, the cumulative reservoir of human experience, and religion.

Principles Derived From Reason

Sample principles that are relevant to the study of global families include values such as love, altruism, truth-telling, human dignity, equality, individual freedom, social order, democracy, self-determination, autonomy, and family or community solidarity. Additional principles identified by international social service providers include social and economic justice, peace, and nonviolent conflict resolution (Estes, 1992).

At times, these lofty sounding moral principles may actually conflict with one another. For example, families around the world struggle with the tension between individual autonomy on the one hand and family solidarity on the other. One way of resolving this value conflict is to force a choice between them, thus rank-ordering values in their descending order of importance (Hardina, 2004). An illustration of this is seen in feminist approaches to ethics:

> *Fully* feminist approaches to ethics are committed first and foremost to the elimination of women's subordination . . . in all its manifestations. A feminist approach to ethics asks questions about power—that is, about domination and subordination—even before it asks questions about *good* and *evil, care* and *justice,* or maternal and paternal thinking. (Tong, 2003, p. 12)

In addition to rank-ordering competing values, one might also attempt to hold competing values and principles in creative tension. For example, is it possible to maintain a dialectic between the principles of individual well-being on the one hand and collective solidarity on the other? Sherif (2004) describes this tension in the context of Islamic family life:

> Even in relatively nonreligious families strong social pressures constantly reinforce conformity and discourage rebelliousness of any sort, at least in public. . . . A young child quickly learns that it is shameful to disregard parental directives. Conformity to parent authority extends to all spheres of life, such as the choice of a major in college and, at times, the choice of a spouse. Decisions that most Americans consider individual choices are, for Muslims, the result of extensive group discussions and negotiations. The individual may make the final decision but only after a great deal of familial input. (p. 187)

The same tension between individualism and community is seen in countries like Somalia, where female circumcision is a cultural rite of passage. What would be gained if one were able to free individual girls from this torturous procedure? Their individual freedom would, in many cases, deprive them of solidarity and identification with the group. By not participating in the traditional puberty ritual, they would miss the opportunity to be formally admitted into adulthood in their own society.

The tension between individual well-being and collective solidarity is further seen by the fact that uncircumcised girls often fear that they have diminished their marriage prospects (Ecker, 1994). A Somali man living in Washington, DC, confirms this fear: "If the lady is 'open,' her chance of marriage is lost" (French, 1992, p. F4). Any recommendation to discontinue ritual circumcision would ideally incorporate the value for collective solidarity along with that for individual freedom. This might be accomplished by creating alternative festivals and rituals to be celebrated during the traditional circumcision months that "promote positive traditional values while removing the danger of physical and psychological harm" (Amnesty International, 1998, p. 3).

An interesting variation on the theme of competing principles and values is seen in the case of child prostitution in Thailand. Instead of two different values in competition, this is a case where the conflict lies between two parties laying claim to the same value: human rights. In Thailand, 63 percent of children under 16 who are brought to brothels are brought by their parents (Skrobanek, 1991).

While child prostitution was traditionally associated with poverty in Thailand, it appears this is less the case today. Instead of being a strategy for economic survival by peasant families, it is now seen more as providing access to consumer goods. It reflects "a yearning for a better standard of living by parents who are not always the poorest of the poor" (Skrobanek, 1991, p. 45). Girls refusing to comply are "regarded as ungrateful and irresponsible by parents and neighbors" (p. 45). Indeed, there are reports of girls being visited at the brothels by teachers and community leaders in order to solicit donations for their pet community development projects. In a position paper describing this phenomenon, Skrobanek argues that parents' rights over their children "should be removed" in order to safeguard the rights of children over their own bodies. The critical issue here becomes whose rights prevail: parents' or their children's?

Principles Derived From Human Experience

A second approach to deontological ethics is to identify principles derived from human experience. As one looks around the world, what family-related principles seem to transcend time, space, and culture? What values enjoy relatively broad, universal consensus? It has been suggested that a worldwide consensus may be gaining momentum around the issue of family violence (Balswick & Balswick, 1995; Lachman, 1997). In the past, violence against women was quite pervasive, occurring in up to 85 percent of traditional societies (Balswick & Balswick, 1995). By way of contrast, the authors believe there is now an "emergent worldwide recognition of violence against women" that discourages pervasive violence:

> The emergence of feminist theory invites us to identify such acts of physical abuse of one spouse by the other as undesirable to marriage and as acts of violence in any cultural system. In the name of cultural relativism, some may seek to normalize marital violence by showing that it is sanctioned by the wider

cultural system of which the marital system is a part. The lesson to be learned from feminist and other so-called value-laden theories, is that so-called value-free theories of marital power must be challenged. (p. 309)

Many values and principles that are widely embraced are eventually codified by the international community. Documents that address the needs and vulnerabilities of women, children, and families, and that have been ratified by such bodies as the United Nations, would be prime examples. Sample documents include the Universal Declaration of Human Rights, the UN Convention on the Elimination of Discrimination against Women, the Convention on the Rights of the Child, and the Declaration on the Elimination of Violence against Women (Amnesty International, 1998). Appealing to international documents such as these broadens the conversation beyond the idiosyncratic critique and biases of a lone family scientist.

Among other commitments, these documents are typically grounded in a broad-based, universal consensus regarding human rights. Indeed, the whole notion of using human rights as a criterion for evaluating traditional family practices sounds quite logical to the Western ear. However, we sometimes forget what a challenge it has been to bring the global community into compliance with such a standard. The former human rights director for UNESCO in Paris suggests that the only reason the UN was able to gain such consensus was that countries were not forced to agree over the fundamental *reasons* behind the Universal Declaration of Human Rights (Senarclens, 1983). According to him, it would have been "illusory to try to reconcile ideologies, philosophies and spiritualities which were over and beyond this fragile point of convergence" (p. 9).

When family scientists in the West attempt to apply human rights principles to specific cultural contexts, it is imperative that they do so with great care and humility. The concept of human rights is after all the product of European liberalism (enlightenment thought). It is an integral part of the framework for philosophical, political, and judicial values affirmed in Europe since the Renaissance (Senarclens, 1983).

Westerners who uncritically embrace the principles of human rights, individualism, equality, democracy, and freedom don't fully appreciate how far these ideological foundations deviate from those of cultures placing a higher value on hierarchy, social control, and community. Indeed, human rights are perceived as extremely subversive in certain social, economic, and political systems (Senarclens, 1983). Lesdema, a Venezuelan law professor, notes that many South Americans associate the human rights agenda with the Western political propaganda machine (1983).

Other cultures have also dragged their feet en route to the human rights table. Daoudi, a Syrian law professor, notes that in Arab countries the teaching of human rights cannot be envisioned if it goes against Muslim dogma for fear of being considered contrary to public order (Daoudi, 1983). In Islam, according to Daoudi, "Man has no rights, for all rights belong to God, and human beings are the reflection of God's rights. Man cannot, therefore, become free except by submission to God" (p. 69).

Despite the obvious challenge of garnering broad support for international human rights documents, the fact remains that the Universal Declaration of Human Rights has been "adopted by the international community" as both a moral compass and an "incontestable juridical authority. It has become the reference for innumerable UN resolutions. It has been the source of inspiration for many national constitutions, laws, and conventions" (Senarclens, 1983, p. 9). Vehicles like the Declaration of Human Rights provide family scientists with external frames of reference for evaluating the merits and shortcomings of particular global family practices.

Principles Derived From Religion

In addition to reason and human experience, deontological ethics is also informed by religion. Nussbaum (1999) argues that religion should be treated with deference, due to her belief that all religions, at some level, care about reforming and improving the conduct of life:

> Furthermore, it would not be too bold to add that all the major religions embody an idea of compassion for human suffering, and an idea that it is wrong for innocent people to suffer. All, finally, embody some kind of a notion of justice. (p. 20)

When looking to religion for ethical principles and guidelines, one might consider religious history and tradition, broad theological themes, and sacred writings.

Religious History and Tradition

Americans can be remarkably ahistorical in their perspectives. European tourists sometimes chuckle at our revered "historical sites," some of which are a scant 50 to 100 years old. In much of Europe, such buildings would not stand a ghost of chance to merit a historic marker. At Oxford University in England, for example, New College was built some years after the university was established, in approximately 1379 AD (Prest, 1993)!

It is not intuitive for most Americans to look to the past when trying to resolve contemporary relational or family problems. Likewise, identifying historical parallels is not a strategy we typically use to understand family life in other cultures. Yet researching religious tradition can provide insight and collective wisdom for responding to and evaluating particular family practices. For hundreds of centuries, family-related issues were among those discussed and debated by a variety of religious tribunals and councils. Many culminated in formal resolutions and treatises summarizing carefully argued guidelines and recommendations. These provide fresh perspectives that might otherwise elude those of us situated in the twenty-first century.

Broad Theological Themes

Another linkage between family and religion is to ask how family practices relate to overarching theological themes or foundational worldviews of particular religions. It has been suggested, for example, that a theology of family in the Christian tradition views family more as a covenantal relationship than a contractual one (Balswick & Balswick, 1989). It is argued that covenant is a central theme in both Jewish and Christian theology. When applied to marriage, the concept of covenant places less emphasis on defending one's own personal rights than on entering into a mutually accountable relationship where commitment may not, in exchange theory terms, always strive to maximize personal rewards and minimize personal costs (Strong et al., 2005, p. 51).

Another overarching theological theme in Jewish, Muslim, and Christian traditions is that of the value, dignity, and worth of the human person (Nussbaum, 2000). The Jewish Talmud records a debate in the second century AD where Ben Azzai argued that since all human beings are created in God's image, they must be treated with dignity and respect, regardless of whether one *feels* love for them (Matalon, 2002). In describing how this overarching theme relates to family caregivers, Matalon writes,

> In practice, Jewish law reflects a hierarchy of values in which the commandment to save a life, Pikuah nefesh, precedes the requirement to love. While the inner quality to our actions is important, it is the deed itself [that] takes precedence. According to Maimonides, it is better if the mitzvah of tzedakah (charity) is performed with love, but it is still an obligation even if it not performed with love. For the [caregiver], Judaism requires efforts to rescue the patient's dignity even when the patient is off-putting, or difficult to relate to. The main task of the caregiver is still "to save a life," even when all efforts to awaken love and

positive feelings fail. Performing a mitzvah is the very act of loving God and loving fellow. In the words of Abraham Joshua Heschel, "by doing the finite we come into contact with the infinite." (p. 2)

A similar affirmation of human dignity is found in Muslim theology. The prophet Muhammad taught that all "children of Adam" are born with dignity and nobility (Mattson, 2002). In the words of the Qur'an, "We have dignified the children of Adam, and borne them over land and sea, and provided them with good and pure things for sustenance, and favored them far about a great part of Our creation" (17:70). This inherent dignity extends across the human life cycle, despite the fact that humans begin and end their lives in a state of helplessness (Mattson, 2002). Even in the most vulnerable state of advanced illness, Islamic tradition teaches that the human person is to be treated with dignity and respect. For example, the religion does not permit family members to force medical treatment on unwilling members of their family. It is said that

> the Prophet Muhammad was angry at his family when they forced him to drink some medicine as he lay on his bed in the last days of his fatal illness. Indeed, when he regained some strength for a short time after that, he made his family drink the medicine themselves—to experience how humiliating it is to be forced to take a medicine one does not want. (Mattson, 2002)

This same theme of human dignity figures prominently in Roman Catholic thought, as well. Feminist Sidney Callahan (2002), professor of moral theology at St. John's University, notes that

> all humans are made in the image of God and as morally equal cannot be discriminated against or denied care. No one earns their intrinsic dignity which is a gift from God. All human beings no matter what their abilities or stage of growth possess an inalienable dignity granted by the Creator. (p. 1)

In summary, overarching theological themes such as human dignity would suggest that traditional family practices that oppress or erode the value and integrity of individual family members are highly problematic.

Sacred Texts and Writings

At times deontological ethics also appeals to principles and ethical guidelines imbedded in sacred texts and writings. The practice of the levirate is one such example. This practice required a widow to marry the brother of her deceased husband. The tradition has been embraced by various cultures including Afghans, Hebrews, Hindus, and Native Americans (Ingoldsby, 1995). In the case of the Hebrew people, an appeal was made to their sacred scriptures to support the practice:

> If brothers are living together and one of them dies without a son, his widow must not marry outside the family. Her husband's brother shall take her and marry her and fulfill the duty of a brother-in-law to her. The first son she bears shall carry on the name of the dead brother so that his name will not be blotted out from Israel. (Deut. 25:5–6)

Muslims, likewise, appeal to their sacred writings. They appeal not only to the Qur'an, for ethical guidance, but also to the *shari'a,* its "legal interpretation" (Sherif, 2004, p. 185), and *sunna* or "practices" (p. 186). According to Fluehr-Lobban,

> The shari'a has developed specialized topics that reflect the highly protective attitude of the *Qur'an* toward minors and aged parents. Specifically, the primary legal relationship centers on adequate maintenance of dependent children and needy parents. The economic and social welfare of children is a major parental responsibility enforceable under Islamic law. (as cited in Sherif, 2004, p. 186)

In using sacred writings, there are several cautions. One is that sacred texts can be distorted and manipulated to support almost any idea to which a person takes a fancy. Sherif (2004) observes that the Qur'an has at times been used selectively:

> Contemporary scholarship has shown that, rather than determining attitudes about women, parts of the Qur'an are only used at certain times to legitimate particular acts or sets of conditions that concern women. This selective use is part of the way in which gender hierarchy and sexuality are negotiated and enforced. It does not explain gender roles; instead, it is part of a constant process of gender role negotiation. (p. 184)

In exploring ways that sacred writings might inform ethical reflection, it is also important to distinguish between folk expressions of a religion and official articulations of the same. Not all ideas people associate with a religion are actually affirmed by religious scholars, rabbis, and clerics of that religious group. Returning to the case of female circumcision, Leeder (2004) notes that in countries where it is common, "it is practiced by both Muslims and Christians" (p. 135). She goes on to emphasize there is no evidence female circumcision is prescribed by Jewish or Christian scriptures. While many Muslim laypeople assume circumcision is taught or required by Islam, interviews with a series of respected Muslim leaders, however, reveal otherwise ("Africa: A Ritual," 1992; Amnesty International, 1998; Leeder, 2004).

Nussbaum (2000) offers a helpful summary of the challenges related to using religious texts and writings in ethical reflection:

> Religions are intertwined in complex ways with politics and culture. Even when a religion is based on a set of authoritative texts, culture and politics enter in complex ways into the interpretation of texts and the institutionalized form of traditional practice. Jews differ about where to draw the line between what is genuinely religious in the tradition and what is the work of specific contextual and historical shaping. Similar debates arise in Christianity and Islam. . . . Where Hinduism is concerned, the absence of scriptural authority makes it all the more difficult, if not virtually impossible, to identify a necessary religious core distinct from layers of history and culture, all powerfully infused with imperfect people's desire for political power. (p. 194)

Care Ethics

The third ethical framework useful for evaluating global family practices is care ethics, often viewed as a subset of character or virtue ethics. Care ethics places a value on meeting others' needs and on caring relationships lived out in a context of mutual trust and responsiveness (Held, 2004, p. 145). This framework reflects a feminist vision for a "new way of seeing and interacting with the world" (Riley, Torrens, & Krumholz, 2005, p. 91). It is often claimed to have "assumptions, goals and methods" (Held, 2004, p. 143) that differ from those of the dominant ethical theories described earlier in the chapter:

> Among the characteristics of the ethics of care is its view of persons as relational and as interdependent. [Deontological] and consequentialist moral theories focus primarily on the rational decisions of agents taken as independent and autonomous individuals. . . . In contrast, the ethics of care sees persons as partly constituted by their relations with others. It pays attention primarily to relations between persons, valuing especially caring relations. (p. 143)

One advocate of the care orientation is feminist Carol Gilligan (1982). She suggests that women's narratives reflect a different voice and a different morality (Hollinger, 2002). Their orientation tends to be more "contextual and narrative rather than formal and abstract" (Gilligan, 1982, p. 19). As such, care ethics focuses more specifically on "context, relationship and compassion," rather than on "truth, rights and fairness" (Hollinger, 2002, p. 50).

Many advocates of the care approach recognize that justice and care each "have a place in moral development and ethical reflection" (Hollinger, 2002, p. 50); however, exclusive reliance on one over the other can be highly problematic. An overemphasis on justice ethics has created a global "culture of neglect" by systematically devaluing "interdependence, related-ness, and positive involvement in the lives of distant others" (Robinson, 1999, p. 7). As such, an ethic of justice that fails to give attention to care is "clearly deficient" (Hollinger, 2002, p. 50).

On the other hand, care should not be the primary criterion upon which to base ethical decision-making. "In the opinion of Loewy (1996) it would be as dangerous to blindly obey the rules and regulations as it would be to base one's ethical decision-making solely on one's emotions and urge to care" (Botes, 2000, p. 1073). Some would argue that in an ideal world, both would be affirmed:

> Both the fair and equitable treatment of all people (from the ethics of justice) and the holistic, contextual and need-centered nature of such treatment (from the ethics of care) ought therefore to be retained in the integrated application of the ethics of justice and the ethics of care. (Botes, 2000, p. 1071)

Stage 4: Social Action

Following an intentional process of ethical reflection, there are times when family scientists feel compelled to become catalysts of social change and transformation. As long as education remains a cerebral exercise, there is little sense of urgency to become engaged in the lives of real flesh and blood families or in cultural practices that might be deemed harmful. While it is true that action at this stage is fraught with many potential perils and misunderstandings, passive acquiescence to violence, oppression, and exploi-tation is not an honorable option either.

In considering one's potential role in advocating for social change or in community organizing, Hardina (2004) stresses the importance of develop-ing guidelines, frameworks, and best practices for this advocacy work. Strategic interventions should be weighed in terms of their relative costs and benefits and their short-term versus long-term effectiveness as well as their potential to "violate social norms" (Hardina, 2004, p. 599).

Spheres of Influence

As the family scientist weighs the potential spheres of influence through which to implement social change or transformation, there are many possibilities. These might include working through local education, development, health care, or religious institutions. At times it may be desirable to initiate change at the level of law or public policy. It has been observed that legislative change is most effective when consistently integrated throughout the entire legal code. A training manual distributed by Amnesty International offers the following advice:

> Ensure that FGM [female genital mutilation] programs are integrated into all relevant areas of state policy. Departments of health should clearly prohibit medicalization of FGM, and move to incorporate this prohibition into professional codes of ethics for health workers. Departments of education, women's affairs, immigration and development should all include FGM programs, as well as addressing the underlying factors which give rise to FGM such as access to education. (1998, p. 5)

As a general rule, the greater the number of institutions and spheres of influence engaged, the more significant the long-term change. For example, changes in the legal code will be more far-reaching "if accompanied by a broad and inclusive strategy for community-based education and awareness-raising" (Amnesty International, 1998, p. 2).

Guiding Principles

There are a number of general principles to keep in mind when strategizing for social change or transformation.

1. An *attitude of humility* is of critical importance (Marks, 2000; Weaver, 1999). Such humility rejects the paternalistic notion that we, the advantaged ones, are there to "restore" those less fortunate than ourselves (Marks, p. 614). "Epistemological humility" recognizes that even after careful ethical reflection, ones' beliefs should be held with a small amount of hesitation (Applebaum, 1996). In other words, family scientists are keenly aware of their own fallibility and potential for mistakes in judgment. Epistemological humility allows one to say,

> I believe I am right and insofar as I do, I believe you are wrong, but I grant that I might be wrong on this matter just as I have been shown to be on many others. (Gardner, 1992, p. 79)

It is hoped that open-minded humility will enable us to affirm clear value commitments, while becoming more astute and sensitive when interacting with those whose viewpoints or approaches differ from ours (Applebaum, 1996).

2. A second principle is an overarching *commitment to family well-being* (Brock, 1993). Anthropologists have long been skeptical of efforts to define quality of life in universal terms (Wilk, 1999), recognizing that cultures differ quite dramatically in their visions of individual and family well-being (Gough, 2004). Pioneering anthropologists like Bronislaw Malinowski and Margaret Mead challenged conventional wisdom that quality of life is somehow tied to personal income and material abundance. These founding anthropologists

> invented the concept of "cultural relativism" as a critique of what most felt was excessive materialism, loss of meaning, and decay of kinship and community that inevitably followed Westernization and modernity. Their portraits of other cultures were meant to remind the literate West that there are other sets of values, deeper and more meaningful than money, by which to assess the texture of a life. (Wilk, 1999, p. 91)

Despite the ever-present danger of linking quality of life to free-market economics and material prosperity, it still seems appropriate that family scientists be motivated by a passion to ensure basic quality of life standards for all world families. As such, there would be great interest in determining the bare social minimum or threshold below which "truly human functioning is not available to citizens" (Nussbaum, 2000, p. 6).

3. Yet another related principle is a *commitment to beneficence or to doing no harm*. Practitioners working with global families may have the most generous of spirits and selfless of intentions, but in the rush to do good, they must remain alert to their own potential for doing harm:

> Virtually every caring system we have keeps its eye on the good it hopes to accomplish and blinks at the harm it is doing. As a result, hundreds of thousands—perhaps millions—of people are violated every day of their lives by the encroachments of their ostensible benefactors. (Glaser, 1978, p. 165)

Family scientists should attempt to anticipate "how interventions [will] impact participants and their families" (Leigh, Loewen, & Lester, 1986, p. 579). At the very least, potential risks should be identified. For example, risks one may encounter by refusing to participate in female circumcision rituals might include "ostracism, ridicule, and other social pressures" (Leeder, 2004, p. 135).

4. The fourth guiding principle is that of *family empowerment* (Kagitcibasi, 1996). It is so easy to assume that one knows best what other people need, particularly if one is an expert with formal academic training in

family dynamics and well-being. The challenge is to balance this expert knowledge base with families' very real need for "self-determination and empowerment" (Hardina, 2004, p. 595). Indeed, professionals involved in community organizing often cite "constituent self-determination [as] one of the primary goals" (p. 596).

Strategies of Intervention

Having noted some broad principles for initiating social change, the final section highlights selected strategies one might employ in intervention. There have been many attempts to identify practical skills and strategies for effecting social change and transformation. Some are more relevant for work with families than others. These might include the following:

1. Conducting *background research*. Before embarking on planned social action, it is important to do your homework. You should seek to understand the issue in as holistic a way as possible. With regard to an issue like FGM, Amnesty International advises that

> information is particularly needed on its prevalence, physical and psychological effects, social attitudes and religious requirements. Research should also review the impact of efforts to date. In particular work needs to be done to study the prevalence of FGM outside Africa, especially in the Middle East, Latin America, and in many countries where it is practiced among immigrant communities. (Amnesty International, 1998, p. 4)

Disciplining oneself to do relevant background reading and research will ensure that strategies employed will be more thoughtful and well conceived.

2. A *collaborative approach* is also much wiser than embarking on a solo mission to change the world. The collective wisdom of a multidisciplinary team can round out the perspective and skill set of a family scientist. The team might be composed of "human rights activists, educationalists, health professionals, religious leaders, development workers and many others" (Amnesty International, 1998, p. 3).

3. Close *cooperation with grassroots leaders* and movements can also enhance one's chances of success. Even when appealing to internationally agreed upon standards of human rights, "Those best placed to set the direction of the campaign are the grassroots activists and community workers with a presence in the areas" (Amnesty International, 1998, p. 3) where the tradition in question is practiced.

4. In addition to collaborating with multidisciplinary teams and with grassroots leaders, it is important to *consult closely with local families* themselves. There is a great danger that one might be consulting with everyone else about the problem but the people directly involved. Rhodes (1991) has observed this tendency in social work practice where the client's point of view is sometimes overlooked. Here, casework

> emphasizes clients' psychodynamics and excludes serious consideration of their values or their opinion about how to solve problems. Clients sometimes report that they have never been asked by their workers how they would solve a problem; workers simply assumed that as workers they were in the best position to decide. (Rhodes, 1991, p. 51)

Nussbaum (2000) notes that by simply informing people of what is good for them, "We show too little respect for their freedom as agents (and in a related way, their role as democratic citizens). People are the best judges of what is good for them, and if we prevent them from acting on their own choices, we treat them like children" (Nussbaum, 2000, p. 51).

Doherty (2000) echoes this sentiment by challenging family scientists to shift their focus away from a "trickle down model of research and practice" (p. 319). In this model, serious knowledge about families is seen to be generated from academic researchers, who dispense their wisdom down through practitioners to families. In the process, real flesh-and-blood families are rarely invited to identify problems or organize to solve them. Doherty rejects the trickle-down approach in favor of one where family scientists work "as catalysts for families to be active shapers of their [own] communities and their destinies" (p. 321). As such, family scientists' intentions are not to "stifle families' own wisdom and initiative" (p. 322).

5. Another useful strategy for addressing difficult and controversial family practices is to begin by *searching for common ground* (Bennett, 1993). It is reasonable to assume that one could hypothetically construct common goals with every culture of the world (Rhodes, 1991). Celebrating common values and commitments can create a climate of trust before tackling the more difficult discussions related to areas of difference. Rhodes (1991) provides the example of working with a culture to celebrate common values related to human dignity, equality, and community as a backdrop for later discussions on issues where views might diverge.

6. Closely related is the suggestion to begin by *acknowledging family strengths and capacities*. It is so tempting when working with diverse families to equate difference with a deficit model of family functioning. Kagitcibasi

(1996) discusses this deficiency model in his work with the Turkish Early Enrichment Project. He notes that rejecting a deficiency model

> does not imply that the existing conditions are optimal for the development of children. If this were so, there would be no need for intervention. It rather means that the agent of change builds on the existing strengths in changing the conditions to promote optimal development. (p. 173)

By highlighting family strengths, the hope is to "strengthen what is adaptive in order to change what is maladaptive" (Kagitcibasi, 1996, p. 173).

7. A *fertile imagination* can be a wonderful asset in strategizing for social change. Feminist scholars typically place a high degree of importance on the role of imagination (Nussbaum, 2000). Unfortunately, our imagination is often limited by our own cultural backgrounds (Rosaldo, 2000). Rhodes (1991) notes that "too often we limit our inquiry to an established set of questions or assume constraints imposed by society and therefore limit the possibilities of creative and satisfactory solutions to ethical problems" (p. 51). A helpful antidote might be planned exposure to a broader range of societies and cultures so that we are able to think outside the box of our own culture and to experience "a rich contextual imagining of particular lives and circumstances" (Nussbaum, 2000, p. 250).

8. In addition to a fertile imagination, it is helpful to adopt *strategies that are nonconfrontational*. It is quite easy to allow the ends to justify the means by endorsing tactics of coercion, violence, terrorism, deceit, or personal humiliation (Hardina, 2004). In selecting appropriate intervention strategies for work with global families, one might ask whether the strategies are ethical and whether they sacrifice long-term substantive change for short-term benefits (Hardina, 2004).

Conclusion

The foregoing developmental model has particular application for faculty and students processing complex family issues in the university classroom. It was designed in response to expanding globalization of the family science curriculum. The paradigm is offered as one possible response to the vexing ethical dilemmas implied by various traditional family practices. As a process model, it moves students through a four-stage developmental sequence with each stage building off the last. It reflects a larger vision of mentoring future family scientists along a trajectory from ethnocentric thinking through constructive ethical reflection and ultimately to responsible social action.

Several years ago the Carnegie Foundation published a report in which it challenged higher education to restore its "original purpose of preparing graduates for a life of involved and committed citizenship . . . [since] by every measure . . . today's graduates are less interested and less prepared to exercise their civic responsibilities" (Newman, 1985, p. xiii). It is hoped that the developmental model presented here might be a useful pedagogical tool for faculty and might inspire future family scientists to become more intentional about their journeys toward responsible global citizenship.

References

Adams, R. A., Dollahite, D.C., Gilbert, K. R., & Keim, R. E. (2001). The development and teaching of the Ethical Principles and Guidelines for Family Scientists. *Family Relations 50*, 41–48.

Africa: A ritual of danger. (1992, Fall). *Time*, p. 39.

Aldous, J. (1978). *Family careers*. New York: Wiley.

Aldous, J. (1990). Family development and the life course: Two perspectives. *Journal of Marriage and the Family, 52*, 571–583.

Altergott, K. (Ed.). (1993). *One world, many families*. Minneapolis, MN: National Council on Family Relations.

Amnesty International. (1998). *Female genital mutilation: A human rights information pack*. London: Author.

Applebaum, B. (1996). Moral paralysis and the ethnocentric fallacy. *Journal of Moral Education, 25*(2), 185–200.

Asia: Discarding daughters. (1990, November 1). *Time, 136*(19), 40.

Augsburger, D. (1986). *Pastoral counseling across cultures*. Philadelphia: Westminster.

Balswick, J. O., & Balswick, J. K. (1989). *The family: A Christian perspective on the contemporary home*. Grand Rapids, MI: Baker.

Balswick, J. O., & Balswick, J. K. (1995). Gender relations and marital power. In B. Ingoldsby & S. Smith (Eds.), *Families in multicultural perspective* (pp. 297–315). New York: Guilford.

Benedict, R. (1934). *Patterns of culture*. Boston: Houghton Mifflin.

Bengston, V. L., & Allen, K. R. (1993). The life course perspective applied to families over time. In P. Boss, W. Doherty, R. LaRosa, W. Schumm, & S. Steinmetz (Eds.), *Sourcebook of family theories and methods: A conceptual approach* (pp. 469–498). New York: Plenum.

Benjamin, M. L. (2003). 10th anniversary of the International Year of the Family—2004. *NCFR Report, 48*(1), 5–6.

Bennett, M. J. (1993). Toward ethnorelativism: A developmental model of intercultural sensitivity. In R. M. Paige (Ed.), *Education for the intercultural experience* (2nd ed., pp. 1–51). Yarmouth, ME: Intercultural Press.

Botes, A. (2000). A comparison between the ethics of justice and the ethics of care. *Journal of Advanced Nursing, 32*(5), 1071–1075.

Bredehoft, D. J., & Walcheski, M. J. (2005). *Family life education: Integrating theory and practice*. Minneapolis. MN: National Council on Family Relations.

Brock, G. W. (1993). Ethical guidelines for the practice of family life education. *Family Relations, 42*(2), 124–128.

Burns, J. (1998, May 11). Though illegal, child marriage is popular in parts of India. *New York Times*, p. A1.

Callahan, S. (2002, March 22). Spirituality, religious wisdom, and care of the patient. *Yale Journal for Humanities and Medicine* [Electronic version]. Retrieved September 16, 2005, from http://info.med.yale.edu/intmed/hummed/yjhm/spirit2003/dignity/scallahan2.htm

Coll, S. (1994, March 22). Asian prosperity spawns conspicuous consumption. *Washington Post*, p. A1.

Cultural relativism. (2005). Retrieved August 12, 2005, from http://www.anthrobase.com/Dic/eng/def/cultural-relativism.htm

Daoudi, R. (1983). Teaching of human rights in Arab countries. In A. Eide & M. Thee (Eds.), *Frontiers in human rights education*. Oslo, Norway: Universitetsforlaget.

DeGenova, M. K. (1997). *Families in cultural context: Strengths and challenges in diversity*. Mountain View, CA: Mayfield.

DeSensi, J. T. (1994). Ethnocentric and ethnorelative stages of intercultural sensitivity in sport: An analysis. *Research Quarterly for Exercise and Sport, 65*(1), 94.

Doherty, W. J. (2000). Family science and family citizenship: Toward a model of community partnership with families. *Family Relations, 49*(3), 319–325.

Duvall, E. M. (1957). *Family development*. Philadelphia: Lippincott.

Ecker, N. (1994, January). Cultural and sexual scripts out of Africa. *SIECUS Reports*, 16–21.

Estes, R. (Ed.). (1992). *Internationalizing social work education: A guide to resources for a new century*. Philadelphia: University of Pennsylvania School of Social Work.

Fine, M. A. (1993). Current approaches to understanding family diversity. *Family Relations, 42*, 235–237.

Fitzpatrick, J. (2005). International year of the family (IYF): United Nations' millennium development goals. *NCFR Report, 50*(3), 8, 12–13.

Fluehr-Lobban, C. (1987). *Islamic law and society in the Sudan*. London: Frank Cass.

French, M. A. (1992, November 22). The open wound. *Washington Post*, p. F4.

Gardner, P. (1992). Propositional attitudes and multicultural education or believing others are mistaken. In J. Horton & P. Nicholson (Eds.), *Toleration: Philosophy and practice*. Orebro, Sweden: Aldershot Avebury.

Getting to know you. (1987, August 10). *Time, 130*(6), 23.

Gilligan, C. (1982). *In a different voice: Psychological theory and women's development*. Cambridge, MA: Harvard University Press.

Glaser, I. (1978). Prisoners of benevolence: Power versus liberty in the welfare state. In W. Gaylin, I. Glasser, S. Marcus, & D. Rothman (Eds.), *Doing good: The limits of benevolence* (pp. 97–170). New York: Pantheon.

Glenn, D. (2004, April 30). A dangerous surplus of sons? *Chronicle of Higher Education, 50*, A14.

Gough, I. (2004). Human well-being and social structures. *Global Social Policy, 4*(3), 289–312.

Greeley, A. (1969). *Why can't they be like us? Facts and fallacies about ethnic differences and group conflicts in America.* New York: Institute of Human Relations Press, American Jewish Committee.

Hamon, R., & Ingoldsby, B. (Eds.). (2003). *Mate selection across cultures.* Thousand Oaks, CA: Sage.

Hardina, D. (2004). Guidelines for ethical practice in community organizing. *Social Work, 49*(4), 595–605.

Headley, R., & Dorkenoo, E. (1992). *Child protection and female genital mutilation.* London: Department of Health.

Health effects of female circumcision: Training course in women's health (Module 5). (1986). Chapel Hill, NC: Institute for Development Training.

Held, V. (2004). Care and justice in the global context. *Ratio Juris, 17*(2), 141–155.

Hernandez, H. (1989). *Multicultural education: A teacher's guide to content and process.* Columbus, OH: Merrill.

Hillman, E. (1975). *Polygamy reconsidered.* Maryknoll, NY: Orbis.

Hollinger, D. P. (2002). *Choosing the good.* Grand Rapids, MI: Baker.

Husband, C. (2000). *The politics of diversity education for transcultural health care practice.* London: Department of Health.

Hutter, M. (Ed.). (2004). *The family experience: A reader in cultural diversity* (4th ed.). Boston: Pearson.

India: Till death do us part. (1990, November 1). *Time, 136*(19), 39.

Ingoldsby, B. (1995). Mate selection and marriage. In B. Ingoldsby & S. Smith (Eds.), *Families in multicultural perspective* (pp. 143–160). New York: Guilford.

Ingoldsby, B., & Smith, S. (Eds.). (1995). *Families in multicultural perspective.* New York: Guilford.

Kagitcibasi, C. (1996). *Family and human development across cultures.* Mahwah, NJ: Erlbaum.

Kauffmann, N., Martin, J., & Weaver, H. (1992). *Students abroad, strangers at home: Education for a global society.* Yarmouth, ME: Intercultural Press.

Lachman, P. (1997, June–July). *Ethical and practical issues for the mandatory reporting of child abuse in developing countries.* Presented at the 5th International Family Violence Research Conference, University of New Hampshire, Durham, NH.

Leeder, E. (2004). *The family in global perspective: A gendered journey.* Thousand Oaks, CA: Sage.

Leigh, G. K., Loewen, I. R., & Lester, M. E. (1986). Caveat emptor: Values and ethics in family life education and enrichment. *Family Relations, 35,* 573–580.

Leininger, M. M. (Ed.). (1995). *Transcultural nursing: Concepts theories, research and practices.* New York: McGraw-Hill.

Leo, J. (2002, July 22). Professors who see no evil. *U.S. News & World Report, 133*(3), 14.

Lesdema, H. (1983). The study and teaching of human rights in Latin America. In A. Eide & M. Thee (Eds.), *Frontiers of human rights education* (pp. 73–81). Oslo, Norway: Universitetsforlaget.

Levey, B. (1994, April 4). When yuppieism bursts out of control. *Washington Post,* p. D20.

Loewy, E. H. (1996*). Textbook of healthcare ethics.* New York: Plenum Press.

Mahoney, S., & Schamber, J. F. (2004). Exploring the application of a developmental model of intercultural sensitivity to a general education curriculum on diversity. *Journal of General Education, 53*(3/4), 311–335.

Marks, S. P. (2000). Teasing out the lessons of the 1960's: Family diversity and family privilege. *Journal of Marriage and the Family, 62*(3), 609–622.

Matalon, J. R. (2002, September 6). Love and the care of the patient. *Yale Journal for Humanities in Medicine* [Electronic version]. Retrieved September 16, 2005, from http://info.med.yale.edu/intmed/hummed/yjhm/spirit2003/love/rmatalon.htm

Mattson, I. (2002, July 17). Dignity and patient care: An Islamic perspective. *Yale Journal for Humanities in Medicine* [Electronic version]. Retrieved September 16, 2005, from http://info.med.yale.edu/intmed/hummed/yjhm/spirit/dignity/imattson.htm

McPeck, J. E. (1990). *Teaching critical thinking: Dialogue and dialect.* London: Routledge.

Miller, B. (1987). Female infanticide and child neglect in rural North India. In N. Scheper-Hughes (Ed.), *Child survival* (pp. 95–112). Dordrecht, Holland: D. Reidel.

Muslim Women's League. (1999, April). *Position paper on "honor killings."* Retrieved September 12, 2005, from http://www.mwlusa.org/publications/positionpapers/hk.html

Newman, F. (1985). *Higher education and the American resurgence.* Princeton, NJ: Carnegie Foundation for the Advancement of Teaching.

Nussbaum, M. (1999, February). *Religion and sex equality* (Occasional Paper Series, Women and Human Development, The Fifth Annual Hesburgh Lectures on Ethics and Public Policy). Notre Dame, IN: The Joan B. Kroc Institute for International Peace Studies, University of Notre Dame. Retrieved October 18, 2006, from http://kroc.nd.edu/ocpapers/op_16_2.pdf

Nussbaum, M. C. (2000). *Women and human development.* Cambridge, UK: Cambridge University Press.

Okie, S. (1993, April 13). Female circumcision persists: Tribal rite worries Kenyan health officials. *Washington Post,* p. Z09.

O'Toole, K. (1999, May 26). Theories of relativity: Okin, Rorty assess students' moral views at ethics teach-in. *Stanford on-line report.* Retrieved September 12, 2005, from http://news-service.stanford.edu/news/1999/may26/ethics-526.html

Partington, G. (Ed.). (1987). *Multicultural education: A book of readings.* Doubleview: Western Australian College of Advanced Education.

Paul, R. (1992). Teaching critical reasoning in the strong sense: Getting behind world views. In R. Talaska (Ed.), *Critical reasoning in contemporary culture* (pp. 135–156). Albany: State University of New York Press.

Powell, L., & Cassidy, D. (2001). *Family life education: An introduction.* New York: McGraw-Hill.

Prest, J. (Ed.). (1993). *The illustrated history of Oxford University.* Oxford, UK: Oxford University Press.

Pusch, M. (Ed.). (1979). *Multicultural education: A cross cultural training approach.* LaGrange Park, IL: Intercultural Network.

Queen, S., Habenstein, R., & Quadagno, J. (1985). *The family in various cultures* (3rd ed.). New York: Harper & Row.

Rhodes, M. L. (1991). *Ethical dilemmas in social work practice.* Milwaukee, WI: Family Service Association.

Riley, J., Torrens, K., & Krumholz, S. (2005). Contemporary feminist writers: Envisioning a just world. *Contemporary Justice Review, 8*(1), 91–107.

Robinson, F. (1999). *Globalizing care: Ethics, feminist theory, and international relations.* Boulder, CO: Westview.

Rosado, C. (1994). *The concept of cultural relativism in a multicultural world.* Philadelphia: Rosado Consulting for Change in Human Systems. Retrieved August 12, 2005, from http://www.rosado.net/articles-relativism.html

Rosaldo, R. (2000). Of headhunters and soldiers: Separating cultural and ethical relativism. *Issues in Ethics, 11*(1). Retrieved August 12, 2005, from http://scu.edu/ethics/publications/iie/v11n1/relativism.html

Senarclens, P. (1983). Research and teaching of human rights: Introductory remarks. In A. Eide & M. Thee (Eds.), *Frontiers of human rights education.* Oslo, Norway: Universitetsforlaget.

Sherif, B. (2004). Islamic family ideals and their relevance to American Muslim families. In M. Hutter (Ed.), *The family experience: A reader in cultural diversity* (4th ed., pp. 183–189). Boston: Pearson.

Skrobanek, S. (1991). Child prostitution widespread in Thailand. *Women's International Network News, 17*(3), 44–46.

Smith, S., & Ingoldsby, B. (1992). Multicultural family studies: Educating students for diversity. *Family Relations, 41*(1), 25–30.

Srinivasan, P., & Lee, G. R. (2004). The dowry system in Northern India: Women's attitudes and social change. *Journal of Marriage and Family, 66*(5), 1108–1117.

Strong, B., DeVault, C., & Cohen, T. (2005). *The marriage and family experience* (9th ed.). Belmont, CA: Wadsworth.

Taylor, C. (1992). *Multiculturalism and the "politics of recognition."* Princeton, NJ: Princeton University Press.

Thiroux, J. P. (1990). *Ethics: Theory and practice* (4th ed.). New York: Macmillan.

Tong, R. (2003). Feminist ethics. In *Stanford encyclopedia of philosophy* [Electronic version] (pp. 1–19). Retrieved August 31, 2005, from http://plato.stanford.edu/entries/feminism-ethics

Ufland, H., & Ufland, M. (Producers), & Gilbert, B. (Director). (1991). *Not without my daughter* (Videocassette). Culver City, CA: MGM/UA Home Video.

Waiarda, H. (1985). *Ethnocentrism in foreign policy: Can we understand the Third World?* Washington, DC: American Enterprise Institute for Public Policy Research.

Walking, P. H. (1980). The idea of a multicultural curriculum. *Journal of the Philosophy of Education, 14*(1), 87–95.

Weaver, H. N. (1999). Indigenous people and the social work profession: Defining culturally competent services. *Social Work, 44*(3), 217–225.

White, J. M. (1991). *Dynamics of family development: A theoretical perspective.* New York: Guilford.

White, J. M. (2003). Family development theory. In J. J. Ponzetti, R. Hamon, Y. Kellar-Guenther, P. Kerig, T. Scales, & J. White (Eds.), *International encyclopedia of marriage and family* (2nd ed., Vol. 2). New York: Macmillan.

Wilk, R. (1999). Quality of life and the anthropological perspective. *Feminist Economics, 5*(2), 91–93.

Wolfe, A. (1999). The revival of moral inquiry in the social sciences. *The Chronicle of Higher Education, 46*(2), B4.

Concluding Observations

The chapters in this volume illustrate the complexity of trying to study, analyze, and understand families in our highly heterogenous society. While family scholars have developed greater sensitivity toward including and studying culturally diverse families, there is still much work that needs to be accomplished. Methodological concerns, questions about the adequacy of existing theoretical frameworks, and charged emotional and political contexts in which discourse needs to take place are a few areas that need to be addressed in order to advance understanding of diverse families.

A plethora of methodological issues currently muddle the field. First, concepts need to be clearly defined and used appropriately. For instance, when and under what conditions should we use the term *families of color*? Ethnicity? Race? Culturally diverse? Nativist versus immigrant? When selecting a particular term over another, do we thereby exclude some groups and include others that may not belong? As evidenced in each of the preceding 14 chapters, culturally diverse families exhibit many nuances not currently captured under our categorizations by race and ethnicity. National origin, timing of arrival in the United States, regionality, education, and many other characteristics make it difficult to generalize about groups. Hopefully, this volume amply illustrates that categorizing individuals and families by race does little to inform us about the variability of lives and experiences. Yet, we cannot ignore race, as it plays an integral part in American society, both historically and today.

Second, what research methodologies and samples are most appropriate for this type of discovery? Given that both family science and mainstream journals tend to favor quantitative work, researchers, under pressure to publish, often comply with popular notions of what is to be studied and how research is to be conducted. However, much of the existing scholarship on culturally diverse families has been qualitative in nature and is often published in lesser-known, smaller journals or book chapters. Thus, we need family scholars willing to facilitate a greater interface between various disciplines, methodological approaches, and scholarly publication outlets. So, too, our samples tend to focus on the most accessible groups, in large part due to the orientation of the researchers themselves. For example, we have been unable to resolve the question as to the legitimacy of studying groups to which we ourselves do not belong. This is compounded by the issues of accessibility; it is often difficult to gain entrance to culturally diverse groups, particularly if the researcher is not a member of that group, due to suspicions about motives for the study. While these methodological realities contribute to the lack of studies on diverse populations, we must overcome obstacles associated with lending voice to these groups.

Third, what are the questions that we should be asking? What are the most helpful topics to be studied? Despite their distinct and unique qualities and characterizations, culturally diverse families often deal with very similar issues to those of mainstream families related to such things as mate selection, marital relations, parenting, aging, and divorce. Often, as many of the preceding chapters illustrate, culturally diverse families share more commonalities with families at their same socioeconomic level than with those with whom they are grouped due to race or ethnicity.

The discussion and incorporation of diversity into our scholarly dialogue is also sometimes thwarted due to the fact that we currently lack adequate theoretical frameworks that allow us to capture variability in family experiences in the United States. When it comes to the study of families, we still currently employ conceptual perspectives developed for the study of middle-class White families. Interestingly, there has been little advancement in social theory in general to understand the rapid flow and the constantly changing nature of social life. Most of our popular theoretical perspectives were developed in the mid- to late nineteenth century under very different societal conditions. We have modified these assumptions and frameworks, but, strikingly, few new orientations have developed in the last century.

Given our highly charged emotional and political climates, as evidenced by strident debates on issues like illegal immigration, affirmative action, and multicultural education, civil discourse can be challenging. Listening to the other's point of view, identifying the other's strengths and contributions to family and the larger society, and considering ways to empower the others in meeting their individual and familial needs should be priorities. Family science researchers and practitioners are uniquely positioned to model informed positions, cultural humility, and respectful and civil discourse in promoting conversation on important topics having to do with cultural diversity.

With its commitment to discovery (i.e., research) and application, family science has the capacity to be at the forefront in identifying and understanding some of these rapid developments both in the United States and abroad. As we unravel the mysteries of increasingly diverse and complex families through research, the applied aspects of family science allow us to translate research findings into effective pedagogical strategies and messages, sensitive and sensible policy initiatives, and responsive human and family service delivery practices. Armed with skills in research and practice, as well as a desire to integrally link the two, family scientists are well situated to lend voice and capacity to diverse families.

—Bahira Sherif Trask and Raeann R. Hamon

Index

About the Editors

Bahira Sherif Trask, PhD, is a faculty member in the Department of Individual and Family Studies, University of Delaware, and a policy scientist in the Center for Community Research and Service. She has a PhD in cultural anthropology from the University of Pennsylvania and a BA in political science from Yale University. Her research addresses issues of cultural diversity from national and international perspectives. Specifically, Dr. Trask is interested in the interrelationship of work, gender, and belief systems in culturally diverse families, the conceptualization and redefinition of non-Western families when compared to Western families, and the pivotal role of economics in families. She has published and spoken extensively on these topics in the United States and Europe and has served as an expert witness and national commentator on challenges facing American families. Dr. Trask recently coedited *The Greenwood Encyclopedia of Women's Issues Worldwide* (Greenwood Press, 2003) and is working on a new book, *Globalization and Families* (Kluwer/Springer, forthcoming).

Raeann R. Hamon, PhD, CFLE, is Distinguished Professor of Family Science and Gerontology and chair of the Department of Human Development and Family Science at Messiah College in Grantham, Pennsylvania. She received her PhD in family and child development and her graduate certificate in gerontology from Virginia Polytechnic Institute and State University. Dr. Hamon has numerous publications and presentations on topics such as filial responsibility, family relationships in later life, parents' experience of their adult children's divorces, intergenerational service learning and relationships, and Bahamian family life. She coedited *Mate Selection Across Cultures* (Sage, 2003), served as an associate editor for a four-volume *International Encyclopedia of Marriage and Family* (Macmillan Reference, 2004), and edited *International Family Studies: Developing Curricula and Teaching Tools* (Haworth Press, 2006). A Certified Family Life Educator, Dr. Hamon teaches such courses as Dynamics of Family Interaction, Marital Relationships, Strategies of Family Intervention, and Sociology of Aging.

About the Contributors

Katherine R. Allen, PhD, is professor of family studies in the Department of Human Development and a faculty affiliate in both the Center for Gerontology and the Women's Studies Program at Virginia Polytechnic Institute and State University in Blacksburg. Her academic interests are in family diversity over the life course, feminism and family studies, and qualitative research methods. Dr. Allen is author and coeditor of several books and numerous journal articles and book chapters. She serves on the editorial boards of *Journal of Marriage and Family, Journal of Family Issues, Family Relations,* and *Journal of GLBT Family Studies.* She is a charter fellow of the National Council on Family Relations and a fellow of the Gerontological Society of America. She received her PhD from Syracuse University and undergraduate degree from the University of Connecticut.

William D. Allen is a licensed marriage and family therapist practicing privately in Minneapolis, Minnesota. His research interests include the intersection of families and ethnicity and the important roles males play in family life across the life span. Dr. Allen is an adjunct professor in the Family Social Science Department of the University of Minnesota and consults with both public- and private-sector institutions in relation to family mental health and well-being. He has written and presented nationally on cultural influences on parenting practices, cultural competence, males in families, and, more recently, practical approaches for building healthy marriages. Dr. Allen has served on the boards of the Minnesota Association of Black Psychologists, the Minnesota Association of Marriage and Family Therapists, and the University of Minnesota's Consortium on Youth and Families as well as the National Council on Family Relations. His written work describing his research and practice with families of color includes several journal articles and book chapters on African American families and an upcoming exploration of culture's influence on parenting practices.

Ben K. Beitin, PhD, is assistant professor of marriage and family therapy in the Department of Professional Psychology and Family Therapy at Seton Hall University in South Orange, New Jersey. His academic interests are in Arab American families, social justice and family therapy, and qualitative research methods. Dr. Beitin is the author of journal articles on working with Arab American couples and families. He is in private practice in Florham Park, New Jersey, and works with couples and families on a multitude of issues. He received his PhD from Virginia Polytechnic Institute and State University in marriage and family therapy.

Teresita Cuevas, MPA, is a research associate at the Center for Disabilities Studies at the University of Delaware, where she also received her master's degree in public administration. She has been involved in the evaluation of human service, parent education, and early childhood programs. She is particularly interested in the diverse ways in which Latina children and their families cope with the cultural stresses and expectations associated with living in the United States.

Fabienne Doucet is an assistant professor in the Department of Teaching and Learning at the New York University Steinhardt School of Education. She has a PhD in human development and family studies from the University of North Carolina at Greensboro. Her research interests include the schooling experiences of immigrant and U.S.-born children of color; family, school, and community partnerships; and parental values and beliefs about education. Other areas of interest include racial and ethnic identity, gender, and social-class issues as they pertain to the schooling and life experiences of immigrants and people of color, as well as qualitative methodology and teaching for social justice. Dr. Doucet's previous work has examined African American preschoolers' engagement in academically relevant activities as well as African American parents' and caregivers' beliefs, values, and practices surrounding the preparation of preschool children for the transition to school.

Larissa V. Frias earned her master's degree in psychology from the University of the Philippines and is currently a PhD student in the Department of Child Development and Family Studies at Purdue University, majoring in developmental studies. Her research is focused on culture and parenting, parent-child relationships, family communication, and parent and child understanding of peace and war. She has worked in Purdue Extension since 2003 assisting Dr. Judith Myers-Walls with evaluation of parenting programs and producing educational materials about children and families with multicultural backgrounds.

Deborah B. Gentry, EdD, CFLE, CFCS, is professor of family science and associate dean of the College of Applied Science and Technology at Illinois State University in Normal. An experienced educator and scholar of teaching and learning, she has presented and published on the scholarship of teaching and learning, family life education, and family conflict. She has served in numerous leadership roles within the National Council on Family Relations, the Family Science Association, the Groves Conference on Marriage and Family, and the American Association of Family and Consumer Sciences.

Katia Paz Goldfarb is an associate professor and department chair of Family and Child Studies in the College of Education and Human Services at Montclair University in New Jersey. She completed her PhD in family and child ecology at Michigan State University in 1994, has a master's degree in sociology of education from Eastern Michigan University, and has an undergraduate degree in education with a minor in gender studies from the Hebrew University of Jerusalem. Dr. Goldfarb is the chair-elect of the Ethnic Minorities Section of the National Council on Family Relations. Her research and publications have addressed an array of topics with a focus on the relationships between immigrant families, family dynamics, sustainability, schools, teacher education, and communities.

Kimberly A. Greder is an assistant professor and extension specialist in human development and family studies at Iowa State University. Her primary areas of research and extension education include parenting education and food insecurity within a framework of promoting family resilience and shaping family policy. She has authored more than 50 parenting curricula, extension publications, videos, manuscripts, and Web sites focused on these topic areas. She provides leadership for national trainings for parenting educators including an online parenting education training program and an annual satellite program focused on various parenting topics.

Tammy L. Henderson, PhD, director of the Gerontology Institute and associate professor in human development and family sciences at Oklahoma State University, conducts research in the area of family policy and law. She completed her doctoral studies in human development and family sciences at Oregon State University and earned her other degrees from Louisiana State University. Dr. Henderson has published articles on grandparent rights and responsibilities, foster care, and family policy instruction. Her current research is examining the impact of Hurricane Katrina on aging adults. She has worked on several policy-oriented projects: childcare needs in Montgomery County, kinship care issues in the state of Virginia, homelessness and neighborhood redevelopment in Baton Rouge, and improving the capacity of historically Black colleges and universities to address health disparities.

Mary Ann Hollinger is dean of external programs at Messiah College in Grantham, Pennsylvania. She holds a master's in child development and family relations from Montclair State University in New Jersey and a doctorate in family studies from Columbia University in New York. She has done postdoctoral studies at Oxford University in England. Currently Dr. Hollinger gives leadership to the experiential and contextual learning programs for Messiah College and teaches several courses in the Department of Human Development and Family Science. Dr. Hollinger's research interests include international families, ethical reflection in family science, families in religious perspective, and family mediation and conflict resolution. She has served as president and program chair of the Family Science Association, program chair for the DC Sociological Society, board member of the Indiana Council on Family Relations, Public Policy committee member of the National Council on Family Relations (NCFR), and chair of both the International and Family Science sections of NCFR.

Rona J. Karasik, PhD, is the director of the gerontology program and a professor of community studies at St. Cloud State University in St. Cloud, Minnesota. She regularly teaches undergraduate and graduate courses in aging, including the areas of health, dementia, community, and housing for older adults. Her research interests are varied and focus on issues of aging families, housing for older adults, and intergenerational service learning.

Seongeun Kim, PhD, is an assistant professor of human development and family studies at Pennsylvania State University, Delaware County. She earned her BA and MA at Seoul National University in South Korea and her PhD at the University of Delaware in the United States. She regularly teaches courses on diversity and families, family relationships, and adulthood. Her research focuses on how gender is negotiated and reconstructed within Korean immigrant families in an immigration context, and she has published articles on work and the reconstruction of Korean motherhood and on Korean parenting and religion. Currently, she is conducting qualitative research on Christianity and gender relations among working-class Korean immigrant families in the United States.

Julie M. Koivunen, PhD, is an assistant professor in the Human Development and Family Studies Department at the University of Wisconsin–Stout. She earned a PhD in family studies from the University of Delaware, an MA from Western Michigan University in counseling with a specialization in marriage and family therapy, and a BGS from the University of Michigan with a concentration in psychology. She has worked as a counselor and marriage and family therapist with individuals, couples, and families. Dr. Koivunen's research interests include gender roles in the family, feminism in marriage, and the transition to parenthood. Her work has been published in *Family Relations, Family Science Review,* and *The Journal of Teaching in Marriage and the Family: Innovations in Family Science Education.*

Ramona Marotz-Baden, PhD, is professor emerita at Montana State University. She coauthored or coedited six books and is known in the profession for her identification of the implicit use of the deficit family model and her work with families in rural settings. She received her PhD from the University of Minnesota and was recognized as one of the top 100 graduates of the College of Human Ecology at the University of Minnesota. She served in the first group of Peace Corps volunteers that included women, directed the Mexican phase of the University of Minnesota Family Study Center's cross-national research project on parental socialization of adolescents for social change, and was head nutritionist and social science consultant for the University of Minnesota Laboratory of Physiological Hygiene's Multi-Risk Factor Intervention Trial (MRFIT) for coronary heart disease.

Judith A. Myers-Walls, PhD, CFLE, is an associate professor and extension specialist in the Department of Child Development and Family Studies at Purdue University. She teaches classes on working with parents and families and is coeditor or coauthor of several books on parent education and peace studies for young people. Her research focuses on parenting education techniques, parents and children across cultures, and how children and parents communicate about peace and political violence. She has created Web pages regarding children and terrorism (www.ces.purdue.edu/terrorism) and effective ways for childcare providers to work with parents (www.ces.purdue .edu/providerparent).

Pearl Stewart, PhD, MSSA, is an assistant professor in the Department of Family and Child Studies at Montclair State University in New Jersey. Dr. Stewart holds a master's degree in social work and worked with therapeutic foster care families and children prior to her entry into academia. She has written in the areas of family diversity, African American families, and the cultural connections between African American and West African families. Her interests include examining the importance of incorporating culture into work with and interventions for families and children.

Donald G. Unger, PhD, is a professor in the Department of Individual and Family Studies, University of Delaware. He received a master's degree in child and family studies at the Merrill-Palmer Institute and a doctoral degree in clinical/community psychology at the University of South Carolina; he also completed a fellowship at Yale University School of Medicine. He has directed, evaluated, and collaborated with numerous community-based human service programs for families with young children or teenagers with and without disabilities. His publications focus on family stress and coping and the development and evaluation of family support programs.

Paula M. Usita, PhD, is associate professor in the health promotion division of the Graduate School of Public Health at San Diego State University. Previously, she was on the child development and family studies faculty of Purdue University. Her teaching and research activities largely focus on family relationships in adulthood, aging of ethnic minorities and immigrants, and gerontological health. She also has research and teaching interests in behavior change and injury prevention across the life course. Dr. Usita received her BA and MS degrees in psychology from the University of Puget Sound and Western Washington University, respectively, and her PhD in human development and a graduate certificate in gerontology from Virginia Polytechnic Institute and State University.

Tara Woolfolk, PhD, is a research associate in the Department of Individual and Family Studies at the University of Delaware, where she recently completed her doctorate in human development and family studies. Her research focuses on parent-child relationships within African American families. She also has collaborated in the development and evaluation of family support programs in community-based settings.